Chinese Transnational Migration in the Age of Global Modernity

D1743256

The term "circulatory transnational migration" best describes the unconventional migratory route of many contemporary Chinese migrants – that is an unfinished set of circulatory movements that these migrants engage in between the homeland and various host countries. "Return migration", "step migration" to a third destination, and the "astronauting" strategy are all included within this circulatory migration movement wherein "returning" to the country of origin does not always mean to settle back to the homeland permanently; while "step migration" also does not necessarily mean to re-migrate to a third destination country for a permanent purpose.

Liu takes a longitudinal perspective to study Chinese migrants' transnational movements and looks at their transnational migratory movements as a family matter and progressive and dynamic process, using New Zealand as a primary case study. She examines Chinese migrants' initial motives for immigrating to New Zealand; the driving forces behind their adoption of a transnational lifestyle which includes leaving New Zealand to return to China, moving to a third country – typically Australia – or commuting across borders; family-related considerations; inter-generational dynamics in transnational migration; as well as their future movement intentions. Liu also discusses Chinese migrants' conceptualisation of "home", citizenship, identity, and sense of belonging to provide a deeper understanding of their transnational migratory experiences.

Liangni Sally Liu is a Senior Lecturer in the School of Humanities at Massey University, New Zealand. She was previously a Postdoctoral Fellow in the "Asian Migration Cluster" of the Asia Research Institute, National University of Singapore (2013–2014), and a Postdoctoral Fellow in the Research Office, Auckland University of Technology. Dr. Liu's research interest is in Chinese transnational migration. Her broader research interests also include the intersection of migratory mobility and sexuality, ethnic relations between migrants and mainstream/ indigenous people, and the media influence on ethnic relations. Her research work has been published widely in the forms of book chapters and research article in high-ranked peer-reviewed journals. She has been awarded the Marsden Fund (Fast-Start) from the Royal Society of New Zealand in 2016 and is conducting a project entitled "Floating families? New Chinese migrants in New Zealand and their multi-generational families".

Routledge Studies in Asian Diasporas, Migrations and Mobilities

For the full list please refer to URL: www.routledge.com/Routledge-Studies-in-Asian-Diasporas-Migrations-and-Mobilities/book-series/RSADMM

Chinese Transnational Migration in the Age of Global Modernity

The Case of Oceania

Liangni Sally Liu

Routledge
Taylor & Francis Group

LONDON AND NEW YORK

First published 2018
by Routledge

2 Park Square, Milton Park, Abingdon, Oxfordshire OX14 4RN
52 Vanderbilt Avenue, New York, NY 10017

Routledge is an imprint of the Taylor & Francis Group, an informa business

First issued in paperback 2019

British Library Cataloguing-in-Publication Data
A catalogue record for this book is available from the British Library

Library of Congress Cataloging-in-Publication Data
A catalog record for this book has been requested

ISBN: 978-1-138-21805-5 (hbk)
ISBN: 978-0-367-37566-9 (pbk)

Typeset in Galliard
by Apex CoVantage, LLC

I dedicate this book to
My grandmother who brought me up and always
encouraged me to pursue higher education, but passed
away in the year when I finished my PhD study
And
My daughter, Anni who is the most important person
in my life

Contents

Tables

Figures

Acknowledgments

First and foremost, I would like to take this opportunity to thank the unsung heroes in this study – the participants. Without them, this book would not have been possible.

Sincere thanks go to Emeritus Professor Manying Ip, Associate Professor Ward Friesen, Robert Didham, and Emeritus Professor Richard Bedford, for their constant encouragement, kind support, and guidance along all of these years.

For the most practical of reasons this book would not have been possible without the generous financial support of a number of institutions and organisations, including the Marsden Fund (Fast-Start) from the Royal Society of New Zealand, New Zealand Asia Studies Society, Asia: New Zealand Foundation, the Social Policy Evaluation and Research (SPEaR) Linkage Fund from the Ministry of Social Development, the Building Research Capacity in the Social Sciences Network (BRCSS II), and the University of Auckland Doctoral Scholarship.

Lastly and most importantly, thanks also go to my parents for their emotional supports from far away China.

Foreword

In October 2017 Immigration New Zealand (INZ), the government agency responsible for the development and implementation of the country's immigration policy, closed the parent category. This means that immigrants who were born overseas, and whose parents are living overseas, can no longer plan to have their parents living in New Zealand. In effect this policy change makes it virtually impossible for immigrants who plan make New Zealand their home to care for their parents in-country, as they get older. By definition, closing off options for parents of adult immigrants to live in the same country as their children, requires immigrants to practice "circulatory transnational migration" – a form of mobility that Dr Liangni Liu has termed "an unconventional migratory route of many contemporary Chinese migrants".

Dr Liu's book, *Chinese Transnational Migration in the Age of Global Modernity: The Case of Oceania*, contains a detailed analysis of contemporary Chinese migration to and from New Zealand, focusing on the period since August 1986 when a century-long restriction on immigration from China was lifted as part of a major review of immigration policy. Between 1986 and 2016 the ethnic Chinese population in New Zealand increased almost 10-fold, from 26,500 to almost 260,000. Around 75 percent of the increase is accounted for by immigration of Chinese born in countries in Asia. The great majority of these immigrants were younger Chinese men and women – people aged between 20 and 39 years. These were the people prioritized by the points-based selection system that New Zealand introduced in 1990. A very significant proportion of the immigrants were the only child in their families reflecting the impact of China's "one-child" policy that prevailed through the 1980s and 1990s.

Dr Liu is one of these immigrants to New Zealand – the only child of parents living in China. She sets the scene for a very comprehensive analysis of contemporary Chinese migration to New Zealand by reflecting on her own circulatory transnational migration – a migration behavior that is no longer a voluntary choice, as far as maintaining physical contact with her parents is concerned. As noted above, the option of bringing her parents to New Zealand to live here is no longer open now that the parent category in the family sponsorship stream is closed.

Dr Liu's analysis draws on more than a decade of intensive research into contemporary Chinese migration. In collecting the evidence for her argument she carried out field work in New Zealand, Australia and China. She also had almost two years as a Postdoctoral Fellow at the National University of Singapore working with colleagues who are amongst the world's leaders in research on contemporary Chinese migration. Her findings challenge many notions that underpin conventional thinking about international migration as a process that leads to permanent relocation of families overseas. She gives a useful early hint to the reader about the unconventional perspective she brings to her analysis when she observes in the Introduction that "home" for her is not linked with a particular place or country – "home" for her can be involved with movement and is multi-located. Yet, she goes on to stress that for her, "home" represents a family unit, a sense of security and identity and emotional belonging. It is a "safe and secure place or space where family members can truly relax and share both thoughts and emotions".

The contradictions that surround contemporary international migration are profound, as Douglas Massey pointed out more than two decades ago. In the case of New Zealand these contradictions are nowhere more starkly evident than in the policy settings that encourage talented, young people from any country to consider moving to New Zealand to further their education and to work here, while at the same time making it very clear that their parents are not welcome, except as tourists or visitors, unless they qualify for entry under the skilled migrant category. In negotiating these contradictory signals about immigration, young Chinese migrants, often the only child their parents have, must weigh up the costs and benefits of living transnational lives if they wish to remain true members of families that comprise children, parents and grandparents.

Dr Liu has provided us with a powerful, nuanced analysis of the ways Chinese migrants are negotiating the challenges and contradictions of contemporary international migration through "circulatory transnational migration" – a process that is no longer one of choice in many parts of the world but is one that destination country policies relating to immigration of parents and other adult family members now makes mandatory. This is not how it was in the past in what have often been called the "traditional countries of immigration" that lie on the Pacific Rim – Australia, Canada, New Zealand and the United States.

Richard Bedford
Emeritus Professor
University of Waikato and Auckland University of Technology

Abbreviations

AIIB	Asian Infrastructure Investment Bank
BIC	Business Investment Category
BIP	Business immigration Policy
CBD	central business district
EIP	Entrepreneur Immigration Policy
GIC	General Investment Category
GSC	General Skilled Category
IELTS	International English Language Testing System
INZ	Immigration New Zealand
IT	information technology
JSV	Job Search Visa
LTBA	Long Term Business Visas
NZAMI	New Zealand Association for Migration and Investment
NZIP	New Zealand Immigration Programme
NZIS	New Zealand Immigration Service
NZRP	New Zealand Residence Programme
MMP	Mixed-Members-Proportional
OPL	Occupation Priority List
PFM	Prospective Founding Members
POL	Priority Occupation List
PLT	permanent and long-term
PRC	People's Republic of China
RRV	Returning Resident's Visa
SCV	Special Category Visa

1 Introduction

A personal journey – approaching the topic

One result of China's enormous transformation during the past few decades has been the migration outflow of its population to some "White Settler" countries, including New Zealand. Such migratory movement is one of many evidences to tell that today's China is enthusiastically engaging in mobilising all relevant resources from outside world for further development, including resources from its diasporic population. While China has been traditionally viewed as a migrant source country (Skeldon, 1996, 2004), this view requires reassessment as the increasing number of migrants and return migrants to China from a variety of countries has become a significant social phenomenon in recent years. The reasons are mainly centred on work opportunities, trade, business, and education (Pieke, 2012). China's rising prominence at the international stage and its geopolitical power and fast integration into the international community have resulted in a significant shift and change in the world migration system. The economic advancement of China not only increases its emigration flow, but also draws its diasporic population back to home and engenders bilateral and even multilateral movements between China and different relevant places.

The "China factor" has played an increasingly significant role in influencing and re-balancing global labour demand and supply as well as global governance (Zhu, 2013). Under the force of globalisation and opposite to the scenario in 1960s and 1970s, China has moved forward fast to realise the importance of reaching out to seek a wider and deeper connection with other major economies not only in the economic realm but also in the people-to-people contacts. New Zealand has been listed as one of a few favourite immigration destination countries for many Chinese nationals.

On the other hand, the twenty-first century is remarkably characterised by a geo-political shift in global power relations towards Asia, particularly China (Ang, 2015). This has urged New Zealand to recognise China and Asia as its important neighbours. In terms of trade, knowledge, science and technology exchange, cultural integration, economic links, and political co-operation, New Zealand has been building a comprehensive strategic partnership with China (Elder & Ayson, 2012; New Zealand Foreign Affairs & Trade, 2015). New Zealand is the first developed country that entered into a Free Trade Agreement (FTA) with China in 2008. So far most of the provisions in the FTA have come fully into force, although tariffs relating to a small number of items have yet to phase down to the agree end-point (zero in almost all cases) between 2016 and 2019 (New Zealand Contemporary China Research Centre, 2015). Along with the further upgrade in the FTA between these two countries, the previous Prime Minister of New Zealand, John Key, launched the NZ Inc China Strategy in February 2012, aiming to develop an ambitious five-year plan for the relationship with China (New Zealand Contemporary China Research Centre, 2015). People-to-people contacts through short-term visits and temporary immigration are an inescapably part of this ambition. Chinese international students remain the largest single group of New Zealand's overseas students, while the number of Chinese tourists rapidly increased in recent years, with the 300,000 mark being exceeded in April 2015 and a growth rate of 26 per cent year-on-year, which makes now China as New Zealand's second largest tourist market. New Zealand is also the only country in the world to offer a working holiday scheme to citizens from China (New Zealand Contemporary China Research Centre, 2015) and the first developed western country joining the negotiation to set up the Asian Infrastructure Investment Bank (AIIB)[1] and membership (English, 2015).

It is fair to say that these two countries, although do not completely follow each other's assumption in terms of ideology, policies, and perceptions, at least have found room to explore opportunities and accommodate each other (Brady, 2008). Compared with the prevailing perception that views China's rise as a threat (Broomfield, 2003), New Zealand merely runs interests against China, and so does China towards New Zealand. This kind of cordial mentality in the relationship between these two countries certainly has great implications in propelling immigration, especially under the circumstance that Chinese citizens nowadays have more resources to allow them to seek new and more desirable spaces and contexts. New Zealand is one of their many options.

Similar to other "European settler" societies on the Pacific Rim (such as Canada, the US, and Australia), transnational migration has been recognised widely as a remarkable feature among the new Chinese migrants[2] from the People's Republic of China[3] (PRC) in the New Zealand context and attracted considerable policy and academic attention (Ip, 2011; Liu, 2011). The terms of "circulatory transnational migration" (Ip, 2011, p. 6) can be used to best describe the unconventional migratory route of the new Chinese migrants – that is an unfinished set of circulatory movements that these migrants engage in between the homeland and the immigration host countries. "Return migration", "step migration" to a third destination, and "astronauting"[4] strategy are all included into this circulatory migration movement within which "returned" to the country of origin does not really mean to settle back to the homeland permanently; while "step migration" also does not mean to re-migrate to a third destination country for a permanent purpose.

This book aims to illustrate the on-going migratory movement patterns of new Chinese migrants from the PRC based on the New Zealand context. The research has taken a longitudinal perspective to study PRC migrants' transnational movements and looks at their transnational migratory movements as a progressive and dynamic process. It has examined PRC migrants' initial motives for immigrating to New Zealand; the driving forces behind their adoption of a transnational lifestyle which includes leaving New Zealand to return to China, moving to a third country or commuting across borders; family-related considerations; inter-generational dynamics in relation to transnational migration; as well as their future movement intentions. The book will also discuss PRC migrants' conceptualisation of "home", citizenship, identity, and sense of belonging to provide a deeper understanding of their transnational migratory experiences.

By studying transnational migration of the PRC Chinese migrants, a renewed process of domination, co-cption, subversion, and resistance in the global migration system can be revealed. New Zealand is a small country with a population of around 4.6 million but is ideal for studying many aspects of migration since over a quarter of the population is foreign-born (Statistics New Zealand, 2014a), and the exchange of people between New Zealand and other countries is both large and diverse, with a rapidly growing diasporic population between 600,000 to 850,000; namely, the range is one in five to one in seven New Zealanders live overseas (Bedford, 2001; Butcher, 2010). The implications drawn by this study in the New Zealand context can be extended beyond this country. The subject of this research – transnational PRC Chinese migrants of New Zealand – is an important component of the "global citizens" in the modern world, and a great force that is actively participating in the transnational circulation of human capital (Liu, 2014, 2015). With their transnational habitats, they have developed strong connections with their homeland, while they might have multiple citizenship and permanent residence in various countries. The scenarios of transnational migration among this migrant group pose intriguing questions in Chinese migration studies. It is believed, perhaps overly simplistically, that other traditional Chinese immigrant-receiving "white societies" share similar positioning as New Zealand in the world migration system. These Chinese immigrant-receiving countries (i.e. Australia, Canada, and the US) face challenges to develop effective policy to accommodate and retain their skilled Chinese immigrants. At the same time, China, the homeland, actively engages with its diasporic population because this population plays a vital role in connecting China with the international community. The policy of China with respect to its diaspora reflects a multi-layered and complicated relationship between this re-emerging world power and the global North, a term referencing developed economies. How China enhances its international status and reputation through a mediated group of migrants illustrates one aspect of this country's ambition of contributing more to the global governance (Zhu, 2013).

Another advantage of studying Chinese return migration in the New Zealand context is that New Zealand serves as "a social laboratory to examine migration" (Ip, 2011, p. 22). First, the immigration policy is generally transparent and immigration control is openly administered in this country. Second, New Zealand is surrounded by oceans and remains relatively inaccessible to illegal migrants; therefore, immigration statistics can be easily and accurately collected. Last, New Zealand and China have a long history of contact at various levels, and the relationship between these two countries is largely cordial without any significant political conflict. Based on these factors, data derived from a country like this "is more likely to reveal clear results uncontaminated by other socio-political factors" (Ip, 2011, p. 23).

Approaching the research topic – a personal journey towards "home"

Walking along the streets of Central Paris in November 2007, I realised that I missed home badly. The "home" I referred to, like it or not, was determined by a space or place that I recognised as the best place for my infant daughter to grow up and where I felt was the most suitable location for my personal aspirations as well as my family's needs at that stage in our lives. It quickly also became obvious that my perspective of "home" was quite different from the recurring perceptions of "home" for many immigrants. That perception was either a physical household in a particular geographic locale back in the homeland or a conceptual notion of what their national country was like (Basu, 2004; Mallett, 2004; Waetjen, 1999; Wiles, 2008). My perspective of "home", however, was not China – the place of my origin. It was not New Zealand – the immigration destination country I had chosen, even though my house was in Auckland. Parallel to recent discussions of the concept of "home" (Ahmed, 1999; Blunt & Dowling, 2006; Bowlby, Gregory, & McKie, 1997; Mallett, 2004; Rapport & Dawson, 1998; Wiles, 2008), "home" for me was more than a territorial attachment and an overlapping of the meaning of family. It was more likely a psychological concept – a safe and secure place or space where family members can truly relax and share both thoughts and emotions.

In this sense, even though my "home" is located in a particular geographic locality, that geographic locality does not represent my complete idea of "home". I see my "home" as that space where personal, family, and social meaning are fully grounded. It is an emotional "place" or terrain that is there, irrespective of either physical household or geographical locations. My conceptualisation of "home" is not a static but rather a dynamic process that involves seeking personal security and emotional peacefulness and/or making a private living space available where similar ideas and values are shared by family members. "Home" for me can be involved with movement and multi-located. It can be located in different geographic localities if reality requires us to move. Essentially, my conceptualisation of "home" is not tied to the boundaries of a physical territory and a geographical dwelling; rather, it represents family unity, a sense of security and identity, and emotional belonging. A dwelling can be a physical carrier of my sense of belonging and security, but that physical location is not essential. As an ethnic Chinese, I know too that in Chinese culture, "home" can quite often mean where one's elders are and what one's roots are, which of course implies an original homeland from which people migrate and sometimes seek to return to eventually.

My memory returns often back to 2004, when I went back to my hometown to visit my parents for the first time after several years of continuous stay in New

Zealand. It was also the first time that I travelled back to China on my newly acquired New Zealand passport. When my father picked me up at the airport, he greeted me with a very formal "welcome home". I felt warm, but odd. On one hand, it was wonderful to see my father and family. On the other hand, I was anxious, because I knew that the "home" I conceptualised at that time differed significantly from what my father referred to often. As many parents keep for their children, my parents' place, a three-bedroom apartment, would always be open to me as my "home" where I could return and seek comfort whenever I needed it. Even though they certainly knew that I had my own life far away from them, a shared collective concept of "home" was really important to them. It was perhaps a kind of emotional comfort for them and gave them a feeling of still holding me close as their only baby daughter, and affirmed their intimate connection and relationship with me. Yet for me, since my life had changed significantly while I was far away from the shelter of my parents, my concept of "home" was not the one I was used to calling "home". I had gone to a new land, New Zealand, in 2000. I had completed my undergraduate and postgraduate studies there, established my academic career, and started my own family. I had set a new life course and thus re-examined my priorities, values, identity, and perceptions toward my homeland – China. This identity I re-examined and re-formed was a much more independent one from what my parents and family used to expect of me. More importantly, the time when I felt that I really had become mature was not while I was under my parents' shelter, but rather when I stood on my own two feet. Therefore, my real "home" now is no longer that three-bedroom apartment in China owned by my parents. That three-bedroom apartment is only my old family home, defined perhaps now as my home away from home.

At that same time, I had read some of the literature that spoke of "home" and "homeland". However, I knew that all of the academic theories and comments would be inadequate if I tried to use them to convince a traditional Chinese father that his daughter now conceptualised her "home" differently. During my one-month stay with my parents, I sensed that they recognised the changes in me in terms of life perspective, values, and worldview. In their eyes, after living in a Western country for several years, I might not be as Chinese as I used to be or as they still expected. My father was particularly disappointed about my choice of acquiring New Zealand citizenship. For him, the relinquishment of my Chinese citizenship meant a rejection of identifying myself as a Chinese. He seriously reminded me that "you are a Chinese, and will always be" several times, to which I finally lost my patience and replied cynically, "I am a New Zealander, and my home is in Auckland". I felt upset not because I really thought I was a New Zealander. Actually, I always will feel that I am a Chinese deep down. I was upset just because my parents, my closest family members, could not understand that I had gained new perspectives by being away from "home", and yet still tried to impose what they thought to be right from my past on me. Afterwards, although I regretted my action and recognised that I had hurt my father's feelings, I knew I should not disguise my true feelings, not even from him.

That time, however, as the chilly evening wind of Paris started to moan, I was once again certain about my sense of "home", a reality that was distant from what my parents continuously wished that I embrace. This journey happened back near the end of 2007 when I had a holiday trip to Paris, which I had looked forward to for a long time. Paris, the cultural and arts centre of Europe, is a place full of excitement, elegance, and romance and attractive to everybody. I enjoyed Le Louvre, Notre Dame, the River Seine, and the authentic French cuisine. Like many travellers, I was amazed by the charms Paris offered. However, throughout the days that I was there, I experienced many differences and prospects that were beyond my expectations and abilities to relate to easily. Walking along the streets, I felt we were total foreigners because of the language, the street culture, the manner of the restaurant waiters, and all sorts of small details that made up everyday life in Paris. Perhaps in the eyes of French, it was strange to hear a young woman of Asian appearance announcing that she was from New Zealand rather than from an Asian country. To be certain, Paris is not my home. I had never imagined I would miss Auckland so badly. That year, from what I can remember, the Paris winter was cold and windy, while I knew the summer in Auckland was long and full of sunshine. My daughter and I had to be away from our "home" in Auckland for a while because I needed to head back to China to do the fieldwork for my PhD research on transnational Chinese migrants from China to New Zealand.

After a two-week stay in Paris, I went to Chengdu, my hometown, the inland capital city of Sichuan Province in Southwest China where it bordered with the Tibetan, and lived there for a week to prepare for the subsequent intensive field interviews with some return Chinese immigrants in Shanghai and Beijing who had obtained New Zealand permanent residence or citizenship but then returned to China to live and work. I also needed to bring my baby daughter there so that my parents could take care of her when I was in other cities of China to conduct the fieldwork. Today of course, high speed jet travel made my journeys easy. After a 14-hour flight, I landed at Chengdu. The city came into my view as unchanged from my past impression of it as a locality that was smoky and crowded. Everything seemed to be unchanged, apart from the newly built skyscrapers, motorways, tunnels, and subways. The ride into the CBD (central business district) where my parents' apartment was located was joyful. I was very familiar with the dialect the taxi driver used and the jokes he made. Both the Westernisation and local signs in this city were a contrast and interesting. Mum talked about which of my favourite foods she had prepared for dinner, while dad talked about his plan for decorating the new house he had recently bought.

However, the subsequent stay in Chengdu frustrated me. I was unhappy with the safety conditions for my baby girl in their household. I did what I could to improve the safety conditions with extensive furniture re-arrangement. I was also irritated by traffic jams, the driving manners of local people, awful parking at the supermarkets, and the restricted access of baby strollers in shopping malls. I was very critical about people's behaviour and the everyday life in the city, despite it being my hometown. It was where I was born, brought up, and had previously felt so comfortable. The conversation between my parents and I also started to become difficult. I was not happy about my father's requests to visit all the relatives of the paternal extended family one-by-one within just a week. He believed that visiting the elderly relatives of the family proactively was expected and showed the proper manners that ought to be maintained by the younger generation. However, the preparation for my fieldwork was very intensive, and I expected my father to understand my commitment and allow me to make my research as my first priority and postpone family business until I returned from my fieldwork.

After all these confrontations, I quickly started to doubt whether I could really cope with all my trips around China and deal well with the complicated interpersonal relationships of Chinese society and be able to establish positive and harmonious relationships with my interviewees. After several years of being absent from China, my social skills might be off key. I might overlook important social rules and assumptions that govern interpersonal interactions. These were essential for me to conduct my fieldwork in China productively. More importantly, I wondered whether I could successfully conduct the fieldwork interviews in terms of fully understanding the return migration journeys that were pursued by many PRC Chinese migrants who used to reside in New Zealand.

Even though the economy of China is rapidly growing, the social and environmental conditions in China are not comparable to New Zealand. Why did the migrants leave New Zealand, the country of their choice? What propelled them to return to China? These were the two central questions of this fieldwork. I quickly realised that I was going through the so-called "reverse culture shock" caused by returning to a homeland where the reality could not meet one's expectations. This reverse culture shock not only hit me in terms of my confidence toward my research; it also hit me in other ways and more than I expected. Indeed, by the time I landed in Chengdu, my hometown, which I had constantly longed for in my dreams, my vision of it had all but fractured. I was depressed because I knew I could no longer relate to this place and its people in the same way as I had before. The life experiences, expectations, and memories, whether pleasant or not, had all been disrupted for me through the passage of time. I was depressed because I knew I was no longer who I had been; yet other people there still viewed me in the old way. I was also frustrated about the feelings of being so foreign in the place I had called "home".

The "home" in my memory was all about familiarity, comfort, and intimacy. However, that "home" fell short of what I had envisioned before my temporary return. I could not feel the very emotions for which I had longed. I also noticed changes in my own worldview, especially when it did not match the worldview of those around me. I wished I could bend myself to fit into the current scene rather than conflicting with it. I wished I could engage the locally lived world and my globally experienced world simultaneously. I noted that to re-enter China to live and work as a temporary return migrant actually required me to smoothly and frequently pass across two different cultural worlds. However, I found it was very difficult to effect a seamless change between the Western world and a completely different world that was China. Certainly, Chengdu was not my "home" anymore; rather, it was just my "hometown".

Aware of that discomfort and no time to reflect on my emotions and experiences, I headed to Shanghai and Beijing to start my fieldwork interviews with Chinese migrants who had returned to China from New Zealand. It quickly became apparent that there were important similarities between Shanghai, Beijing, and Chengdu. The booming economy, the busy atmosphere, and the Westernisation amidst the old parts of the cities were obvious and refreshing for me. I then started to understand the experiences my interviewees had been through because of my daily interactions with them. Actually, my own feelings at the outset of the journey during the research trip paralleled the experiences of my interviewees. The same depression, discomfort, insecurity, and uncertainty had all been unfolded and shared, reflecting the power relations that are today reinforced by globalisation. The experiences and perceptions that those individuals had had in New Zealand and China undoubtedly shifted from one angle to another because of the perspectives that were available to those who had to view their original homes from a distance. By concentrating on getting to know my interviewees and experiencing these cities in China, I noticed my depression lifting, and I felt a reconnection happening. I also started to feel the power of the cities and could not resist immersing myself fully into them.

After about two months of fieldwork in Shanghai and Beijing, I returned to Chengdu for the Chinese New Year. Finally I had my own personal time to meet again my old friends, classmates, and colleagues. Some of them had also studied in New Zealand. Through daily interaction with them, I started to understand the dilemma they had before they left New Zealand and after they returned to China. With their encouragement and friendly company, I also started to go out more and re-explored the city that I had been so familiar with earlier. I became more tolerant and understanding of everything I experienced in my old hometown and started to feel comfortable there. The familiar network of friendships, lifestyle, even the diet with all of their memories came back to me and seamlessly reached out to me from the past to the present. If toleration and understanding were now emerging, then they came from knowing again the physical places, but it was actually a result of re-connecting with the people first. I observed them, listened to them, and talked to them. Eventually, when this journey came to an end, I found that I was yet just one of them.

When I look back on this journey now, I realise it was not simply an academic research journey; it was a personal and emotional journey as well. It forced me to re-identify myself and constantly reminded me of my Chinese identity and where my heart truly belongs. For a while, I had been very ambivalent and confused about my Chinese identity. However, this research trip became a journey that inscribed that Chineseness firmly onto my identity. After more than ten years in a Western country, I realised that my Chineseness is a perpetual feature of who I am. It is always and will continue to be as a significant part of how I identify myself. This re-confirmation of my Chinese identity took place as this research journey started in my home country – China, paralleling my long-term immigration settlement in New Zealand and many transitions across the course of my life. Even now, although the issue of how I identify myself still bothers me sometimes, I no longer feel insecure about my true identity. Yet two core questions I asked my interviewees, "who are you" and "where is your home", are still difficult for many people to answer, for globalisation is speeding up everywhere in this world and transnationalism essentially today must denote a different and newer meaning of "home" being split.

The reason for starting this book of my personal journey from Oceania to Europe and then to Asia is first because this journey gave me new personal insight toward the overall research project. It heavily influenced the development of my personal ideas and my perceptions for the research topic. Through this journey, I obtained an emotional strength through which I could identify myself more confidently and comfortably as a first-generation migrant with a strong Chinese allegiance. This affirmation consequently contributed significantly to building my intellectual understanding of the research topic. Second, telling my story about my research trip to China offered me a unique opportunity to build social bridges with my interviewees. It is the similarities between these interviewees and me as migrants from the same country that led to my keen interest in this research topic. Finally, the shared experiences that occurred between the interviewees and myself upon re-entering China gave a sense of practical reality to the concepts of transnational migration in the setting of globalisation. To be sure, I am Chinese, but I am also a New Zealander, and a female academic conducting research on transnational new Chinese migrants from China. When I am writing this book, I can also surely claim that I am a transnational migrant, given the fact that my working and life experience have been across several countries. I first immigrated to New Zealand from China for my postgraduate study 17 years ago. Second, I moved to Singapore to work for two years after I graduated with my PhD degree. In 2015, I came back from Singapore to New Zealand to take up my first tenured position and since then have been working in the position for three years. Like many of my interviewees, I move transnationally from place to place for career development as well as for personal preferences.

However, it is necessary to point out that my personal narrative involved into this research project does not necessarily mean that I consider myself an "insider" or "outsider". Instead, I position myself as a researcher who is able to understand my participants more deeply from a distance by sharing the same cultural background, similar life experiences of re-entry, and status as transnational migrants. My personal conceptualisation of "home" was accounted into my research journey. It provided an entry point that paved the way for me to understand more clearly the migrant identity in a transnational world. Within humanistic geography and more recently within feminist geography, "home" has been an important subject to study to understand human movement (Ahmed, Castaneda, Fortier, & Sheller, 2003; Blunt & Dowling, 2006; Blunt & Varley, 2004; Collins, 2009; Pratt, 2004). A number of scholars have used the notion of "home" as "a powerful motif" in their work to (re)locate the relationship between "home" and migration, and identity and belonging (Ahmed, 1999;

Blunt, 2005; Butcher, 2003; Mallett, 2004; Wiles, 2008). In the field of trans-nationalism, Al-Ali and Khoser (2002) pointed out that the relationship between migrants and their homes is always changing, and as such, that changing relation-ship is "a quintessential characteristic of transnationalism" (p. 1). Blunt (2005) found that migrants or multi-locational individuals frequently experience home as being synonymous with identity.

In Chinese terms, the character home (*jia* 家) is analogous to family or a place of inhabitation where a family universe lies. The term is usually used in combina-tion with other characters as phrases that can connote different meanings. For example, *jiaxiang* 家乡 means hometown, *jiating* 家庭 means family, *jiaguo* 家国means homeland or national home. Even though these phrases carry different meanings, they all connote a meaning of belonging or emotional attachment to managed objects or social units. In doing this research, I believe that the idea of "home" and its relevant interpretation and explanation actually structure the experience of migration and re-location of my researched subjects – PRC trans-national migrants. The notion of "home" is heavily embedded into this research project. It is hoped then that the examination of the journey between "home here" and "home there" can provide the contours of a belonging space, and PRC Chinese transnational migration can thus be examined in a fresh and different way.

A research gap identified

I have chosen to study the "transnational migration of new PRC migrants", what has been considered in the literature to be one of the most salient features of new Chinese migrants (Hugo, 2005; Ip, 2000; Skeldon, 2006). In the New Zealand context, Chinese immigrants from Hong Kong, Taiwan, and the PRC are three major sources of New Zealand's Chinese immigrant intake after the enactment of the open-door immigration policy in 1987. These three groups plus other Chinese from other regions are all categorised as new Chinese immigrants. In most literature of New Zealand's immigration studies, terms such as Hong Kong Chinese/immigrants, Taiwanese/Taiwan immigrants, and PRC Chinese/ immigrants are often used to differentiate the different origins of New Zealand's recent Chinese immigrants. Over the last two decades, the constant mobility of new Chinese migrants has attracted much academic attention; however, there is a clear research gap that can still be identified. First, the exodus of Hong Kong and Taiwan Chinese that took place from the late 1980s to the mid-1990s was widely evidenced in certain immigration countries, such as Canada, Australia, and New Zealand. This exodus has been widely regarded as a response to the political fear surrounding the takeover of the former British colony of Hong Kong by the Chi-nese government and in particular the Chinese Communists (Ho, Ip, & Bedford, 2001; Ip, 2003a; Skeldon, 1994a, 1994b, 1996, 2006). This large migration flow and its associated counter flow toward the homeland and step-migration toward third destinations has attracted much academic attention and propelled detailed micro studies of the various manifestations of transnational migration strategies in these two related cohorts.

Considerable attention has been given to the settlement issues of these two migrant groups, their reasons for leaving their homeland, the process of their migration decision-making, their frequent commuting habits, and their future settlement intentions (Beal, 2001; Chiang, Hibbins, & Chui, 2006; Ho, 2003; Ho, Bedford, & Goodwin, 1997; Ho et al., 2001; Ip, 2000, 2001; Ip & Friesen, 2001; Pe-Pua, Mitchell, Iredale, & Castles, 1996; Waters, 2002, 2005). Such research often provides rich data from detailed empirical studies conducted within certain migrant groups in a particular social setting. However, such research was largely limited to just research "snapshots" of the components for the scenario of transnational migration.

What is lacking still is a full picture of the landscape of Chinese transnational migration. Without enough longitudinal studies, the on-going patterns and continuing trends of transnational migration are still largely overlooked. For example, much research has focused on the "astronauting" strategy that many Hong Kong and Taiwan migrants adopted toward balancing family economic survival with the need for obtaining a foreign passport or for gaining their children's education in a less pressured educational system. This phenomenon is evidenced as a short-term transnational strategy but only one of many mani-festations of Chinese transnationalism (Ho & Bedford, 2008; Huang, Yeoh, & Lanm, 2008). It is fair to say then that the early literature on and the inter-pretation of Chinese transnational migration overlooks the full picture of what transnationalism really means. In this research, I propose a non-linear model for understanding Chinese transnational migration. Transnational migration is an on-going and continuing process, actually an extension of the initial migra-tion of leaving the homeland that is prompted by a combination of varied personal reasons and macro-level forces. Movement under this transnational framework is a circular cycle that follows its own logic of departure, arrival, and further later movement.

The second rationale for conducting this research on PRC migrants is because of the size of this immigrant group in New Zealand and the relative paucity of data regarding the group in academic immigration studies within the New Zea-land context. Unlike the immigrants from Hong Kong and Taiwan, who first arrived in the early 1990s, the PRC immigrants' arrival in significant numbers began in the mid-1990s. By that time, the number of immigrants from Hong Kong and Taiwan had already dropped sharply because of a combination of immigration policy changes in 1995 and the onset of the Asia economic crisis in 1997 (Ip, 2003b). From that time on, the number of PRC immigrants to New Zealand climbed rapidly, and China became one of the top sources of New Zea-land's overall immigrant intake (Liu, 2011). Table 1.1 shows that China is one of ten major immigrant source countries (i.e. China, India, South Korea, Philippine, Great Britain, South Africa, the US, Fiji, Samoa, and Tonga) from 1997/98 to 2015/16. During the period, the total residence approvals under the New Zea-land Residence Programme (NZRP)[5] were 819,693, of which nearly 14 per cent was granted for migrants from China. This percentage ranks China as the second largest immigrant source country just after Great Britain with about 17.3 per

Table 1.1 Approvals for residence by nationality, 1997/98–2015/16

Nationality	Total approvals	% residents approved
Asia		
China	114,064	13.9
India	89,695	10.9
South Korea	25,130	3.1
Philippine	44,310	5.4
Sub-total	**273,199**	**33.3**
Pacific		
Fiji	47,103	5.7
Samoa	38,082	4.6
Tonga	18,410	2.2
Sub-total	**103,595**	**12.6**
Others		
Great Britain	141,700	17.3
South Africa	64,895	7.9
USA	21,962	2.7
Sub-total	**228,557**	**27.9**
Total top 10 countries	**605,351**	**73.9**
Total all countries	**819,693**	**100**

(Source: Excel data of R1 – Residence decisions by financial year from Immigration New Zealand, 2016 www.immigration.govt.nz/about-us/research-and-statistics/statistics)

cent residence approvals. India was ranked as the third largest immigrant source country with about 10.9 per cent of the total New Zealand residence approvals.

In terms of the absolute number of the PRC Chinese population in New Zealand, the 2013 census shows that the usually resident population of New Zealand was 4,433,000, including 171,411 (or about 4 per cent) people of Chinese ethnicities living in this country. Among the Chinese population, just over half (89,121 or 52 per cent) were born in China. The second largest group were New Zealand-born Chinese, which numbered 65,979 (38 per cent) (Statistics New Zealand, 2014b). The new PRC Chinese migrants came to New Zealand as skilled middle-class immigrants who were financially secure, well-educated, and qualified the criteria of entering New Zealand under the skill immigration category (Liu, 2009).

Although the increase in the "China born" cohort was dramatic, any study of this cohort appears to be limited within the New Zealand's national boundary. A few micro-level studies on immigrants from the PRC have been conducted, such as Henderson's research on the New Settlers Programme, which looked at PRC immigrant English language proficiency and their generally unsuccessful employment experience in New Zealand (Henderson, 2003; Henderson, Trlin, Pernice, & North, 1997; Henderson, Trlin, & Watts, 2001). A limited number of research on PRC immigrants by using a transnational approach to explore their return movement to China and step migration to a third destination only came very recently (Ip, 2006; Liu, 2011, 2013, 2014, 2015, 2016; Liu & Lu, 2015). Thus, there remains a clear research gap in the understanding of New Zealand's second-largest cohort of immigrant residents.

With their distinctive Chinese cultural heritage and the dynamic current eco-political position of China, PRC new migrants have significantly different characteristics from other Chinese migrants in terms of their motivation for migration, settlement strategies, movement patterns, and future settlement intentions. One of the most salient features of many PRC new migrants not yet scrutinised closely is their constant mobility. In recent years, similar to migrants from Hong Kong and Taiwan, PRC migrants have demonstrated considerable transnational mobility. A recent report from New Zealand Ministry of Business, Innovation and Employment (2013) on the long-term absentees[6] shows that China is ranked as 6th on the list, with 20 per cent (8,450) of the total approved permanent residents (41,577) (see Appendix 1). The immediate question arising here is where they are and whether they have returned to their places of origin or moved to another country. As a part of a worldwide trend of ethnic Chinese people on the move, the initial movement of PRC immigrants to New Zealand and their subsequent movement elsewhere both connect to the recent liberalisation of the New Zealand Immigration Act of 1987, the changing economic and political atmospheres and power relation between these two countries, and the worldwide globalisation process.

In the above section, I briefly examined the development of the research on Chinese transnational migration and identified certain research gaps in this field in terms of both approach and focus. It is hoped that this book can address the paucity of the literature and provide a critique with reference to the New Zealand local context for the literature surrounding transnationalism. In this way, this study will contribute to a more comprehensive understanding of contemporary Chinese transnational migration and its changing characteristics.

The research approaches

Recent Chinese migrants, as Ip and Friesen (2001) argue, are neither "settlers" nor "sojourners". The former term indicates a one-way migration from the country of origin to the immigration destination country followed by permanent settlement (Yang, 1999). The latter term usually refers to the historical pattern of overseas Chinese during the gold-rush years who made a living overseas as long-term labourers without organising any permanent residence and always expecting an eventual return to the homeland for retirement (Yang, 2000). However, many of the new Chinese migrants do not fit precisely into either of these categories because of their constant mobility. Ip (2000) points out that there is an increasing number of migrants who behave in a pattern that is a mixture of migration models. For example, migration to any particular host country is quite often the beginning of a "step-migration" to a third destination. Even for those Chinese who recently returned to China, their re-settlement in the homeland may not be permanent; rather, it may be only a periodic visit or stay followed by further movement.

This migration trend requires a shift in the traditional approach to understand the patterns, trends, and reasons for these migrants to stay in the country of immigration relatively permanently, return to the places of their origin, continue commuting between place of origin and immigration destination country, or further immigrate to a third country. Therefore, this research proposes a non-linear approach for examining Chinese migrant mobility. "Return migration", "step-migration", or frequent commuting between different countries is only one part or phase of Chinese migrants' on-going transnational trajectories and the varied manifestations of their multi-locational transnational characteristic. To apply this research approach into methodology, the qualitative interview questions and the quantitative questionnaire that used to collect data were designed to check the migratory movement history as well as the ongoing movement plan and intentions for the near future. This longitudinal approach applied in the qualitative interviews also involves revisiting previous participants about 6 years after the first interview.

Secondly, since migration across borders usually involves family considerations, this research recognises the significant influence coming from family that may govern decision-making during the migration and re-location processes. For example, young adult migrants, either with their immediate families or not, often came to New Zealand as principal applicants. Later they found that job opportunities were more abundant in a third country or in their homeland where they had accumulated considerable social networks and economic and cultural capital. This realisation often determines their further movement to a third country or the return to their country of origin. Homeward movements are often necessitated by the fact that aging parents require long-term care because of declining health. For the children of return Chinese migrants, once they reach school age, many of their returnee parents consider bringing them back to New Zealand for their education because the education system in New Zealand is more stimulating and more liberal. This educational perspective may also produce a family split where one spouse stays in New Zealand to supervise the children while the other works outside New Zealand to support the family financially. The older generation, usually the parents of the principal applicants, might go to New Zealand to enjoy their retirement in a relatively peaceful and less pressured environment or be asked to come to New Zealand to look after their grandchildren. Quite often, when their adult children are driven to return to their country of origin by the economic attractiveness of the homeland, these parents will instead stay in New Zealand. They no longer like or need a bustling urban atmosphere, and New Zealand's peaceful environment is more suitable for them. To recap, these migrant families are required to function in a transnational social space (Faist, 2000), in which lives of different family members span geographic, cultural, linguistic, and political boundaries and are under a constant state of convergence and divergence resulting from their spatial separation and dislocation.

Of all of these possibilities, it is important to recognise that family units may be geographically split or extended over different continents and yet remain "a family" in the truest essence of the word. Further, where individual members of a family are located can have a strong impact on the mobility patterns of other members. Most significantly, where the older generation is located will affect the younger generation's sense of "home". This often impacts the younger generation's decision to re-locate or undertake an ultimate longer term "settlement". Children's education has also emerged as a particularly important factor that provides a strong impetus for families to go transnational (Waters, 2005).

Taking these factors into account, instead of looking at each individual migrant as a research unit, this research considers families as the major units of investigation. This research approach is applied especially when a substantial new PRC Chinese migrant community has evolved and formed after three decades of immigration and settlement. The existing of this migrant community is evidence by the presence of many multi-generational families including parents, grandparents, and grandchild generations (Liu, 2016). Therefore, a three-generation framework that encompasses first generational migrant parents, their children and their elderly parents, has been developed and employed to investigate the role that a requirement for multi-country residence plays in the experiences of PRC migrant families in New Zealand.

In doing so, the qualitative interviews were conducted with PRC migrant families whose members are living in multiple locations, including New Zealand, China, and Australia. The latter two countries are often the destinations for new PRC migrants who embark on further migratory movements, either onward or back to China. All three generations of the chosen families were interviewed individually if applicable. The interview questions and the quantitative questionnaire that used to collect data in this research were particularly designed to check the location and movement of three generations in the family: the principal applicants and their spouses, the elderly parents, and the children (1.5 generation[7] and second generation)[8]. This means of asking questions remedies the importance of previously overlooked family factors. Instead of asking the interviewees' own intentions, commitment, and the degree of satisfaction with their decision-making, this research asks how decision-making takes place within the family, how the movements of family members differ from each other, and what the input of other family members was in the decision-making processes.

Although the detailed research methodologies will be discussed in greater detail in Chapter 3, it is worth highlighting here the general characteristics of the methodologies. In summary, qualitative in-depth interviews, quantitative on-line survey, and data analysis on New Zealand official immigration data are used, drawing on widely used and tested approaches in the social sciences, anthropology, and human geography (Crang, 2002; Crick & Geddes, 1998; Flick, 2002; Fontana & Frey, 1994; Hay, 2005; Hughes & Sharrock, 2007; Robson, 2002; Schweizer, 1998; Trift, 2000). Guided by the multi-method research approach, the use of both qualitative and quantitative methods for this research was determined by the belief that multiple data collected by using different strategies is "likely to result in complementary strengths and non-overlapping weaknesses" (Johnson & Onwuegbuzie, 2004, p. 18). In other words, the qualitative method provides rich and in-depth insights, while the quantitative method provides hard and general data (Sieber, 1973). To illustrate the character of transnationality and the multi-locational movements of PRC new migrants, multi-sited ethnographic interview (Hannerz, 1998; Marcus, 1995) was employed to collect the qualitative data from chosen PRC migrant families whose family members were pursuing different transnational trajectories and locating in different countries. The quantitative online survey was virtually multi-locational because it targeted Chinese immigrants with New Zealand permanent residence or citizenship worldwide.

Hypotheses and positioning

The research hypothesises that the forces determining the movement of new Chinese migrants from the PRC are multi-layered, and it is far too simplistic to try to examine these forces in the traditional model of "permanent settlement". The transnational behaviour of new Chinese migrants is instead associated with a variety of macro and micro factors and the forces of globalisation and economic and political transformations in both New Zealand and China, the "Greater China"[9] region and beyond. Out of necessity and/or out of choice, new migrants will employ multi-locational strategies to suit the different stages of their own life cycle, as well as the particular needs of their family members. This research also hypothesises that family is no longer a tight integral unit in contemporary immigration flow. Family members are spatially scattered, but they remain connected by only loose, yet resilient, networks. Particular needs and family links across continents and likely dictate the locations of individual family members.

This book proposes then that the kaleidoscopic facets associated with contemporary Chinese immigration and transnational migration have been frequently examined, but under-theorised. The traditional approach, such as neo-classical economics[10] and the new economics of migration,[11] which regard migration processes as economically driven, are inadequate to explain the complex phenomenon of contemporary Chinese immigration and re-migration. While permanent migration has been an enduring feature of immigration practice, transnational migration seems to be more in line with the multi-faceted nature of contemporary Chinese migration. As discussed earlier, the complexity of current Chinese immigration to New Zealand requires a shift in approach to understand the migratory movements of the researched cohort.

This book takes shape within a growing body of literature on transnationalism. With the size of current migration flows and the extent of homeland and destination linkages, transnationalism deserves new significance in any understanding of immigration (Bartley, 2003; Spoonley & Macpherson, 2004). As Hugo (1999) suggests, through the first decade of the twenty-first century, the importance of "temporary" migration, as distinct from the classic "settler" migration of the previous century, will become ever more obvious to researchers and policy makers. In the particular case of focusing on the new Chinese migrants in the New

Zealand scene, the powerful forces of globalisation seem to be complicating their permanent settlement in a local society. The phenomenon of many of these newcomers keeping a tie to their homelands or with the trans-Pacific region is very much alive and actually a current facet of world economic trends and technological advancements that range beyond the borders of individual nations and affect communities in broadly similar ways.

Organisation of the book

This book consists of eight chapters. The first introductory chapter is followed by a discussion of the contemporary trend for Chinese migration to New Zealand from early 1990s onwards with an emphasis on migration from the PRC. The discussion traces the shifting approach to migration in both sending countries (i.e. China) and receiving countries (i.e. New Zealand). China's changing policy perspectives regarding international emigration since the late 1970s and its changing geo-political circumstances have resulted in Chinese nationals being able to participate in international migration movements. New Zealand's approach has shifted since 1987 from a highly-selective policy based on race and national origin to one that approaches migration as rational economic subjects within a neoliberal immigration regime (Simon-Kumar, 2015). This policy change opened the door to migrants from a wider region, especially immigrants from Asian sources.

Chapter 3 offers a theoretical and methodological framework for the analysis and the discussion. The key theoretical assumptions that inform and guide the research are outlined in this chapter. They are based on a principal literature review of transnationalism as the theoretical framework for understanding the practices and experiences of transnational Chinese migrants from China. Considerable attention is given to tracing the original theoretical articulation of this theory, its conceptual refinement, theoretical reformulation, and recent development in relation to those issues immediately associate with transmigration, such as citizenship, identity, sense of home, and belonging. The insights obtained from this literature review are then integrated into the discussion of how the theory of transnationalism in migration studies is relevant to and used in this research project. The second part of this chapter briefly introduces the methodological approach, which consists of both the qualitative and quantitative techniques used to collect the data and arrive at an overall precise understanding of the research topic.

Chapters 4 and 5 present the qualitative interview results, and Chapters 6 and 7 present the quantitative findings. Based on multi-sited ethnographic fieldwork interviews in China, Australia, and New Zealand with transnational PRC migrant families, Chinese who stepped into Australia, Chinese who commute between New Zealand and China or other places frequently, and Chinese who have had no prolonged absence from New Zealand but have kept strong ties with immediate migrant family members outside of New Zealand, Chapter 4 focuses on revealing the physical transnational migratory trajectories of the PRC migrants, the underlying reasons and its related family and inter-generational issues. Chapter 5 however, specifically unveils the emotional experience of highly mobile Chinese migrants, including their conceptualisation of "home" and sense of identity and belonging in association with their perceptions towards citizenship. Chapter 6 focuses on examining trans-Tasman migration of PRC Chinese migrants based on the results from a quantitative online survey and analysis of the Permanent and Long-term (PLT) departure and arrival data from Immigration New Zealand (INZ).[12] Based on the same PLT data set, Chapter 7 however compares return migration pattern of the PRC migrants with four other major non-white migrant groups from the Asian-Pacific region (i.e. Korea, Taiwan, India, and Pacific Island region including Fiji, Samoa, and Tonga). It is through comparison that the distinct feature of return migration pattern of the PRC migrants can be shown.

The final chapter of this book (Chapter 8) draws together the contextual and theoretical discussions offered with the data presented in previous chapters to delivers a discussion and a conclusion. Based on the most significant findings of the research, this chapter offers summarising remarks about the recent trends of Chinese international migration and transnational migration, and a reflection of these new trends to the vastly changing global situation, and rethinks about notions like Chinese modernity, globalisation, translocality, Chineseness, and hybridity.

Notes

1 The Asian Infrastructure Investment Bank (AIIB) is an international financial institution that aims to support the building of infrastructure in the Asia-Pacific region. It was proposed as an initiative by the government of China in October 2013, and started operation after the agreement entered into force on 25 December 2015. The incentive to establish the AIIB is mainly because the Chinese government has been frustrated with the slow pace of joining some major global institutions established like the World Bank and Asian Development Bank, and insignificant input in these institutions. Major economies that have not become the Prospective Founding Members (PFM) include Japan, the US, and Canada which applied for membership on 23 September 2016.

2 "New Chinese migrants" in the New Zealand context is a term that usually refers to Chinese who emigrated to New Zealand after the introduction of the Immigration Act 1987, which abolished the "traditional origin" preference term that favoured British migrants. Among the new Chinese migrants the three major sources are migrants from Hong Kong, Taiwan, and the PRC. These three groups plus Chinese from other countries (e.g. Malaysia, Indonesia etc.) are all categorised as new Chinese migrants in New Zealand. New Chinese migrants are distinct from the earlier Chinese migrants in New Zealand. The earliest Chinese migrants to New Zealand were almost exclusively males, with little or no education, originating from rural Southern China, either directly or by way of other countries, and they migrated primarily for the economic opportunities found in the gold mines in the Western world and the tin mines and plantations in Central America. The majority of contemporary Chinese migrants are ethnically more diverse, as well as highly educated and possess specialised skills or financial capital, which lets them qualify and meet the entry criteria of New Zealand.

3 In the book, the terms People's Republic of China (PRC) and China refer to the same country. These two terms are used interchangeably in the book.

4 The term "astronauting" refers to the phenomenon that occurs among some new Asian migrant families, in which usually the wife and children stay in the immigration receiving country, while the husband returns to the Asian homeland to work to provide financial support and only makes periodic trips to visit his family. The adoption of the "astronauting" strategy largely is one way to cope with the persistent frustration and dilemmas that confront many well-qualified professionals and business entrepreneurs who unable to find suitable employment or business opportunity in their new country.

5 New Zealand Residence Programme (NZRP) was renamed from New Zealand Immigration Programme (NZIP) in July 2006. The programme provides a package of immigration options to better manage immigration in New Zealand and improve the labour market contribution of temporary and permanent migration.

6 In the report by New Zealand Department of Labour, long-term absentees are defined as those who have spent a period or periods of time overseas for more than six months since their arrival as residents.

7 "1.5 generation" refers to migrants' children who accompanied or followed their first generation migrant parents to immigrate to a country when they were young.

8 "Second generation" refers to migrants' children who were born in an immigration destination country.

9 The idea of "Greater China" is one of those products derived from speculation on the re-emergence of China as a powerful actor in world politics and economy. There has been no precise definition of the concept. Whether the term should cover Hong Kong, Macao, Taiwan, and all of the People's Republic of China (PRC) or only parts of it depends on which aspects are emphasised in a particular context. If this term derives from a political perspective, it may refer to a future unified China when Hong Kong, Macao, Taiwan, and the PRC are brought together. If this term is from an economic perspective, it may only refer to the Southern coastal provinces, Hong Kong and Taiwan, which represent the South China Economy Periphery. If this term is from a cultural perspective, it may refer to the tradition of Chinese civilisation and what has transformed that culture in modern times. In this way, many ethnic Chinese now residing abroad might find this idea of a cultural "Greater China" more possible to identify with quite easily.

10 Neoclassical economics assumes that people move permanently abroad to maximize their lifetime earnings. The concept focuses on differentials in wages and employment conditions between countries and also on migration costs.

11 New economics of migration conceptualises migrant movements as temporary measures designed to overcome market deficiencies in the homeland and undertaken as a household decision to minimise risks to the family income.

12 Immigration New Zealand (INZ), formerly the New Zealand Immigration Service (NZIS), is the agency of the New Zealand Ministry of Business, Innovation and Employment responsible for issuing travel visas and managing immigration to New Zealand.

References

Ahmed, S. (1999). Home and away: Narratives of migration and estrangement. *International Journal of Cultural Studies, 2*(3), 329–347.

Ahmed, S., Castaneda, C., Fortier, A. M., & Sheller, M. (2003). Introduction: Uprootings/regroundings: Questions of home and migration. In S. Ahmed, C. Castaneda, A. M. Fortier, & M. Sheller (Eds.), *Uprootings/Regroundings: Questions of Home and Migration* (pp. 1–19). Oxford: Berg.

Al-Ali, N., & Khoser, K. (2002). Transnationalism, international migration and home. In N. Al-Ali, & K. Khoser (Eds.), *New Approaches to Migration Transnational Communities and the Transformation of Home* (pp. 1–14). London: Routledge.

Ang, I. (2015). At home in Asia? Sydney's Chinatown and Australia's 'Asian century'. *International Journal of Cultural Studies, 19*(3), 257–269.

Bartley, A. (2003). *"New" New Zealanders, or Harbingers of A New Transnationalism? 1.5 Generation Asian Migrant Adolescents in New Zealand.* (PhD), Massey University, Albany, Auckland.

Basu, P. (2004). My own island home: The Orkney coming. *Journal of Material Culture, 9*(1), 27–42.

Beal, T. (2001). Taiwanese business migration to Australia and New Zealand. In M. Ip (Ed.), *Re-Examining Chinese Transnationalism in Australia-New Zealand* (pp. 25–44). Canberra: CSCSD, Australia National University.

Bedford, R. (2001). Reflections on the spatial odysseys of New Zealanders. *The New Zealand Geographer, 57*(1), 49–54.

Blunt, A. (2005). *Domicile and Diaspora: Anglo-Indian Women and the Spatial Politics of Home.* Oxford: Blackwell Publishing.

Blunt, A., & Dowling, R. (2006). *Home.* London: Routledge.

Blunt, A., & Varley, A. (2004). Introduction: Geographies of 'home'. *Cultural Geographies, 11,* 3–6.

Bowlby, S., Gregory, S., & McKie, L. (1997). 'Doing home': Patriarchy, caring and space. *Women's Studies International Forum, 20*(3), 343–350.

Brady, A. (2008). New Zealand-China relations: Common points and differences. *New Zealand Journal of Asian Studies, 10*(2), 1–20.

Broomfield, E. V. (2003). Perceptions of danger: The China threat theory. *Journal of Contemporary China, 12*(35), 265–284.

Butcher, A. (2003). *No Place Like Home? The Experiences of South-East Asian International Students in New Zealand and Their Re-Entry Into Their Countries of Origin.* (PhD), Massey University, Albany, New Zealand.

Butcher, A. (2010). Demography, diaspora and diplomacy: New Zealand's Asian challenges. *New Zealand Population Review, 36,* 137–157.

Chiang, L. N., Hibbins, R., & Chui, W. H. (2006). Immigrant Taiwanese women in the process of adapting to life in Australia: Case studies from transnational households. In D. Ip, R. Hibbins., & W. H. Chui (Eds.), *Experiences of Transnational Chinese Migrants in the Asia-Pacific* (pp. 69–86). New York: Nova Science Publishers.

Collins, F. L. (2009). Connecting home with here: Personal homepages in everyday transational lives. *Journal of Ethnic and Migration Studies, 35*(6), 839–859.

Crang, M. (2002). Qualitative methods: The new orthodoxy? *Progress in Human Geography, 26*(5), 647–655.

Crick, M., & Geddes, B. (1998). Introduction. In M. Crick, & B. Geddes (Eds.), *Research Methods in the Field: Eleven Anthropological Accounts* (pp. 1–15). Geelong, VIC: Deakin University Press.

Elder, C., & Ayson, R. (2012). *China's Rise and New Zealand's Interests: A Policy Primer for 2030* (Discussion Paper No. 11). Wellington: Centre for Strategic Studies, New Zealand Victoria University of Wellington.

English, B. (2015). *New Zealand Formally Joins Asian Infrastructure Investment Bank.* Retrieved March 22, 2017 from www.beehive.govt.nz/release/new-zealand-formally-joins-asian-infrastructure-investment-bank

Faist, T. (2000). Transnationalization in international migration: Implications for the study of citizenship and culture. *Ethnic and Racial Studies, 23*(2), 189–222.

Flick, U. (2002). Qualitative research – state of the art. *Social Science Information, 41*(1), 5–24.

Fontana, A., & Frey, J. H. (1994). Interviewing: The Art of Science. In N. Denzin, & Y. Lincoln (Eds.), *Handbook of Qualitative Research* (pp. 361–376). London: Sage.

Hannerz, U. (1998). Transnational research. In H. R. Bernard (Ed.), *Handbook of Methods in Cultural Anthropology* (pp. 235–256). Walnut Creek, CA: Altamira Press.

Hay, I. (2005). *Qualitative Research Methods in Human Geography.* South Melbourne, VIC: New York: Oxford University Press.

Henderson, A. M. (2003). Untapped talents: The employment and settlement experiences of skilled Chinese in New Zealand. In M. Ip (Ed.), *Unfolding History, Evolving Identity: The Chinese in New Zealand* (pp. 141–164). Auckland: Auckland University Press.

Henderson, A. M., Trlin, A., Pernice, R., & North, N. (1997). English language requirements and immigration policy in New Zealand, 1986–1997. *New Zealand Population Review, 23*(1/2), 19–44.

Henderson, A. M., Trlin, A., & Watts, N. (2001). Squandered skills? The employment problems of skilled Chinese immigrants in New Zealand. In R. Starrs (Ed.), *Asian Nationalism in An Age of Globalization* (pp. 106–123). Richmond, Surrey: Curzon Press Japan Library.

Ho, E. (2003). Reluctant exiles or roaming transnationals? The Hong Kong Chinese in New Zealand. In M. Ip (Ed.), *Unfolding History, Evolving Identity: The Chinese in New Zealand* (pp. 165–184). Auckland: Auckland University Press.

Ho, E., & Bedford, R. (2008). Asian transnational families in New Zealand: Dynamics and challenges. *International Migration, 46*(4), 41–62.

Ho, E., Bedford, R., & Goodwin, J. (1997). Astronaut families: A contemporary migration phenomenon. In W. Friesen, M. Ip, E. Ho, R. Bedford, & J. Goodwin (Eds.), *East Asian New Zealanders: Research on New Migrants, Aotearoa/New Zealand Migration Research Network Research Papers* (pp. 20–39). Palmerston North: Department of Sociology, Massey University.

Ho, E., Ip, M., & Bedford, R. (2001). Transnational Hong Kong Chinese families in the 1990s. *New Zealand Journal of Geography*, 24–30.

Huang, S., Yeoh, B. S. A., & Lanm, T. (2008). Asian transnational families in transition: The liminality of simultaneity. *International Migration, 46*(4), 3–13.

Hughes, J. A., & Sharrock, W. W. (2007). *Theory and Methods in Sociology: An Introduction to Sociological Thinking and Practice.* Basingstoke, New York: Palgrave Macmillan.

Hugo, G. (1999). A new paradigm of international migration in Australia. *New Zealand Population Review, 25*(1 & 2), 1–39.

Hugo, G. (2005). The new international migration in Asia. *Asian Population Studies, 1*(1), 93–120.

Ip, M. (2000). Beyond the 'settler' and 'astronaut' paradigms: A new approach to the study of new Chinese immigrants to New Zealand. In M. Ip, K. M. Kang, & S. Page (Eds.), *Migration and Travel Between Asia and New Zealand, Aotearoa/New Zealand Migration Research Network Research Paper* (pp. 3–17). Palmerston North: Department of Sociology, Massey University.

Ip, M. (2001). Chinese business immigrants to New Zealand: Transnationals or failed investors? In M. Ip (Ed.), *Re-Examining Chinese Transnationalism in*

Australia-New Zealand (pp. 45–59). Canberra: Centre for the Study of the Chinese Southern Diaspora, Australian National University.

Ip, M. (2003a). Chinese Immigrants and Transnationals in New Zealand: A Fortress Opened. In J. C. Ma, & C. Cartier (Eds.), *The Chinese Diaspora: Space, Place, Mobility and Identity* (pp. 339–358). Lanham: Rowman & Littlefield Publishers, Inc.

Ip, M. (2003b). Seeking the last Utopia: The Taiwanese in New Zealand. In M. Ip (Ed.), *Unfolding History, Evolving Identity: The Chinese in New Zealand* (pp. 185–210). Auckland: Auckland University Press.

Ip, M. (2006). Returnees and transnationals: Evolving identities of Chinese (PRC) immigrants in New Zealand. *Journal of Population Studies, 33*, 61–102.

Ip, M. (2011). Rethinking contemporary Chinese circulatory transmigration: The New Zealand case. In M. Ip (Ed.), *Transmigration and the New Chinese: Theories and Practices From the New Zealand Experience* (pp. 21–56). Hong Kong: The Centre of Asian Studies of the University of Hong Kong.

Ip, M., & Friesen, W. (2001). The new Chinese community in New Zealand: Local outcomes of transnationalism. *Asian and Pacific Migration Journal, 10*(2), 213–240.

Johnson, R. B., & Onwuegbuzie, J. O. (2004). Mixed methods research: A research paradigm whose time has come. *Educational Researcher, 33*(7), 14–26.

Liu, L. (2009). Home is calling? Or home is on the move? Return Chinese immigrants of New Zealand as transnationals. *New Zealand Journal of Asian Studies, 11*(2), 164–171.

Liu, L. (2011). New Zealand case study of PRC transnational migration: Returnees and trans-Tasman migrants. In M. Ip (Ed.), *Transmigration and the New Chinese: Theories and Practices From the New Zealand Experience* (pp. 57–101). Hong Kong: The Centre of Asian Studies of the University of Hong Kong.

Liu, L. (2013). A search for a place to call home: Negotiation of home, identity and sense of belonging among new migrants from the people's republic of China (PRC) to New Zealand. *Emotion, Space and Society.*

Liu, L. (2014). PRC Chinese transnational migration in the case of New Zealand: Returnees and trans-Tasman migrants. *The International Journal of Diasporic Chinese Studies, 6*(1), 41–71.

Liu, L. (2015). Examining trans-Tasman migration of New Zealand's new immigrants from the People's Republic of China: A quantitative survey. *Asia Pacific Viewpoint, 56*(2), 297–314.

Liu, L. (2016). Intergenerational dimensions of transnational Chinese migrant families in New Zealand. *Journal of Chinese Overseas, 12*(2), 216–250.

Liu, L., & Lu, J. (2015). Contesting transnational mobility among New Zealand's Chinese migrants from an economic perspective: What does an online survey tell? *Journal of Chinese Overseas, 11*(2), 146–173.

Mallett, S. (2004). Understanding home: A critical review of the literature. *The Sociological Review, 52*(1), 62–89.

Marcus, G. E. (1995). Ethnography in/of the world system: The emergence of multi-sited ethnography. *Annual Review of Anthropology, 24*, 95–117.

New Zealand Contemporary China Research Centre. (2015). *New Zealand's China Policy: Building a Comprehensive Strategic Partnership.* Sydney: Australia-China Relations Institute (ACRI), University of Technology Sydney.

New Zealand Foreign Affairs & Trade. (2015). *Opending Doors to China: New Zealan's 2015 Vision.* Retrieved March 21, 2017 from www.mfat.govt.nz/assets/_securedfiles/NZ-Inc-stategy/NZ-Inc-China/NZInc-Strategy-China.pdf

New Zealand Ministry of Business Innovation and Employment. (2013). *Migration Trend and Outlook 2012/2013*. Wellington, New Zealand: New Zealand Ministry of Business, Innovation and Employment.

Pe-Pua, R., Mitchell, C., Iredale, R., & Castles, S. (1996). *Astronaut Families and Parachute Children: The Cycle of Migration Between Hong Kong and Australia*. Wollongong, Australia: Centre for Multicultural Studies, University of Wollongong.

Pieke, F. (2012). Immigrant China. *Modern China, 38*, 40–77.

Pratt, G. (2004). *Working Feminism*. Philadelphia: Temple University Press.

Rapport, N., & Dawson, A. (1998). The topic and the book. In N. Rapport & A. Dawson (Eds.), *Migrants of Identity: Perceptions of Home in a World of Movement* (pp. 3–18). Oxford: Berg Press.

Robson, C. (2002). *Real World Research: A Resource for Social Scientists and Practitioner – Researchers*. Oxford, UK: Blackwell Publishers.

Schweizer, T. (1998). Epistemology: The nature and validation of anthropological knowledge. In H. R. Bernard (Ed.), *Handbook of Methods in Cultural Anthropology* (pp. 39–87). Walnut Creek, California: A Division of Sage Publications, Inc.

Sieber, S. D. (1973). The integration of fieldwork and survey methods. *American Journal of Sociology, 73*, 1335–1359.

Simon-Kumar, R. (2015). Neoliberalism and the new race politics of migration policy: Changing profiles of the desirable migrant in New Zealand. *Journal of Ethnic and Migration Studies, 41*(7), 1172–1191.

Skeldon, R. (1994a). Hong Kong in an international migration system. In R. Skeldon (Ed.), *Reluctant Exiles? Migration From Hong Kong and the New Overseas Chinese* (pp. 21–51). Hong Kong: Hong Kong University Press.

Skeldon, R. (1994b). Reluctant exiles or bold pioneers: An introduction to migration from Hong Kong. In R. Skeldon (Ed.), *Reluctant Exile? Migration From Hong Kong and the New Overseas Chinese* (pp. 3–18). Hong Kong: Hong Kong University Press.

Skeldon, R. (1996). Migration from China. *Journal of International Affairs, 49*(2), 434–455.

Skeldon, R. (2004). *China: From Exceptional Case to Global Participants*. Retrieved August 6, 2009 from www.migrationinformation.org/Profiles/display.cfm?ID=219

Skeldon, R. (2006). The case of Hong Kong. In L. Pan (Ed.), *The Encyclopedia of the Chinese Overseas* (pp. 67–70). Singapore: The Chinese Heritage Centre.

Spoonley, P., & Macpherson, C. (2004). Transnational New Zealand: Immigrants and cross-border connections and activities. In P. Spoonley, C. Macpherson, & D. Pearson (Eds.), *Tangata Tangata: The Changing Ethnic Contours of New Zealand* (pp. 175–194). South Victoria, Australia: Thomson/Dunmore Press.

Statistics New Zealand. (2014a). *2013 Census QuickStats About Culture and Identity – Birthplace and People Born Overseas*. Retrieved March 21, 2017 from www.stats.govt.nz/Census/2013-census/profile-and-summary-reports/quickstats-culture-identity/birthplace.aspx

Statistics New Zealand. (2014b). *Census QuickStats About Culture and Identity – Asian Ethnic Group*. Retrieved December 1, 2016 from www.stats.govt.nz/Census/2013-census/profile-and-summary-reports/quickstats-culture-identity/asian.aspx

Trift, N. (2000). Dead or alive? In I. Cook, D. Crouch, S. Naylor, & J. Ryan (Eds.), *Cultural Turns/Geographical Turns: Perspectives on Cultural Geography* (pp. 1–6). Harlow, Essex: Prentice Hall.

Waetjen, T. (1999). The 'home' in homeland: Gender, national space, and Inkatha's politics of ethnicity. *Ethnic and Racial Studies, 22*(4), 653–678.

Waters, J. (2002). Flexible families? 'Astronaut' households and the experience of lone mothers in Vancouver, British Columbia. *Social and Cultural Geography, 3*(2), 117–134.

Waters, J. (2005). Transnational family strategies and education in the contemporary Chinese diaspora. *Global Networks, 5*, 359–377.

Wiles, J. (2008). Sense of home in a transnational social space: New Zealanders in London. *Global Networks, 8*(1), 116–137.

Yang, P. (1999). Sojourners of settlers: Post-1965 Chinese immigrants. *Journal of Asian American Studies, 2*(1), 61–91.

Yang, P. (2000). The 'Sojourner Hypothesis' revisited. *Diaspora, 9*(2), 235–258.

Zhu, J. (2013). China attracting global top talent: Central and local government initiatives. In G. Wang & Y. Zheng (Eds.), *China: Development and Governance* (pp. 361–368). Singapore: World Scientific Publishing.

2 Chinese modernity and New Zealand's opening up – perspectives from both immigrant sending and receiving countries

Chinese immigrants have made up a significant part of the post-1987 immigrant intake of New Zealand after the enactment of the Immigration Act 1987. Of the new Chinese immigrant intake, Hong Kong, Taiwan, and the People's Republic of China (PRC) are the three main contributing sources (Ho, 2003). Chinese immigrants from the PRC are the most recent arrivals. Unlike the immigrants from Hong Kong and Taiwan who made their presence felt from the early 1990s onward, the presence of the new PRC immigrants in significant numbers occurred later (Ip, 2006b). Most immigrants started to arrive in the mid-1990s, and their numbers increased rapidly in the late 1990s making the PRC become not only the top contributing region for New Zealand's Chinese and Asian immigrant intake but also one of the top sources of New Zealand's overall immigrant intake (see Table 2.1). These patterns are a result of the changing geo-economic situation in both China and New Zealand and also inseparably connected to globalisation processes happening throughout the world.

Based on the China-born[1] specific data from Statistics New Zealand and the Immigration New Zealand (INZ), the objective of this chapter is to illustrate who these new PRC Chinese immigrants are and how this cohort is distinguishable from other ethnic Chinese (such as those from Hong Kong and Taiwan) and other major immigrant groups in New Zealand in terms of time of arrival, migration patterns and pathways, and demographic structure. First, a brief overview is provided for the migration-related policies of both the immigrant sending country (i.e. China) and receiving country (i.e. New Zealand). Since migration is often regarded as a product of discrete pushes and pulls because of changing geopolitics in both the receiving and the sending countries (Liu & Norcliffe, 1996; Ong, 1992; Zolberg, 1989), the perspectives of migration-related polices of both countries should be examined. New Zealand immigration policy after 1986 was conditioned to the arrival of new PRC Chinese immigrants, while changing policy perspectives toward international emigration since the late 1970s in China propelled immigration flows out of that country. I will first consider the conditions in China – its policy perspectives regarding emigration and the changing geopolitical circumstances resulted in Chinese being able to participate in international migration movements. I will then turn to review recent immigration policy changes in New Zealand. Those policy changes are analysed in more detail

Table 2.1 Approvals for residence by nationality and migrant stream/category, 1997/98–2015/16

Nationality	Total Approvals	Total Family Sponsorship	Family Sponsorship Sub-categories					Skilled/Business		International Humanitarian
			Spouse	Parents	Dependent Child	Siblings and Adult Child	Family Quota and Humanitarian	Skilled	Business	
Asia										
China	114064	55322	20149	26588	2205	4815	1565	44699	12799	1244
		48.5%	17.7%	23.3%	1.9%	4.2%	1.4%	39.2%	11.2%	1.1%
India	89695	29316	15168	10063	1044	2634	407	59312	362	705
		32.7%	16.9%	11.2%	1.2%	2.9%	0.5%	66.1%	0.4%	0.8%
South Korea	25130	5703	3368	1243	392	359	341	13432	5775	220
		22.7%	13.4%	4.9%	1.6%	1.4%	1.4%	53.5%	23.0%	0.9%
Philippine	44310	9598	6618	1190	1270	400	120	34252	40	420
		21.7%	14.9%	2.7%	2.9%	0.9%	0.3%	77.3%	0.1%	0.9%
Sub-total	273199	99939	45303	39084	4911	8208	2433	151695	18976	2589
% Asia	33.3%	35.5%	29.0%	51.7%	24.5%	42.7%	22.9%	34.5%	61.1%	2.6%
Pacific										
Fiji	47103	20534	8768	6302	1049	3153	1261	22279	695	3595
		43.6%	18.6%	13.4%	2.2%	6.7%	2.7%	47.3%	1.5%	7.6%
Samoa	38082	16379	7016	2021	6320	648	374	635	0	21068
		43.0%	18.4%	5.3%	16.6%	1.7%	1.0%	1.7%	0.0%	55.3%
Tonga	18410	9673	5432	2025	1005	848	363	1694	21	7022
		52.5%	29.5%	11.0%	5.5%	4.6%	2.0%	9.2%	0.1%	38.1%
Sub-total	103595	46586	21216	10348	8374	4649	1998	24608	716	31685
% Pacific	12.6%	16.5%	13.6%	13.7%	41.8%	24.2%	18.8%	5.6%	2.3%	30.6%

Other countries

Great Britain	141700	39098 27.6%	26552 18.7%	9960 7.0%	964 0.7%	1355 1.0%	267 0.2%	98220 69.3%	3115 2.2%	1267 0.9%
South Africa	64895	9932 15.3%	3412 5.3%	4649 7.2%	792 1.2%	891 1.4%	188 0.3%	53927 83.1%	485 0.7%	551 0.8%
US	21962	8589 39.1%	7525 34.3%	452 2.1%	417 1.9%	153 0.7%	42 0.2%	11843 53.9%	932 4.2%	598 2.7%
Sub-total	228557	57619	37489	15061	2173	2399	497	163990	4532	2416
% Other	27.9%	20.5%	24.0%	19.9%	10.9%	12.5%	4.7%	37.3%	14.6%	1.1%
Total top 10 countries	605351	204144	104008	64493	15458	15256	4928	340293	24224	36690
% res. Approvals	100%	33.7%	17.2%	10.7%	2.6%	2.5%	2.4%	56.2%	4.0%	6.1%
Total all countries	819693	281688	156184	75626	20017	19243	10618	439394	31038	67573
% res. Approvals	100%	34.4%	19.1%	9.2%	2.4%	2.3%	3.8%	53.6%	3.8%	8.2%
% from 10 countries	73.9%	72.5%	66.6%	85.3%	77.2%	79.3%	46.4%	77.4%	78.0%	54.3%

(Source: Immigration New Zealand)

elsewhere (Bedford, Farmer, & Trlin, 1987; Bedford, Ho, & Lidgard, 2005a; Henderson, Trlin, Pernice, & North, 1997; Ip, 1995; Trlin, 1997; Trlin & Kang, 1992); however, some significant changes, especially those relevant to Chinese immigration, are outlined and sketched here to provide an overview of their effects on the new Chinese immigrant inflow. These changes reveal an obvious neoliberal trend of the country's immigration policy development. They are then reviewed alongside an examination of the changing size of the ethnic Chinese population in New Zealand using the national census data from 1986 to 2013. In this way, the influx of new PRC Chinese immigrants can be placed in the context of policy changes since 1987 and the significance of New Zealand's immigration policy change on Chinese immigration is made known.

Secondly, the current characteristics of the PRC immigrant cohort are illustrated by examining the most recent statistical data from the New Zealand Census 2013 and INZ. A critical analysis of the relevant academic literature on new Chinese immigration into New Zealand will also be carried out to assist this overview. This focus exhibits the demographic structure, immigration pathways, and education and employment situations of the China-born population within New Zealand. These parameters can be used to indicate their settlement outcomes and socio-economic integration within the wider New Zealand society.

Migration policies of sending and receiving countries

China's perspective on international emigration

Conditions in countries of origin play a decisive role in the migration process. This section presents a brief discussion of the conditions regarding China's changing social, economic, and political situations and that country's policy towards international emigration. Individual Chinese migrant perspectives and motivations to immigrate to New Zealand are also discussed. The recent favourable economic development and social changes in China may influence immigration decision-making and patterns. On the one hand, these economic and social conditions have the potential strength to hold its residents in China; on the other hand, these same economic and social conditions may provide people with more financial and social capital available for migratory mobility. Since there is limited literature on the topic of China's policies and perspectives on emigration issues, the discussion that follows applies information from a few research articles and my personal empirical observations and knowledge of contemporary Chinese migration from China.

Compared with Hong Kong and Taiwan, whose people started moving overseas in the late 1960s, China came to the migration arena late (Ip, 2006b; Skeldon, 1996, 2004). As Liu and Norcliff (1996) point out, the reason was geopolitical. Even though China was the major source of Chinese immigration historically, the PRC China, a nation-state, established by the Chinese Communist Party after the Communist revolution of 1949, imposed extreme restrictive control over the international movements of its citizens. Like other Communist countries in

Eastern Europe and the Soviet Union, Cold War geopolitics characterised by East-West/socialist-capitalist confrontations led the PRC China to pursue strict border control and be a closed society with rare contact with the West until the late 1970s. Overseas travel was only possible if it was officially sanctioned. Such politicised border control blocked nearly all direct international emigration (Liu & Norcliffe, 1996; Xiang, 2003). The early years of the Cultural Revolution (from 1966 to 1969) further isolated the PRC China from the rest of the world. There were no new diplomatic relations established between China and other countries, and even worse, already established foreign relations were lessened and thus damaged. This situation literally meant the absence of official channels that could link China with immigrant-receiving countries (Liu & Norcliffe, 1996).

That situation started to change in the late 1970s. The Chinese government allowed students and scholars to study overseas beginning in 1978, but in the hope that they would still return to China. Most of these students were either on state scholarships or under institute sponsorship (Gittings, 1989; Luo, Guo, & Huang, 2003). After the implementation of economic reforms and open-door policies in 1979, the market-oriented economic system gradually opened China to contact with the outside world and freed its people's spatial movement, resulting in a gradual acceleration of international migration. The reason for this change was also geopolitical. With the recognition of Mao's foreign policy as perilous, a broken relationship with the Soviet Union, and the serious damage caused by the 10-year Cultural Revolution, China was forced to shift its foreign policy and seek an improvement in Sino-West relations and put an end to its isolation (Liu & Norcliffe, 1996). There were also significant changes in the Chinese government's perspectives on emigration. Xiang (2003) described the change as "a trend toward neutralisation" (p. 22). With this departure from a politicised perspective toward emigration, emigration is increasingly treated as a matter of individual choice and one that is "unrelated to the person's role in the state system" (Xiang, 2003, p. 22). Going to a capitalist country is no longer treated as a "betrayal" or politically incorrect.

Throughout the early 1990s, the Chinese government relaxed its restrictive control over international migration, producing a wave of Chinese people moving overseas. In 1981 the Chinese government formally recognised self-financed overseas study for the first time. That recognition produced a wave of student migration. Most were postgraduate-level students whose academic performance was good enough to secure scholarships at overseas universities (Luo et al., 2003; Skeldon, 1996; Xiang, 2003). This new wave of student migration led to settlement later in some cases, but it is fair to say that direct settlement migration rarely happened immediately. The vast majority of the Chinese population then had not yet been touched by international migration, and there was no official regulation that allowed Chinese citizens to go overseas. From a practical point of view, these were significant blockages in terms of encouraging Chinese nationals to migrate. To obtain a passport, one had to go through a long and complex process. Permission had to be sought from a variety of authorities and sources, and personal contact (*Guanxi* 关系) was crucial in charting such a course through the complex bureaucracy (Skeldon, 1996).

The official trigger for the increasing migration flow was the adoption of the Emigration and Immigration Law in November 1985. It guaranteed the rights of Chinese citizens to travel outside China and allowed those who wished to leave the country for private reasons to do so (Liu & Norcliffe, 1996; Skeldon, 1996). Together with the transformation in immigration policy that was occurring in some developed countries in North America and Australasia, migration from China was reinforced, and complex migration patterns began to appear (Skeldon, 1996). For example, the 1965 Immigration Act in the United States effectively removed all discriminatory quotas; the introduction of a revised immigration regulation in 1962 in Canada terminated the White Canada policy; ten years later, Australia ended its white immigration policy; and New Zealand removed the racial bias from its immigration policy in 1987. These radical changes in immigration policy in these prospective immigrant-receiving countries, together with China's open-door policy to the outside world, allowed some people from China to become part of the international context of transnational population mobility. Apart from student migration, there was also an increasing complexity in the migration patterns, such as settlement migration and labour migration (Skeldon, 1996, 2004; Xiang, 2003).

Following China's international opening-up, there has been significant social transformation and economic development in this country. This development was accompanied by ever increasing geographical mobility of its nationals and more population movement across borders. By the late 1990s, international migration was a growing phenomenon in China. These new Chinese migrants significantly differed from the Chinese migrants of the early nineteenth century. Very little migration took place to traditional destinations in Southeast Asia; instead settler societies in North America and Australasia became preferred choices (Skeldon, 2004). The earlier Chinese migration in the nineteenth century was mainly driven by both pull and push factors, with internal poverty, natural disasters, and warfare being the key factors that propelled that movement across the seas. The early Chinese migrants were mostly uneducated male peasants from rural Southern China, and they migrated primarily because of the economic opportunities found in the gold mines in the Western world and the tin mines and plantations in Central America (Eng, 2006a, 2006b; Skeldon, 1996, 2004).

Compared with these early Chinese migrants, the majority of contemporary Chinese migrants is highly educated and possesses specialised skills or financial capital, which lets them qualify and meet the entry criteria of the receiving countries. Looking for economic opportunities overseas is no longer the primary reason for the Chinese to migrate; rather, their movements are often hastened by non-economic reasons. Searching for "greener pastures" is a significant feature of contemporary Chinese migration. A better lifestyle and living environment, an advanced educational system, and sometimes the securing of foreign passports have propelled this migratory movement (Eng, 2006a). Some new types of migration also took place, such as settlement migration of families or individuals under skilled or business immigration categories. These immigration categories have in fact become the main channel used by many Chinese to migrate overseas (Skeldon, 1996, 2004).

It is important then to recognise that the fast-developing economy of China produces a great means of capital mobilisation for Chinese international migration. By the turn of the twenty-first century, it became clearly apparent that China had the potential to become a future economic superpower. Its official involvement into the World Trade Organization (WTO) in 2001 further accelerated its integration into the global economy. Although China's economic growth is slowing down a bit during the past four years, it is still the fastest-growing market in the world, and its GDP was growing more than three times faster than the USA economy especially in the early 2000s (Zeng & Williamson, 2003). The "One Belt One Road" initiation[2] – a development strategy proposed by Chinese President Xi Jinping that focuses on connectivity and cooperation with Eurasian, Oceania, and North of African countries – underlines China's push to take a larger role in global affairs and the desire to coordinate manufacturing capacity with other countries (Ngai, Sneader, & Zecha, 2016; Phillips, 2017). What happened simultaneously was that China also contributed significantly to those ethnic Chinese on the move. Toward the end of the twentieth century, an estimated 33 million ethnic Chinese were living outside China, Taiwan, and Hong Kong. These 33 million Chinese living overseas actually increased from around 22 million in 1985 and 12.7 million in the early 1960s. Given the general low fertility of overseas Chinese populations and much smaller population pools in other main sources of Chinese migration (i.e. Hong Kong and Taiwan), the significant increase of overseas Chinese population suggests the central role that Chinese people from China have played in Chinese international migration in recent years (Skeldon, 2004).

Meanwhile, the changing attitude of the Chinese government toward international emigration has also contributed significantly towards initialising Chinese nationals' movements internationally. International migration has been increasingly seen by the Chinese authorities as a means to enhance China's integration into the world economy. The Chinese government has shown both an apolitical and a neutral attitude when dealing with migration issues over the last twenty years, compared with earlier times (Xiang, 2003). The stance the Chinese government has taken most recently towards emigration as being non-ideological and non-political has given Chinese citizens an unprecedented freedom of international movement, including immigrating to New Zealand.

A neoliberal trend: New Zealand immigration policy from 1987 to present and its impact on Chinese immigrant intake

The presence of new PRC immigrants in New Zealand is a direct result of the *Immigration Policy Review* 1986 that introduced a proactive immigration policy to recruit talents and economic investment. The policy was refined further with the introduction of a points-based selection system in November 1991. The policy change opened the country to a much wider range of immigrants, irrevocably led to profound changes in New Zealand's migrant source countries (Trlin, 1992), and had a major impact on both the size and characteristics of the Chinese population in New Zealand. The distinguishing feature of New Zealand's immigration policy from the late 1980s onwards has been a consistent emphasis on encouraging the intake of both skilled and business immigrants (Bedford et al., 2005a). The Labour Government[3] initiated this emphasis, and since, it has been carried on by both the National[4] (1990–1999 and 2008 – current) and the Labour (1984–1990 and 1999–2008) governments.

There is another distinguishing feature of New Zealand's immigration policy – that is rather than developing a policy based on long-term social goals and overall planning, policy development has been frequently fine-turned and changed to counteract swings in permanent and long-term arrivals, and the departures and flow in net migration (Bedford & Ho, 1997). Usually, changes occurred to control the numbers of skilled immigrants through the introduction of more restrictive entry criteria as a response to the negative societal backlash provoked by a higher influx of new immigrants (Bedford et al., 2005a). It would appear that when the New Zealand government embarked on a revolutionary step forward towards adopting a colour-blind immigration policy, the society and public were not well enough prepared to encounter the cultural diversity that these new immigrants, especially those from "non-traditional" sources, were to bring into this country.

In the following sections, the reactive and frequent fine-tuning features of the post-1986 immigration policy will be illustrated along with reviews of the immigration policy after 1986. Trans-Tasman migration is also highlighted. Based on the Trans-Tasman Travel Arrangement, New Zealand and Australian citizens were not subjected to controls by the points systems in either country before the Australian policy change in 2001. Hence any policy relaxation in New Zealand that might lead to an increase of uncontrolled flow to Australia always has attracted close scrutiny (Bedford, Ho, & Lidgard, 2000; Hugo, 2004). It is impossible to provide a full policy review here, but a solid grasp of the legal and institutional context for the targeted research cohort (i.e. new Chinese migrants from China) is crucial to a better understanding of this cohort. This section thus highlights some of the significant changes to the structure of the New Zealand immigration policy following the 1986 changes, which had a major impact on the immigration of the research cohort. While the policy changes regarding the skilled and business migration was the focus of the policy review, the policy changes concerning the entry of migrants' family members, especially the elderly parents will be also discussed, as this chapter will later illustrate that the Parent Category of the Family Sponsorship Stream has been used far more frequently by new PRC Chinese migrants compared with other major migrant groups.

Immigration policy changes in the early 1990s and impacts on Chinese immigration

It is well known that New Zealand used to be extremely selective regarding its immigrant source country based on race, in particular preferring Britain (Mckinnon, 1996). Asian immigration was closely regulated, and the entry of Chinese was effectively restricted for a long period of time. However, changes started with the review of immigration policy in 1986 (see Table 2.2), which provided the policy basis for the Immigration Act 1987. This policy review proclaimed a liberal philosophy of selecting immigrants based on an assessment of personal merit, qualifications, and their potential financial and entrepreneurial contributions

Table 2.2 Summary of significant immigration policy changes in New Zealand (1987–2017)

Time	Main feature(s)	Detailed policy changes
1987	Immigration Act 1987	1 Abolished "traditional source country preference"; 2 Started to select immigrants based on 'personal qualities, skills, qualifications, potential contribution to New Zealand and capacity to settle well'.
1991	Point-based System	1 A point-based selection system was introduced in the General Category (GC). There were two sub-categories under the GC: General Skilled Category (GSC) and General Investment Category (GIC). In the GSC, points were given based on age, employability, qualification, and settlement factors (a maximum of 15 points to a tertiary education, 10 points to people aged between 25 and 29, 10 points to those who have 20 years working experience relevant to their qualifications). In the GIC, applicants score points on the basis of capital (NZ\$100,000 – NZ\$300,000) to be invested for at least two years. 2 The Business Investment Category (BIC) was introduced to replace the previous Business Immigration Policy (BIP). Three types of investment were specified: • A passive investment of NZ\$750,000 (e.g. in a bank account, trust fund or listed stocks); • An active investment of NZ\$625,000 in either Auckland or Wellington urban areas; • An active investment of NZ\$500,000 elsewhere in New Zealand.
1995	Policy tightening-up	1 The Business Investor Category replaced the previous Business Investment Category. Under the Business Investor Category, a full point-based ranking system was introduced. It aims to solve the shortcoming of the tendency of passive investment and lack of qualifications of applicants in the previous Business Investment Category; 2 An amended point system was introduced in the GSC. It redressed the bias towards academic qualifications and professional skills, and allowed applicants with trades or technical qualifications to score higher than before; thus, facilitated a broader skills mix; 3 The requirement of a statutory registration before point awarded was enforced for some professional qualifications, such as medical doctors;

(Continued)

Table 2.2 (Continued)

Time	Main feature(s)	Detailed policy changes
		4 Points for investment funds from the GIC was removed;
		5 A minimum Band score of 5 in general Training Modules of the International English Language Test System (IELTS) for adult applicants (over 16 years old) from non-English-speaking background and under the BIC and GC categories was required. NZ$20,000 language bond was applied to spouses and dependants 16 years and over if they failed to meet the English language requirements within the specified time.
2001	Introduction of the managed entry regime	A managed entry regime was introduced. It was deliberately designed to regulate the "economic" and "social" streams of immigrants. Within this managed entry regime;
		1 A Skilled/Business Stream was allocated 60 per cent of the government's total target for residence approvals;
		2 A Family Sponsorship Stream was allocated 30 per cent of the total target for residence approvals;
		3 An International/Humanitarian Stream was allocated 10 per cent of the total target of residence approvals.
2003	New Selection system: EOI	A new Skilled Migrant Category (SMC) was introduced to replace the previous GSC. It replaced the pass mark system with a process whereby people qualify a level of points (at least 100 points) can submit an expression of interests (EOI) into a selection pool, from which they were invited to apply for residence. Points were allocated on the basis of age, qualifications, a skilled job or offer, the regional location of the job offer, work experience and identified skills shortage. Bonus points are granted in certain circumstances and recognise partners' employment and experience, New Zealand qualifications and employment outside of Auckland.
2012	Two-tier system in Parent Category	1 The EOI application system was applied to applicants seeking permanent residence under the Parent Category. Applicants were required to submit an EOI before making a formal application to enter New Zealand as permanent residents;
		2 EOIs must be submitted with reference to criteria applying to two tiers of entry.
		• Tier 1 has the first priority and currently has a queue of around 18 months for applicants awaiting assessment. The key requirement for Tier 1 is that the applicants must have a sponsoring child (or the child's spouse or partner) with a gross income of at least NZ$65,000 per annum or a combined gross income of NZ$90,000.
		• Tier two has lower priority and already has a waiting time for assessment estimated to be up to seven years, Applicants under the Tier 2 scheme mush have a sponsoring adult child who meets a minimum gross income figure (NZ$33,675) and, if they have other adult children, they must be living lawfully and be permanently resident outside the country they come from.

Time	Main feature(s)	Detailed policy changes
2016	Tightening-up of the SMC and closure of Parent Category	1 The number of points required for residence is raised from 140 to 160 points under the SMC; 2 The average band score of the International English Language Testing System (IELTS) has increased from 5 to 6.5. 3 The Parent Category in the Family Sponsorship Stream is closed for at least two years.
2017	Changes on the SMC and Essential Skills Visa category	1 Under the Skilled Migration Category (SMC), two remuneration thresholds are being introduced for applicants applying for residence. The first band would mean those earning under the NZ$49,000 median wage would no longer be considered highly skilled while those earning above the 1.5 times median income threshold of NZ$73,000 would automatically be regarded as high skilled; 2 As for the Essential Skills Visa, a three-year limit would be placed on those visa holders earning below the threshold of NZ$49,000. Moreover, if their partners want to come to live in New Zealand for long term, they have to meet the requirements for a visa in their own right

(Sources: *New Zealand and International Migration: A Digest and Bibliography 1, 2, 3, 4, 5*; Immigration New Zealand)

to New Zealand society (Ip, 1995). With the removal of the traditional source country preference in favour of selection based on "criteria of personal merit without discrimination on grounds of race, national or ethnic origin" (Burke, 1986, p. 11), Asian immigration increased dramatically, and Chinese arrived in unexpectedly large numbers.

It is necessary to point out the social, economic, and political context of the policy change in 1986. First, this immigration policy change was part of the Fourth Labour government's overall economic de-regulation and restructuring programme (Poot, 1992; Trlin, 1992). For more than a decade earlier, New Zealand had suffered a serious economic downturn for a variety of reasons, including a closed economy, loss of Britain as a guaranteed market, growing public debt, and the costs of maintaining a universal welfare system (Ho, Lidgard, Bedford, & Spoonley, 1997). The Fourth Labour Government which came into power in 1984 was determined to embark upon a radical path of economic de-regulation in order to revitalise the country's economy. It is in this context that immigration was encouraged, especially entrepreneurial immigration that "demonstrated ability and investment capital" which could contribute to the process of "economic restructuring and . . . the development of new competitive industries and markets" (Burke, 1986, p. 19). The use of immigration was seen as a positive means to attract more foreign investment capital and stimulate domestic economic growth.

Second, the new immigration policy sought to use immigration to remedy the "brain-drain" that was resulting from steady net migration loss due to the strong out-migration of young educated New Zealanders (Henderson, 2003; Kasper, 1990). During the 1970s and 1980s, New Zealand had been steadily losing people with a net migration loss averaging 18,000 per year (Bedford, Lidgard, & Young, 1995). Therefore, opening the door of the country to immigration was seen as necessary and a major part of New Zealand's social restructuring. The country chose to invite quality immigrants to make a contribution to the society.

Finally, there was a tentative desire to use immigration as a way to link to the Pacific Rim countries of Asia where a booming economic miracle was exemplified by the "Asian Little Dragons"[5] (Henderson, 2003; Ip, 1995; Trlin & Kang, 1992). Upon seeing a competitive global economy that was increasingly influenced by Asian industrial production and markets, New Zealand gradually realised the importance of integrating their country more closely with that part of the world where it was geographically located and of establishing stronger business links with the new powerhouses of Asia. This policy choice partly depended on the human capital that the new immigration policy might allow to enter the country (Trlin, 1992).

As a part of the Labour commitment to a free market economic philosophy and programme, the removal of the traditional source country bias was coupled with the introduction of a new business immigration scheme – the Business Immigration Policy (BIP). The BIP replaced the earlier scheme, known as the Entrepreneur Immigration Policy (EIP) (Poot, 1992; Trlin, 1992; Trlin & Kang, 1992). The priority for selection criteria for the new scheme was an individual applicant's personal merits rather than an investment proposal (see Table 2.2). Poot (1992) indicated that in a 42-month period (September 1986 – March 1990), 2,874 cases involving 10,581 people were approved for residence under the BIP scheme, compared with 225 EIP applications in the same period that only produced 788 successful applicants. The new arrivals under this BIP were also increasingly dominated, from April 1987 onwards, by migrants from Hong Kong and Taiwan (Trlin & Kang, 1992). It was the first time that ethnic Chinese immigrants arrived in New Zealand in large numbers based on an equal selection basis with other immigrants. Since then, ethnic Chinese have become a sizeable cultural group in New Zealand. According to the census, the ethnic Chinese population in New Zealand was just below 19,500 in 1986, and it increased to around 38,000 in 1991. By the next census in 1996, it had doubled yet again to just over 80,000 (Ip, 2006a).

When the National Government came to power in 1990, it maintained the previous Labour Government's programme of economic deregulation, but then accentuated it with a more proactive stance towards international immigration. National's 1991 policy changes primarily featured the introduction of a revised Business Investment Category (BIC) to replace the previous BIP and the encouragement of skilled immigration via a General Category (GC) that involved a point-based selection system (Trlin, 1997) (see Table 2.2). The point system in particular shifted the focus from obtaining immediate economic and financial benefit from new immigrants to a greater determination to secure human capital and quality migrants who had as their objectives making a contribution to the nation's economic growth and strengthening international linkages required for that growth (Birch, 1989; Trlin, 1997). It was supposed to be a " 'key instrument' to attract greater number of 'quality migrants' who would make a positive contribution to economic and social development" (Trlin, 1997, p. 5). This new system favourably targeted people with tertiary education who were young and had a track record of gainful employment (Ip, 1995).

This auto-pass, point-based system had a significant impact on the numbers and composition of the new Chinese immigrant cohort arriving in New Zealand. The Asian presence[6] among the new arrival cohort became even stronger. By 1993, the Asian percentage of all those approved for permanent residency jumped from almost 50 per cent to slightly more than 60 per cent. The major Asian contributions came from Taiwan, Hong Kong, South Korea, and China. In terms of arrival conditions, the GC category, especially the General Investment Category (GIC), a sub-division of the GC category,[7] quickly became the main channel through which Asian applicants gained residency. By 1993, the percentage of Asians under the GIC sub-division reached as high as 86 per cent or almost 58 per cent of the total GC approvals (Trlin, 1997). The numbers of approved applicants under both the BIC and the GC categories from Britain were thus overtaken by Chinese from the three main origin countries (Ip, 2001). It should be noted too that when the government introduced these pro-immigration policies, for example, welcoming applicants with skills and entrepreneurial capital to enter New Zealand, no one foresaw that the policy would lead to such a sizeable influx of ethnic Asian immigrants, including new Chinese immigrants (Ip, 2001).

The effects of these immigration policy changes in the late 1980s and early 1990s took a much longer time to affect the PRC cohort compared with their effects on the Hong Kong and Taiwan cohorts. Of these three main Chinese immigrant intake sources, the Hong Kong arrivals were the earliest and peaked in 1991. They were followed by people from Taiwan whose numbers peaked in 1996. However, the size of the PRC cohort was much smaller than both of the Hong Kong and Taiwan cohorts before the mid-1990s (Ip, 2006b). Migrant totals from the PRC started to catch up with the Hong Kong and Taiwan cohorts after the 1991 policy change and then increased steadily, but cyclically as shown in Figure 2.1. By the late 1990s, PRC migrants became predominant. INZ data can be used as a clear indicator of the trend of Chinese immigration from the PRC to New Zealand. Even when the 1995 policy change reduced the number of Hong Kong and Taiwan approvals significantly, it seemed that this policy change had little effect on the number of immigrants arriving from the PRC (see Figure 2.1).

Of note along with the opening-up of skilled and business immigration, another clear immigration policy objective in the early 1990s was to strengthen families and communities (Burke, 1986). Trlin made a comment on the family reunification immigration policy in the *Immigration Policy Review 1986* "with respect to aged parents, adult children and siblings" (Trlin, 1992: 7). In the 1991 policy, there was a Family Category which covered three situations: marriage to a

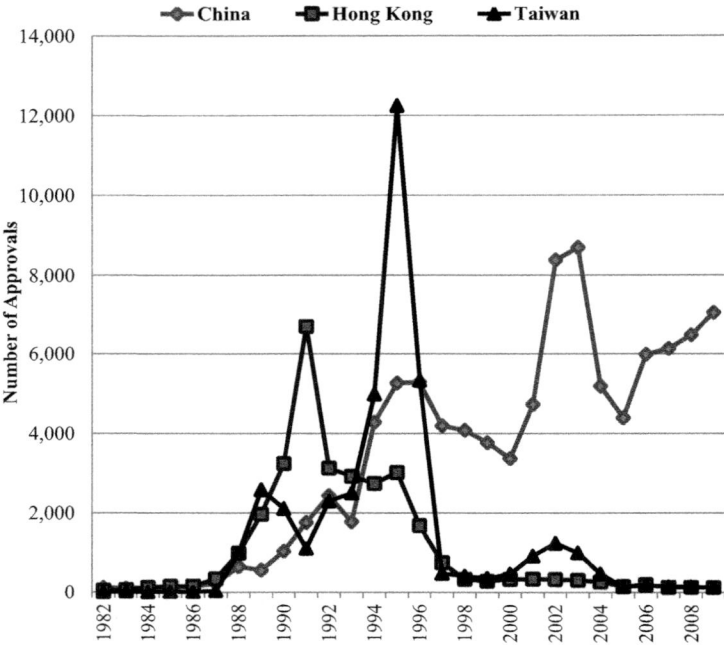

Figure 2.1 Annual New Zealand residence approval number for people from China (PRC), Hong Kong, and Taiwan for 1982 to 2009

(Source: Immigration New Zealand).

New Zealand citizen or resident; a de factor or homosexual relationship; and the case of parents, dependent children, and single adult siblings and children (Trlin, 1997). Obviously, under the New Zealand immigration law, migrants' parents are included into the category of family members who could be brought into this country. This is quite social-liberal compared with other countries where only nuclear family members (i.e. spouse and child) are defined to belong to the family reunification immigration category, such as Sweden, the United Kingdom, and Netherland (Borevi, 2015a; Robinson, 2013). This social-liberal family reunification immigration policy was largely influenced by a social-liberal model of citizenship, emphasising a full range and equal "social rights" for all citizens and even permanent residents (McMillan, Trlin, Spoonley, & Watts, 2005, p. 78). Under this model, immigrants' parents were not only allowed to immigrate to New Zealand but also entitled social services and welfare provision.

The tightening of entry criteria in 1995

The significant increase in the number of new Asian immigrants and their high visibility soon put pressure on New Zealand's immigration system. Although there were immigrant quota "targets" set by the government, and in theory regulated by a "floating" points system prior to the change, the actual intake regularly exceeded the target, resulting in peak migration for the years 1994 to 1996 (Ip & Friesen, 2001). The public's attitude toward Asian immigration was generally negative throughout the 1990s, and a number of opinion polls revealed that there was a consistent anti-Asian sentiment but a welcoming attitude toward immigration from the Great Britain and South Africa (Ip, 2001). Fuelling the public's anti-Asian sentiment was the media's negative representation of new Asian arrivals. An article titled "Inv-Asian", published in the suburban newspaper *The Eastern Courier* in April 1993, presented a stereotypical view of the new Asian migrant and undoubtedly intensified public unease toward the rapid increase of immigrants from those "non-traditional" sources (Ip, 2001). The issue of Asian immigration were also capitalised on by some politicians, including Winston Peters, the leader of the New Zealand First Party.[8] He used an anti-Asian strategy for his party's campaign in the 1996 election. By playing the race card, he made sufficient political capital out of the public concerns over immigration in that election to ensure that his party gained enough seats to secure a coalition agreement with the National Party. His anti-immigrant rhetoric further stirred up great social tension in the months that preceded the 1996 election. Public opinion polls showed that support for the New Zealand First significantly increased from below 3 per cent in February of 1996 to 28 per cent in July of that same year (Ip, 2002).

A combination of immigration policy changes had taken place in October 1995 (see Table 2.2). The October 1995 review of immigration policy brought about a subtle change in the policy, emphasising on maintaining "social cohesion" as an important policy goal, together with the goal of economic growth (Henderson, 2003; Ip, 2001).

This policy revision was a response, as least in part, to the influx of new Asian immigrants. As Bedford and others suggests, migration systems are shaped and re-shaped by links between migration policies and the broad economic and political objectives of a government (Bedford, 2005; Bedford & Ho, 2006). The introduction of the Mixed-Members-Proportional (MMP)[9] voting system in 1996 also made immigration issues more sensitive in the New Zealand political terrain. Since the MMP system offers great opportunities to ethnic minority groups and can guarantee that the places and role of minorities are adequately represented, with the increasing population of new Asian immigrants in New Zealand, dominated by Chinese, the "Chinese factor" started to catch politicians' attention and become a significant consideration in New Zealand politics. First, the advent of Chinese voters could influence the election outcome. More importantly, the MMP electoral system gave the Chinese as a community the chance to be politically represented and potentially influence the nation's politics in a way they would not have been able to under the old electoral system (Ip, 2002). The first practice of the MMP system in the national election of 1996 coincided with the significant presence of many new Chinese in New Zealand, which made the 1995 policy change even more important for the political scene.

During this policy revision, a more challenging criteria for entry was introduced. This tightening-up policy was particularly welcomed in Australia because it reduced their concerns about "back-door" entry[10] from New Zealand of those migrants who otherwise would not have gained direct entry under Australian policy. On the policy level, these changes were introduced to tackle some of the shortcomings of previous policies. In reality, some changes to the entry criteria, especially the English language requirement for both principal and non-principal (over 16) skilled and business migrants was actually a designed strategy to reduce the rapid increase of Asian immigrants (Henderson et al., 1997). It was pronounced as being necessary to enhance the social cohesion of the country and "a key to successful settlement" (New Zealand Immigration Services, 1995, p. 10). In fact, as Henderson argues: "It was hoped that the language requirement would reduce the 'over-supply' of high quality migrants from Asia and alter the migrant mix over time" (Henderson, 2003, p. 145). When the new immigrants surged to 40,000 in the year ending March 1994 and then peaked at 57,520 for the year ending March 1995 where unexpectedly more than half were Asians, the language requirement of attaining Level 5 of the General Module of the International English Language Testing System (IELTS) was set as a bar to restrict the entry of migrants from non-English-speaking backgrounds (Ip, 2001). A NZ$20,000 language bond was applied to spouses and dependants 16 years and over if they failed to meet the English language requirements within the specified time (see Table 2.2).

Ip (2001) argues that "no other settler countries from the Pacific Rim had such rigid and financially punitive English language requirements in the modern age of immigration" (p. 48). The introduction of the English language filter in 1995 was just like the English language reading test of the nineteenth century, both of which were designed to cut back Chinese immigration. Even though well-polished wording like "English is a key to successful settlement" (New Zealand Immigration Services, 1995, p. 10) was used to make the language filter look reasonable at first glance, the similarity to the past policy was notable.

The 1995 policy change took effect quickly and led to a substantial immigration decline in the late 1990s (Bedford, Lidgard, & Ho, 2005b). The number of approvals from Chinese sources declined dramatically. Those from Taiwan and Hong Kong were hit particularly hard (Henderson, 2003; Ip, 2001). The tightening of policy, coupled with the handover of Hong Kong to China on 1 July 1997 and the onset of the Asian economic crisis that began in the second half of the year of 1997 effectively reduced the inflow of migrants from Hong Kong and Taiwan. From 1996 to 2000, the number of immigration applications from Hong Kong and Taiwan dropped from over 10,000 to only a couple of thousand and then further declined to a few hundred per year (see Figure 2.1). By 1997, Hong Kong had dropped to number 10 on the "source regions list", while Taiwan completely disappeared from the "Top Ten" list (Ho, 2003; Ip, 2001).

The 1995 policy change had a particularly strong impact on obtaining business immigrants. Until the mid-1990s, Hong Kong and Taiwan were the two major sources of business migrants to New Zealand. Between 1987 and 1996, over

17,000 Hong Kong and Taiwan nationals were granted permanent residence under the business category. After the policy change in 1995, business migrant intake from the same two sources declined to just 1,000 between 1997 and 2001 (Ho, 2003).

While applications from Hong Kong and Taiwan dropped dramatically, the raised entry criteria in 1995 did not deter the Chinese applicants from China. During the following years, applications and approvals from China steadily increased (see Figure 2.1). The reasons behind this trend were more likely that the China applicants relied on the accrual of points for human capital rather than financial capital. Therefore, the tightening-up of selection criteria on business immigration had little effect on the China cohort. In addition, because China has a huge population base, there were still many applicants from China who were skilled and had good English skills (Henderson, 2003).

Relaxation of entry criteria near new millennium and the launching of the New Zealand Immigration Programme (NZIP) in 2001

Having received sharp criticism to the impact of the 1995 policy change on business immigration and a net migration loss, the government instituted a number of changes to the selection requirements in 1997 to try to remedy the migration decline. The most significant changes included first the abolition of the English language bond for non-principal residence applicants and its replacement with pre-paid English language training in an approved course, and second the introduction of the new categories of entrepreneur/investor migration and long-term visas for business people. Following this, a series of more proactive immigration programmes were introduced at the turn of the new millennium.[11] These resulted in a return to sizeable net migration gains. However, it also led to a high-level political debate about the cost of the unrestricted access of New Zealanders to Australia and their associated entitlement to welfare support. In February 2001, the Australian government introduced stricter controls over access to welfare provisions to New Zealand migrants who arrived in Australia, but not under Australia's immigration programme. The new policy made New Zealand migrants ineligible for most of the social security support in Australia, and sufficiently reduced "back-door" migration. Since then, "back-door" migration has no longer been a major concern in Australia (Bedford et al., 2005a).

In 1999, the Labour Government was back into power, and some new initiatives in immigration policy took place. The most significant initiative during the Labour Government's first term (1999–2002) was the launch of the New Zealand Immigration Programme (NZIP)[12] in October 2001 and the introduction of a managed entry regime (see Table 2.2). Within this managed entry regime, NZIP is divided into three streams, including Skilled/Business Stream, Family Sponsorship Stream, and International/Humanitarian Stream, and each stream is allocated a percentage of the Government's total target for residence approvals. For example, the Skilled/Business Stream was allocated 60 per cent of the Government's total target for residence approvals, while a Family Sponsorship

Stream was allocated 30 per cent and an International/Humanitarian Stream 10 per cent (Bedford et al., 2005a). It was the first time that New Zealand immigration regime started to regulate the "economic" and "social" streams of immigrants based on actually numerical terms (Bedford & Liu, 2013). The emphasis on "economic" migration signalled a clear shift of immigration policy orientation from social-liberalism to neoliberalism which gives focus on economic output from immigration (McMillan et al., 2005; Simon-Kumar, 2015). This shift was also as a response to domestic and global market changes.

Apart from the October 2001 package, there were certain side-stream immigration channels promoted by the Government. The enactment of the Government's initiative for "work to residence" in April 2002 was significant in terms of its high potential to attract highly employable people to become permanent residents. There are two components of this initiative: the "talent visa"[13] and the "POL (Priority Occupation List) work permit".[14] Both aim to attract highly skilled people to New Zealand and "generate value-creating ideas and knowledge in an economy placing increasing emphasis on innovation and technological change in the drive for improved productivity and higher incomes" (Bedford et al., 2005a, p. 20). Later, the Job Search Visa (JSV)[15] was introduced in November 2002. As Bedford and co-authors discuss, all these initiatives show the willingness of the government to facilitate transition for people with temporary work permit status and student visa/permits and wish to obtain residence (Bedford et al., 2005a). The results show that these initiatives worked very well in terms of channelling more skilled/business immigrants into New Zealand by providing a more viable transitional stage. In the year ending June 2000, a total of 34,075 principal applicants were granted work permits. By the year ended June 2002, the total number of principal applicants granted work permits had risen by 74 per cent to 59,148. In the same period, principal applicants who held student permits increased from 28,646 to 73,525, an increase of 158 per cent – more than double the increase in work permits (Bedford et al., 2005a).

These policy developments were highly relevant to the arrival conditions of new Chinese immigrants from China, especially those who obtained their residence after 2003. Since the INZ data shows that a large percentage of Chinese immigrants (including PRC migrants) used the on-shore application process to gain residency (Ho, 2005, 2006), the POL work permits and JSV could be used by most on-shore Chinese as a transitional way to apply for permanent residence. Given the massive increase in the number of Chinese international students from 2000 and 2002, it was highly likely that Chinese applicants from China after 2002 comprised a large number of Chinese international students who then stayed and sought residence after finishing their studies.

Adjustment of the immigration policy between 2000 and 2002 led to a return of sizeable net migration gains and promoted immigration from Asia, especially China. The permanent and long-term (PLT) net migration gains from countries in Northeast, Southeast, and South Asia showed that immigration from all three of these sub-regions reached its highest recorded level in 2002 and 2003. Chinese immigration dominated the Northeast Asian flow with migrants from China comprising the largest share of the net gains since 1996/97. Meanwhile, as previously mentioned, immigration from Hong Kong and Taiwan, the two main sources of Chinese immigrants in the early 1990s, was much less significant after 1996. Between 1989/90 and 1995/96, the net gain was 29,130 for Hong Kong and Taiwan, while only 10,100 came from the PRC. However, the aggregate PLT net gain from the PRC for the period 1996/97 to 2002/03 turned out to be 51,220, compared with only 9,320 from Hong Kong and Taiwan (Bedford et al., 2005b).

The 2001 census data can also be used to demonstrate the significance of Chinese immigration from China from the mid-1990s onwards. It shows that the "China born" population was 38,325, constituting 35 per cent of the total ethnic Chinese population in New Zealand, which stood at 105,054. The China-born Chinese was the largest single group, outnumbering the New Zealand born (25 per cent), Taiwan born (12 per cent), Hong Kong born (10 per cent), and other overseas born Chinese (17 per cent) (see Figure 2.2). The increase of a "China born" population can also be seen in the 2006 census (see Figure 2.3) – that the "China (PRC)-born" population in New Zealand increased further, reaching 52.29 per cent of the total Chinese population, while the Hong Kong-born and Taiwan-born Chinese population shrunk to 4.54 per cent and 7.21 per cent, respectively.

New Zealand's overall immigrant intake, between 1996/97 and 2002/03, showed that immigrants from Great Britain, China, India, and South Africa dominated New Zealand's international migration system (Bedford et al., 2005b). In 1997, for the first time, China (PRC) was featured as the second largest source country for New Zealand's immigrant intake, closely following Great Britain. Immigrants from the PRC continuously increased without any significant slump, especially after the launching of the NZIP in 2001 resulting in an initial peak in 2003 (Figure 2.4).

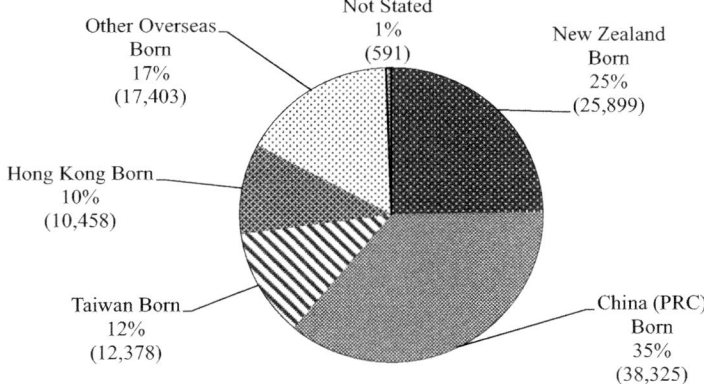

Figure 2.2 Birthplaces of New Zealand Chinese (Total 105,057) in 2001 Census
(Source: Statistics New Zealand, 2002)

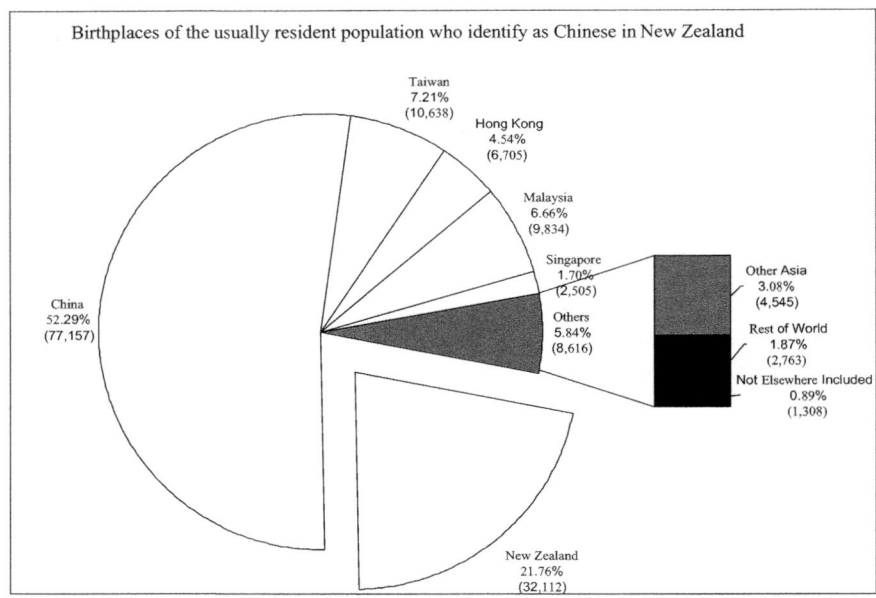

Figure 2.3 Birthplace of the usual resident population who identify as Chinese in New Zealand: The 2006 Census

(Source: Statistics New Zealand, 2006)

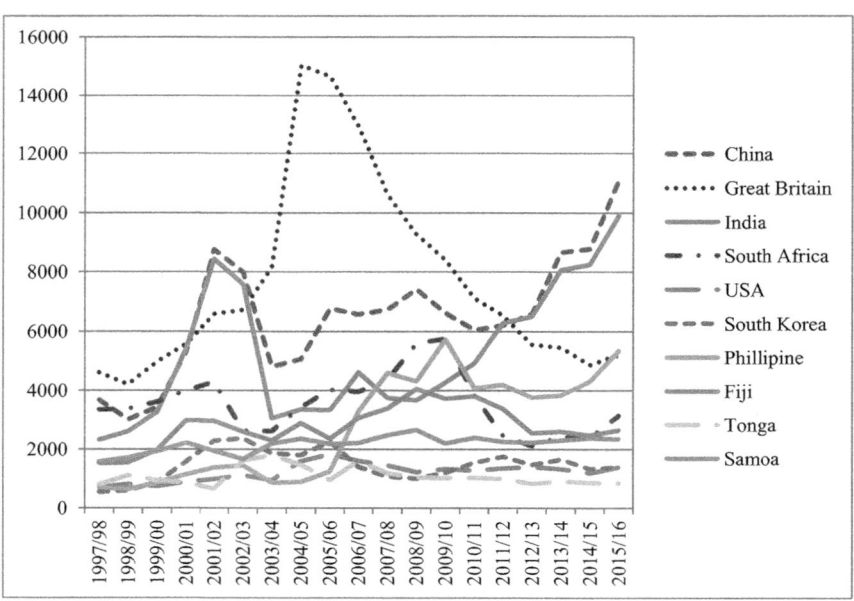

Figure 2.4 Annual residence approvals for the top 10 immigrant source countries, 1997/1998 to 2015/2016

(Source: Immigration New Zealand)

A new selection system in 2003: from a numerical target and
economic outcome to a settlement outcome

The sudden and sharp increase in immigrants after 2000 soon put pressure on the immigration system. The number of resident approvals for skilled/business migrants comprised 68 per cent of the total resident approvals by July 2002, slightly exceeding the target resident approvals (60 per cent) for the "skilled/ business" stream (Bedford et al., 2005a). Even though the overall number of approvals[16] proved to be difficult to obtain, the new immigration wave, together with the arrival of a large number of international students from Asia, did result in an impression of "Asianisation" to many New Zealand locals, especially in the Auckland region. Similarly to what happened in the mid-1990s, these immigration issues were quickly subjected to intense public concern and scrutiny and capitalised on once again by the leader of the New Zealand First Party, Winston Peters, in the 2002 central government election (Spoonley & Trlin, 2004). During this period, significant changes were made to tighten up the immigration entry criteria. First, there was an increase in the "pass" mark for the General Skilled Category (GSC), from 28 to 29 in September 2002, and then to 30 in October 2002. Secondly, higher English language requirements were implemented. The minimum IELTS score for the GSC category increased from an average of 5 to 6.5 across all 4 bands, while the score for business categories increased from an average of 4 to 5. All applicants, including those already under consideration when the policy changes were announced, were required to meet the new criteria. Lastly, there was a tighter, more restrictive requirement and operational control for obtaining JSV and Long Term Business Visas (LTBA) as well as for the Investor Category (Bedford et al., 2005a). These changes, especially the raised English language requirements, resulted in a major outcry from immigration consultants and prospective immigrants, and the New Zealand Association for Migration and Investment (NZAMI) legally challenged the Minister's decision.

Following the tightening of the entry criteria in 2002, the NZIS began to tailor a selection system that would focus much more on ensuring that migrants with skills were actually needed in the labour market rather than merely accepting all those who met a specific point target. In July 2003, the Minister of Immigration suddenly announced that a new Skilled Migrant Category (SMC) would come into force in December 2003 and replace the GSC. The essence of the new selection system was summed up in then Immigration Minister Dalziel's 2003 package of press releases (see Appendix 2).

In general, the new SMC shifts the way the point system worked from the passive acceptance of residence applications to the active selection of skilled migrants. It replaced the "pass" mark system with a process whereby people who qualify above a certain level of points (at least 100 points) can submit an expression of interest (EOI) to a selection pool, from which they are then invited to apply for residence. Points were allocated on the basis of age, qualifications, a skilled job or offer, the regional location of the job offer, work experience, and identified skills shortage. Without wider consultation and no warning, this change was passed under a sense of urgency, struck down the High Court's ruling on the NZAMI case, and made it clear that in the future, all immigration policy decisions to cancel any applications in any category could not be challenged in court. This new system has continued to remain, however it was not applied to the Family Sponsorship Stream until 2012 when the new two-tier system was introduced to this immigration stream.

It should be noted that the introduction of the new selection system took place in the context in which successful settlement outcomes of migrants was recognised by the government as being more important than numerical outcomes. Before 1999, the policy put the emphasis on numerical targets. The political debate around immigration leading up to the national election in 1999 saw an increased emphasis on ensuring successful settlement outcomes. By recognising the difficulties that many new immigrants, especially new immigrants from Asia, were experiencing in obtaining employment, the government realised the importance of assisting new immigrants to settle successfully and attain a better labour market. Several initiatives undertaken by the NZIS's Settlement Information Programme between 1997 and 1999 evidenced this shifting emphasis in policy (see Appendix 3).

The emphasis on successful settlement outcomes was further enhanced after the election of the Labour Government in November 1999, and the appointment of Lianne Dalziel as Minister of Immigration. After the 1999 election, as an initial response to calls for a clearly defined official settlement strategy, the Minister asked the NZIS to develop a budget proposal that sought approval to use funds collected through the migrant levy (part of the fees paid by applicants for residence) for a series of settlement pilots (see Appendix 3) that targeted different groups of refugees and migrants (Ho, Cheung, Bedford, & Leung, 2000). The settlement pilots showed a commitment to assisting refugees and migrants to get the support they needed to settle effectively. Unfortunately, the government's approach toward achieving more successful settlement outcomes did not depend on co-ordinated settlement support; rather, like Bedford and co-authors argue, it lay in the way that the points selection system worked and how migrants were selected (Bedford et al., 2005a). This was how the new EOI selection system was initiated and developed. It is also important to note that the emphasis on settlement outcomes is well aligned with the neoliberal trend of the immigration policy environment where obtaining employment is a precondition for the successful economic outcome of immigration.

In terms of policy effect, a very different policy landscape was in place until 2003 which resulted in a greater mix of approvals from more diverse sources. From 1997 onwards, immigration from China dominated New Zealand immigration flows from Asia, with Chinese migrants comprising the second-largest share of residence approvals closely following Great Britain. After 2003, Great Britain remained the largest source country for New Zealand's immigrant intake, but the number of residence approvals for those from Europe and North America increased, with some reduction in immigrant numbers from China and India

(Bedford, Ho, & Bedford, 2010). The approvals for applicants from China sharply reduced after 2003, but started to climb back again in 2005. This was followed by a short slump between 2008 and 2010, however a quick recovery started from 2011. In 2013, the number of residence approval for China was greater than its previous historical highest level of 2003, and subsequently has increased steadily throughout 2016. The year of 2012 was the first time that the approval number for China was larger than Great Britain (Figure 2.4).

A full formation of a neoliberal immigration regime

As demonstrated above, New Zealand immigration policy has been always refining and re-defining; however, no matter how the policy emphasis shifted, the factors of human capital and economic investment in recruiting immigrants have never been changed much (Bedford et al., 2010). While this neoliberal ideology was well advanced, settlement and integration support was promoted and seen as a key pillar to ensure a better settlement outcome of immigration. Moreover, it was very similar to Australia that Asia together with the immigration issues from that region were increasingly set into the discussion of their association with the state's economic and business success (Ang, 2016; Simon-Kumar, 2015). These trends indeed accelerated a full formation of a neoliberal immigration regime which is in favour of highly skilled and business immigrants over family and social immigrants. This full formation of a neoliberal immigration regime during the past decade is especially of notice in the subsequent changing policy regarding the entry of migrants' family members.

In the *Review of Family Sponsorship Policies* for Cabinet early in 2007, the Minister of Immigration (Hon. David Cunliffe) recommended that "while the [family] stream perform an important social role, it is critical that policies also be considered through an economic lens" (Cunliffe, 2007a, p. 7). This review led a critical policy change with regard to the family sponsorship immigration in May 2007. First, the Family Sponsorship Stream was divided into two sub-streams: Parent, Adult Child(ren), and Sibling Stream (PACS) and Partner and Dependent children Stream. Under the first stream, there were three sub-categories: the Parent Category, Sibling Category, and Adult Child(ren) Category. Under the second stream, there are two sub-categories: the Dependent Child(ren) Category and Spouse/Partners Category. Second, although the overall family sponsorship stream had had a notional ceiling of 30 per cent of all residence approvals before May 2007, there had been no specific cap on the numbers of parents, adult children and siblings. However, the 2007 policy change capped these categories with actual numbers. It meant that when the limit, namely, the cap was reached, no further visas would be granted in that visa class in the programme year. The Parent Category was given approximately 4000 quota per year. In addition, the 2007 policy change also included requirements of a minimum income for sponsors (i.e. NZ$33,675 per year) and an increased length of time a migrant sponsor would have to support their parents without access to benefits (i.e. from two years to five years) (Bedford & Liu, 2013).

These two changes were a deliberate attempt to prioritise the entry of immediately family members, especially overseas-born partners and dependent children, while limiting the entry of other family members who were dependent in relatively low workforce participation and had a high tendency of welfare dependence (Cunliffe, 2007b). For example, older parents of adult immigrants have a greater cost on the health and medical system. The "economic lens" to construct parent sponsorship immigration in New Zealand was further defined and refined the final approval of the enforcement of the two-tier selection system in the Parent Category by Cabinet in May 2011, starting from July 2012.

Similar to the two-stage EOI system that was introduced for skilled immigrant selection in December 2002, people seeking entry under the Parent Category are required to submit an EOI before making a formal application to enter New Zealand. EOIs must be submitted with reference to criteria applying to two tiers of entry, with Tier 1 having a much higher financial requirement for sponsors than Tier 2 (see Table 2.2). The rationale behind the new EOI policy under the capped Parent Category is to monitor the number of EOIs in the pool, quantify the EOIs under the Tier 1 and Tier 2 schemes, and give Tier 1 priority over those submitted under Tier 2 criteria (Bedford & Liu, 2013).

The 2012 policy change in the Parent Category can be thought of a prelude of the 2016 change which completely closed off the Parent Category. Whether this immigration category will be re-opened or not is unknown, depending on further policy review over the next two years (Woodhouse, 2016). Both policy changes aim to tighten up the entry of migrants' parents. The rationale of these changes is that parent migrants impose fiscal costs to New Zealand because most of them are highly likely to have low labour market participation, high rates of benefit uptake, and high health costs (Office of the Minister of Immigration, 2016). The 2016 policy change in the Parent Category aimed at reducing the targeted quota for the capped family categories from 5,500 to 2,000 per year.

Coupled with the policy change with regard to the entry of migrants' parents, there were changes made under the Skilled Migrant Category (SMC) in 2016. First of all, points required for permanent residence has been increased from 140 to 160. Secondly, the average band score of the IELTS has increased from 5 to 6.5. With a high-level of immigration arrivals in the past a few years, changes made in 2016 aimed to reduce the total number of migrants being granted residence to a range of 85,000–95,000 from previous range of 90,000–100,000 over two years (see Table 2.2).

Most recently in April 2017, policy changes on the SMC and Essential Skills Visa category were proposed and will come into effect in August of the same year (see Table 2.2). Under the SMC, two remuneration thresholds are being introduced for applicants applying for residence. The first band would mean those earning under the NZ$49,000 median wage would no longer be considered highly skilled while those earning above the 1.5 times median income threshold of NZ$73,000 would automatically be regarded as high skilled (Immigration New Zealand, 2017b). As for the Essential Skills Visa, a three-year limit would be placed on those visa holders earning below the threshold of NZ$49,000. Moreover, if their partners want to come to live in New Zealand for long term, they have to meet the requirements for a visa in their own right (Immigration New Zealand, 2017a).

All of these changes together highlight the soaring tension between the state's claim for more control in immigrant selection, welfare distribution and increasing demand from migrants of moving out of their countries of origin to seek new lives in "desired places" of the world. New Zealand is one of these places. These policy changes also reflect the fact that contemporary New Zealand immigration regime has progressively pursued a neoliberal immigration discourse in which skilled and business immigration is favoured, while social and family reunification immigration is discouraged (Simon-Kumar, 2015). Such policy discourse is a significant manifestation of a nation's ambition for further economic growth in which skilled and business immigrants are viewed as an important resource to channel in human and financial capital to the immigrant-receiving countries, while low skilled labour immigrants and dependent family members of skilled and business immigrants are regarded as a burden for host countries' welfare and health support systems (Borevi, 2015b; Czaika & De Haas, 2013; DeShaw, 2006b).

What will happen in terms of Chinese immigration in the future remains unknown. The following statistics from INZ perhaps can tell the story. With a more restricted immigration policy enforced under both Skilled/Business Stream and Family Sponsorship Stream, a sharp decline in New Zealand's migrant arrival numbers (including migrants from China) can be expected in the near future.

Building on secondary resources: a profile of PRC migrants in New Zealand

Chinese immigrants from the PRC China are the most recent arrivals among the new Chinese groups. Unlike the earliest Chinese immigrants to New Zealand who were mostly humble peasants from rural Southern China forced to leave by natural disasters and warfare and who then arrived in New Zealand as gold miners, the new PRC immigrants are mainly well educated and highly skilled professionals and urban dwellers (Ip, 1995, 2006b). They gained entry because they were considered by INZ as potential migrants well equipped with useful human and financial capital and able to contribute to New Zealand's economic and social development. They are also quite different from other new Chinese groups.

In this section, both the China-born specific data from the latest New Zealand Census (2013) and data from INZ illustrate the unique characteristics of the PRC new Chinese migrants in terms of their immigration pathway, educational background, labour force performance, and family and community formation. It is necessary to consider New Zealand's other important immigrant groups in the discussion because the distinct feature of the PRC migrant cohort can only be found through a comparative perspective.

Immigration pathways

Table 2.1 shows that the top ten major immigrant sending countries of New Zealand during the period of 1997/98–2015/16. Great Britain was the largest immigrant source country for New Zealand, with China ranked as second. When examining the percentages of residence approvals under different immigration categories by each country, Table 2.1 shows that for people from South Africa, Great Britain, Philippine, India, the US, and South Korea, the Skilled Category was highly used to obtain permanent residence compared to other immigration categories. This is highlighted from all these six countries which had more than 50 per cent residence approvals under the Skilled Category from their total residence approvals. This rank was followed by Fiji and China. Both countries' residence approvals under the Skilled Categories accounted just below 50 per cent of their total residence approvals (46.8 per cent for Fiji, and 40.5 per cent for China). However, when examining the Business Category, people from China used this category to obtain permanent residence far more often than people from Great Britain, South African, and the US, with 11.8 per cent residence approvals for Chinese under the Business Category compared with 2.4 per cent for Great Britain, 0.8 per cent for South Africa, and 4.5 per cent for the US. Only South Korea's percentage of business immigration approvals was more than China, with 23.9 per cent business residence approvals of its total residence approvals. For the three Pacific countries, Philippine and India, the percentages of their business immigration approvals were nominal.

Another dominant feature of the PRC immigration to New Zealand, as shown in Table 2.2, is that China had the highest and outstanding share of its total residence approvals under the Parent Category (20.8 per cent) among all top ten countries, followed by Fiji (13.7 per cent), India (13.1 per cent) and Tonga (12.0 per cent), while South African (7.0 per cent), Great Britain (6.8 per cent), Samoa (6.4 per cent), South Korea (5.3 per cent), and Philippines (3.0 per cent) had rather smaller percentages – all were below the average of 9.0 per cent.

The table shows that the PRC new migrants follow various routes to New Zealand. Many are in the Skilled and Parent Categories, while quite a few entered via the Business Category. This reflects the fact that China's growing economy has played an important role in bolstering its nationals' financial ability to obtain New Zealand's permanent residence. The high percentage of residence approvals under the Parent Category reveals a very important Chinese cultural value – filial piety and family reunification plays a significant role in contemporary Chinese immigration (Li, 2011; Liu, 2016). The actual practice of this cultural value among new Chinese migrant population is that once adult immigrants settle in New Zealand, they would like to sponsor their parents to immigrate to this country and to live with their parents, either in the same household or the same locality (Liu, 2016). This is a common phenomenon of the PRC new immigrants in other traditional immigration-based "White Settler" countries, such as Australia, Canada, and the US (Ip, Lui, & Chui, 2007).

Social indicators: educational background and employment status

The most recent New Zealand Census data (2013) shows that PRC Chinese are one of the best-educated groups in New Zealand, with 33.7 per cent having bachelor's degrees or higher, compared with the New Zealand national average of 20 per cent (Statistics New Zealand, 2014). Unfortunately, their advanced qualifications did not give PRC Chinese an advantage in job-seeking. The 2013 census shows that the percentage of PRC Chinese who are employed full-time and those who are employed part-time are both lower than the national averages, while their unemployment rate is higher than the national average (see Table 2.3). Many studies have found that immigrant performance in the labour market is an important indicator of how well immigrants settle in their adopted locales (Baker, 1994; Miller, 1986; Poot, 1993; Winkelmann & Winkelmann, 1998). Usually, immigrant labour market performance closely relates to immigrant education level, that is, the higher one's educational level is, the better performance one should have in the labour market. However, the PRC Chinese good educational profile has been a serious mismatch with their performance in the labour market, indicating a waste of valuable human capital.

Further, PRC Chinese have a higher percentage of self-employment and not-in-labour-force status than the national average (see Tables 2.3 and Table 2.4). Among those who are not in the labour force, about 34 per cent of them are studying full-time (see Table 2.5). In fact, the PRC group presents the highest full-time study participation percentage among adults over 18 years old – more than six times the national average (see Table 2.5). Even though the high percentages of PRC migrants who are studying and are not-in-labour-force in the census data include Chinese international students, given the fact that international students are highly likely not to participate in the New Zealand Census, these percentages still can be used as an indicator of the poor performance of PRC migrants in the labour market. Since self-employment and additional education are often strategies undertaken to overcome unemployment (Ip, 2001; Waldinger, 1990), when many were rejected for employment in the local labour market, they realised that obtaining a recognised local qualification could give them a better chance to secure employment in the future. Re-training is generally

Table 2.3 Labour market participation by New Zealand residents born in the PRC, Hong Kong, and Taiwan compared to the national average

Labour market participation	China	NZ national average
Employed full-time	40.2%	48.0%
Employed part-time	11.8%	14.3%
Unemployed	5.1%	4.8%
Not in the labour force	42.9%	32.9%

(Source: Statistics New Zealand, 2014)

Table 2.4 Employment status of New Zealand residents born in China compared to the New Zealand national average

Employment status	China	NZ national average
Employee	75.8%	79.4%
Employer	8.3%	6.6%
Self-employed without employees	13.3%	12.1%
Unpaid family worker	2.6%	1.9%

(Source: Statistics New Zealand, 2014)

Table 2.5 New Zealand residents from China over 18 and participating in full-time or part-time study in comparison to New Zealand national average

Study participation	China	NZ national average
Full-time study	33.7%	5.1%
Part-time study	6.9%	5.0%
Total in study	40.7%	10.1%
Not in study	59.3%	89.9%

(Source: Statistics New Zealand, 2014)

perceived by many PRC migrants as a feasible strategy for upgrading themselves or to help them gain employment in New Zealand.

Based on empirical observation and findings, some of PRC migrants take further study in their previous academic or professional areas, while some instead chose completely different areas. This choice may not be their personal choice, but based on job prospects. A better job that can generate corresponding income to sustain living and match one's educational and previous professional background is usually the preferable circumstance for a new migrant of working age. A sense of settlement and commitment to New Zealand is also largely dependent on whether staying and working in the immigration host society does address migrants' and their families' economic well-being.

These features indicate the common difficulties currently present in the wage employment that many new PRC immigrants have encountered and also the overall moderate economic outcomes of PRC migrants within the wage economy. Since PRC migrants are one of the most highly-educated groups in New Zealand and are also comparatively young, their moderate labour market performance is a serious mismatch to their age-education profile. This mismatch represents a "serious wastage of human capital as well as great personal frustration" (Ip, 2006b, p. 76). The experience of unemployment is usually associated with financial cost and loss of self-esteem.

Some scholars suggest that the employment problem may be one of several factors that motivate some PRC migrants to return to China or to move to a third country (Henderson, 2003; Ip, 2006b). Whether that is true or not, it is understandable that the decision to stay or leave the host country for many immigrants may partly depend on whether the economic and social outcomes of immigration meet their initial immigration expectations.

Settlement and family and community formation

As the migration process evolves over time, a substantial new Chinese migrant community has established in New Zealand, evidenced by the presence of many multi-generational Chinese migrant families. Figure 2.5 shows that Chinese migrants' children and their elderly parents make up an important proportion of New Zealand's China-born population.

The usual practice is that after the adult migrants settle down in New Zealand, many of them sponsor their parents to come to New Zealand. These elderly Chinese migrants come to New Zealand in their later life for a variety of purposes, such as retirement, being close with their adult children, or taking care of their grandchildren (Ho, Lewin, & Muntz, 2010).Under New Zealand's previous policies relating to the capped Parent Category of the Family Sponsorship Stream, it was relatively easy for adult migrants to bring their parents to New Zealand. If a migrant who is 18 years of age or over with New Zealand citizenship or permanent residence can provide financial support (the minimum income figure is NZ$31,202.08 per annum) and accommodation for his or her parents,

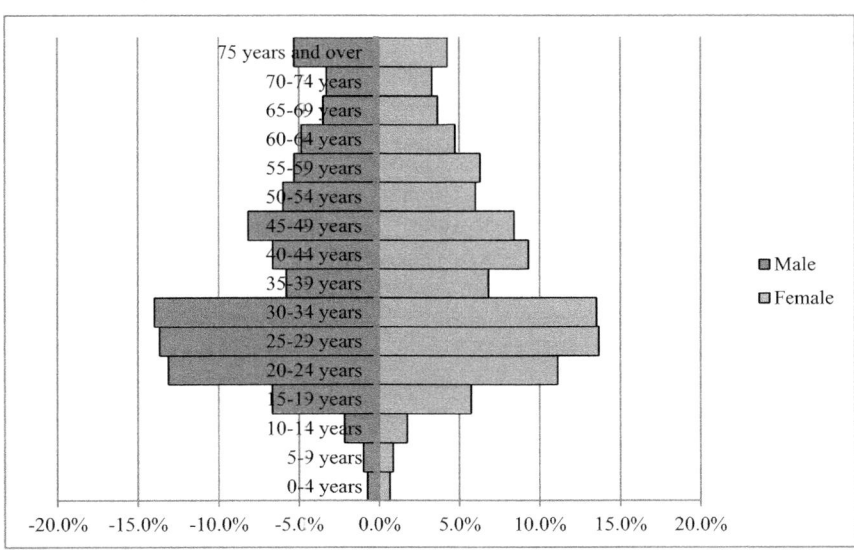

Figure 2.5 Age-sex pyramid for the China-born ethnic Chinese population in 2013 Census

(Source: Statistics New Zealand, 2013)

and can demonstrate that the family's "centre of gravity"[17] is in New Zealand, the parent(s) can be sponsored to come to New Zealand as permanent resident(s) (Trlin, 1992, 1997). It has been noted that New Zealand's family-reunion policy is especially China-friendly by default, given that China's "one-child"[18] policy means that parental applicants can easily demonstrate that their families' centre of gravity is in New Zealand, thus qualifying for family reunification under New Zealand's immigration legislation (DeShaw, 2006a). This is the pre-determined policy condition of how Chinese migrant families have been established.

Adding to this condition is China's inadequate welfare system and the cultural stigma which underpins the family assembly of new PRC Chinese migrants in New Zealand. First, China is not a welfare state in the sense that developed countries are, and the Chinese government started to develop a universal social-security and healthcare insurance system for its citizens rather late. Very recently, in 2012, a universal basic pension system was established, but rural China still faces great challenges in providing for its ageing population. According to official estimates, full pension coverage can be achieved in 2020. The goal to provide minimum livelihood protection for all elderly who live below the local poverty line was set in 2015 (Zhang, 2013). Whether this goal has been achieved or not has not yet been indicated in official statistics. Due to the fact that living standards and the amount of capital per person in China are still significantly lower than the international average and healthcare costs in China are said to be unaffordable (Qiao, 2013), it would seem that a large number of older Chinese will not be able to receive sound care, including those whose adult children have emigrated.

Second, while institutional old-age care facilities are on the rise in China, there is apparently a cultural stigma attached to the utilisation of such institutions, given that it implies lack of filial piety – an important cultural value that posits family-centred care provision for the aged as the preferable approach. Recently, in 2013, a legal amendment was introduced in China requiring adult children to visit their ageing parents each year and stay in touch "often". The amendment does not particularly target China's overseas population, but it has significant implications for it (Liu, 2016). Although the majority of elderly parents of young adult migrants do not need financial assistance from their children, ageing care is nevertheless a moral responsibility for adult migrants. This legal amendment was passed as part of the government's efforts to solve the social problem of the "left behind" (Lin, Yin, & Loubere, 2014) ageing population due to the large volume of China's rural-to-urban migration and the trend of young people moving to big cities for job opportunities but leaving their ageing parents to cope with their late stage of lives alone.

Coupled with this cultural stigma is the legacy of China's "one-child" policy which makes the fulfilment of this moral duty challenging for many adult Chinese nationals, including migrants overseas who are often the only child. If the only child of a family emigrates, his or her ageing parents are simply left behind. Consequently, the migrant families are under tremendous pressure to arrange care for their elderly parents in the homeland – China. Therefore, bringing their elderly parents to New Zealand is one feasible option. Recent research shows that childcare by grandparents is a common strategy that many Chinese migrant families adopt to cope with multiple life transitions in the course of immigration. In return, the adult children assume responsibility for supporting their parents in New Zealand when they are unable to live on their own. In such a way, generations mutually benefit from such multi-generational and transnational arrangements (Ho et al., 2010; Liu, 2016). This is how multi-generational Chinese migrant family and households have typically been formed and sustained.

Notes

1 It should be noted that "country of birth" is the category used for the national census, while INZ data uses "country of origin/citizenship". A small proportion of "China-born" arrivals may hold passports from Taiwan, Hong Kong, or Southeast Asian countries.

2 "One Belt, One Road" initiation is also known as "The Belt and Road (B&R)". This development strategy is two-folded. "One Belt" refers to the Silk Road Economic Belt, a land-based and economically cooperated zone. It includes countries situated on the original Silk Road through Central Asia, West Asia, the Middle East, and Europe. The initiative calls for the integration of the region into a cohesive economic area through building infrastructure, increasing cultural exchanges, and broadening trade. Apart from this zone, which is largely analogous to the historical Silk Road, another area that is said to be included in the extension of this "belt" is South Asia and Southeast Asia. Many of the countries that are part of this belt are also members of the China-led Asian Infrastructure Investment Bank (AIIB). North, Central, and South belts are proposed. The North belt would go through Central Asia, Russia to Europe. The Central belt goes through Central Asia, West Asia to the Persian Gulf and the Mediterranean. The South belt starts from China to Southeast Asia, South Asia, to the Indian Ocean through Pakistan. One Road refers to the twenty-first century Maritime Silk Road, an oceangoing zone as a complementary initiative to "One Belt" that aims at investing and fostering collaboration in Southeast Asia, Oceania, and North Africa, through several contiguous bodies of water – the South China Sea, the South Pacific Ocean, and the wider Indian Ocean.

3 The Labour Government was formed by the Labour Party – a social-democratic political party and one of the two major parties in New Zealand politics. Another major party is the National Party.

4 National, also named as National Party, is a centre-right and one of the two major political parties in New Zealand politics.

5 The "Little Asian Dragons" is a popular term that is used to describe the robust economies of South Korea, Hong Kong, Taiwan, and Singapore.

6 The "Asian" here means people from three Asian regions: North, South, and Southeast.

7 The General Category (GC) is divided into two sub-categories – "General Skilled Category" (GSC) and "General Investment Category" (GIC). Under GSC, applicants are assessed on employability, age, and settlement factors. People who have a tertiary education, preferably with a science, technical, or engineering degree can have a maximum of 15 points. Those who are between 25 and 29 can have a maximum of 10 points. Those who have 20 years of working experience relevant to their qualifications can have 10 points. Under the GIC, applicants score points on the basis of capital (NZ$100,000 – NZ$300,000) to be invested for at least two years.

8 This party was widely regarded as opportunistic, anti-immigrant, and anti-Asian.

9 Under the MMP election system, there are 120 members in a single chamber Parliament. The political parties win seats according their nationwide share of the vote. There are two different kinds of members in parliament: some are "electoral MPs" and some are "list MPs". Sixty-five seats go to the highest polling candidates of the country's 65 electorates (with about 52,000 people each). At the election, every voter can cast two votes: one for the preferred electoral candidate and one for the preferred party. Political parties that win a greater share of the total vote than the actual number of their electorate MPs will "top up" by adding candidates from the parties' ranked lists. This system was introduced partly to guarantee that the place and role of minorities are adequately represented. Under the old system, it was highly unlikely that candidates from ethnic minorities could be chosen by any major parties to be electorate candidates. Parties thus needed to choose candidates who had broad appeal and can draw a majority of votes from the local population – who are mostly of European origin. Under the new MMP system, an ethnic candidate can be picked as a party-list candidate as a focus to appeal for the support of the ethnic community nationwide and be then used as a vote-drawing magnet for the ethnic population throughout New Zealand.

10 It is a negative comment used in Australia referring to the sharp increase of New Zealand citizens' moving to Australia, but born outside of New Zealand.

11 It includes: 1) those who are within five points of the pass mark could apply for an open work permit, thus making it easier for them to accumulate the point necessary for residence while meeting a demand for labour; 2) the language requirements for principal applicants was reduced from a minimum of 5 in each of the four IELTS modules (including listening, speaking, reading, and writing) to an average of five across all four modules.

12 The New Zealand Immigration Programme (NZIP) was renamed as the New Zealand Residence Programme (NZRP) in July 2006.

13 There were two types of talent visa introduced in April 2002. The first was for skilled workers in demand by accredited employers who were prepared to pay a minimum base salary of NZ$45,000 for at least two years. The second was for applicants deemed to have exceptional talent in a declared field of art, culture, and sport, who were being sponsored by reputable New Zealand organisations. In both cases, the visa was issued for two years with the provision that after this period the applicant could apply for residence while still in New Zealand.

14 This permit came into effect in April 2002, specifying occupations in which there was an absolute shortage of labour. This was a refined version of the Occupation Priority List (OPL) that had been a key component of immigration policy during the 1980s. POL work permits could be issued for two years to people meeting pressing labour shortages, and at the end of this period they also could apply for permanent residence.

15 Job Search Visa (JSV) offered to an applicant where his/her qualification(s) is(are) relevant to occupations on the Occupation Shortage List. This policy also applied to those who lodged their applications for residence prior to November 2002 and were waiting to have their applications processed at the time the changes came in.

16 Under a managed entry regime introduced in 2001, overall permanent residence approvals include both "economic" and "social" streams of immigrants. This "economic" stream includes the "skill/business" category, while the "social" stream includes family and humanitarian categories.

17 A family's "centre of gravity" is in New Zealand if: 1) the principal applicant parent has no dependent children, and the number of a couple's adult children lawfully and permanently in New Zealand is equal to or greater than those lawfully and permanently in any other single country, including the country in which the principal applicant is lawfully and permanently resident; or 2) the principal applicant parent has dependent children, and the number of his or her adult children

lawfully and permanently in New Zealand is equal to or greater than those lawfully and permanently in any other single country, including the country in which the principal applicant parent is lawfully and permanently resident, and the number of their dependent children is equal to or fewer than the number of their adult children who are law-fully and permanently in New Zealand.

18 The "one-child" policy was introduced by the PRC government in 1979 to combat China's population problem. The policy decreed that a couple should have only one child and inflicted penalties on couples that have more than one child. This policy has been recently abolished in 2015.

References

Ang, I. (2016). At home in Asia? Sydney's Chinatown and Australia's 'Asian century'. *International Journal of Cultural Studies, 19*(3), 257–269.

Baker, M. (1994). The performance of immigrants in the Canadian labor market. *Journal of Labor Economics, 12*(3), 369–405.

Bedford, R. (2005). International migration and globalization: The transformation of New Zealand's migration system since the mid-1980's. In R. Patman & C. Rudd (Eds.), *Sovereign Under Siege? Globalization and New Zealand* (pp. 129–155). Hants, UK: Ashgate Publishing Limited.

Bedford, R., Farmer, R. S. J., & Trlin, A. (1987). The immigration policy review. *New Zealand Population Review, 13*(1), 49–65.

Bedford, R., & Ho, E. (1997). The population conference: Talkfest or turning point? *New Zealand Population Review, 23*(1&2), 95–106.

Bedford, R., & Ho, E. (2006). Immigration future: New Zealand in a global context. *New Zealand Population Review, 32*(2), 49–63.

Bedford, R., Ho, E., & Bedford, C. (2010). Pathways to residence in New Zealand 2003–2010. In A. Trlin, P. Spoonley, & R. Bedford (Eds.), *New Zealand and International Migration: A Digest and Bibliography, Number 5* (pp. 1–49). Palmerston North, New Zealand: Massey University Printery.

Bedford, R., Ho, E., & Lidgard, J. (2000). *International Migration in New Zealand: Context, Components and Policy Issues* (Discussion Papers No. 37). Hamilton, New Zealand: Population Studies Centre, University of Waikato.

Bedford, R., Ho, E., & Lidgard, J. (2005a). From Targets to outcomes: Immigration policy in New Zealand, 1996–2003. In A. Trlin, P. Spoonley, & N. Watts (Eds.), *New Zealand and International Migration: A Digest and Bibliography, Number 4* (Vol. 4, pp. 1–43). Palmerston North: Department of Sociology, Massey University.

Bedford, R., Lidgard, J., & Ho, E. (2005b). Arrivals, Departures and net migration, 1996/97–2002/03. In A. Trlin, P. Spoonley, & N. Watts (Eds.), *New Zealand and International Migration: A Digest and Bibliography, Number 4* (pp. 44–69). Palmerston North: Department of Sociology, Massey University.

Bedford, R., Lidgard, J., & Young, J. (1995). *Globalisation and Population Change in New Zealand, 1986–1994.* Hamilton, New Zealand: Population Studies Centre, University of Waikato.

Bedford, R., & Liu, L. (2013). Parents in New Zealand's family sponsorship policy: A preliminary assessment of the impact of the 2012 policy changes. *New Zealand Population Review, 39.*

Birch, B. (1989). Immigration policy: Guidelines for 1990. *New Zealand Population Review, 15*(1), 55–59.

Borevi, K. (2015a). Family migration policies and politics: Understanding the Swedish exception. *Journal of Family Issues, 36*(11), 1490–1508.

Borevi, K. (2015b). Family migration policies and politics: Understanding the Swedish exception. *Journal of Family Issues, 36*(11), 1490–1408.

Burke, K. (1986). *Review of Immigration Policy August 1986*. Wellington: Government Printer.

Cunliffe, H. D. (2007a). *Review of Family Sponsorship Policies: Paper for the Cabinet Policy Committee Attached to POL (07) 160, 21 May 2007*. Wellington: New Zealand Ministry of Business, Innovation and Employment.

Cunliffe, H. D. (2007b). *Review of Family Sponsorship Policies: Paper for the Cabinet Policy Committee Attached to POL(07) 160, 21 May 2017*. Wellington: New Zealand ministry of Business, Innovation and Employment.

Czaika, M., & De Haas, H. (2013). The effectiveness of immigration policies. *Population and Development Review, 39*(3), 487–508.

DeShaw, R. (2006a). The history of family reunification in Canada and current policy. *Canadian Issues, 9*.

DeShaw, R. (2006b). The history of family reunification in Canada and current policy. *Canadian Issues,* Spring(9–14).

Eng, K. K. (2006a). Locating the self in the Chinese diaspora: Introductory remarks. *Asian Studies Review, 30*, 217–221.

Eng, K. K. (2006b). Transnational self in the Chinese diaspora: A conceptual framework. *Asian Studies Review, 30*, 223–239.

Gittings, J. (1989). *China Changes Face: The Road From Revolution, 1949–1989*. Oxford: Oxford University Press.

Henderson, A. M. (2003). Untapped talents: The employment and settlement experiences of skilled Chinese in New Zealand. In M. Ip (Ed.), *Unfolding History, Evolving Identity: The Chinese in New Zealand* (pp. 141–164). Auckland: Auckland University Press.

Henderson, A. M., Trlin, A., Pernice, R., & North, N. (1997). English language requirements and immigration policy in New Zealand, 1986–1997. *New Zealand Population Review, 23*(1/2), 19–44.

Ho, E. (2003). Reluctant exiles or roaming transnationals? The Hong Kong Chinese in New Zealand. In M. Ip (Ed.), *Unfolding History, Evolving Identity: The Chinese in New Zealand* (pp. 165–184). Auckland: Auckland University Press.

Ho, E. (2005, Tuesday, October 18). *From Students to Residents: Policy Initiatives, Data Issues and Research Findings in New Zealand*. Paper presented at the The 10th International Metropolis Conference's Workshop on International Students as Immigrants, Metropolitan Toronto Convention Centre, Toronto, Canada.

Ho, E. (2006). Contemporary migration and settlement of Chinese migrants in New Zealand. In D. Ip, R. Hibbins, & W. H. Chui (Eds.), *Experiences of Transnational Chinese Migrants in the Asia-Pacific* (pp. 41–58). New York: Nova Science Publishers.

Ho, E., Cheung, E., Bedford, C. E., & Leung, P. (2000). *The Settlement Assistance Needs of Recent Migrants*. Wellington: New Zealand Immigration Service.

Ho, E., Lewin, J., & Muntz, M. (2010). *Ageing Well in a New Country: Preliminary Findings of a Survey of Older Chinese People in New Zealand*. Hamilton, New Zealand: Population Studies Centre, University of Waikato.

Ho, E., Lidgard, J., Bedford, R., & Spoonley, P. (1997). East Asian migrants in New Zealand: Adaptation and employment. In A. Trlin & P. Spoonley (Eds.), *New*

Zealand and International Migration: A Digest and Bibliography, Number 3 (Vol. 3, pp. 42–59). Palmerston North: Department of Sociology, Massey University.

Hugo, G. (2004). Future immigration policy development in Australia and New Zealand. *New Zealand Population Review, 30*(1&2), 23–42.

Immigration New Zealand. (2017a). *Review of Temporary Migrant Work Settings.* Retrieved June 15, 2017 from www.immigration.govt.nz/about-us/media-centre/news-notifications/review-temporary-migrant-work-settings

Immigration New Zealand. (2017b). *Skilled Migrant Category Changes.* Retrieved June 15, 2017 from www.immigration.govt.nz/about-us/media-centre/news-notifications/skilled-migrant-category-changes

Ip, D., Lui, C. W., & Chui, W. H. (2007). Veiled entrapment: A study of social isolation of older Chinese migrants in Brisbane, Queensland. *Aging and Society, 27,* 719–738.

Ip, M. (1995). Chinese New Zealanders: Old settlers and new immigrants. In S. W. Greif (Ed.), *Immigration and National Identity in New Zealand: One People, Two Peoples, Many Peoples?* (pp. 161–199). Palmerstone North, New Zealand: The Dunmore Press Ltd.

Ip, M. (2001). Chinese business immigrants to New Zealand: Transnationals or failed investors? In M. Ip (Ed.), *Re-Examining Chinese Transnationalism in Australia-New Zealand* (pp. 45–59). Canberra: Centre for the Study of the Chinese Southern Diaspora, Australian National University.

Ip, M. (2002). Chinese political participation in New Zealand: The role of Taiwan migrants *Essays on Ethnic Chinese Abroad, Volume 2* (pp. 223–240). Taipei: Academia Sinica.

Ip, M. (2006a). New Zealand. In L. Pan (Ed.), *Encyclopedia of Chinese Overseas* (pp. 286–291). Singapore: Curzon.

Ip, M. (2006b). Returnees and transnationals: Evolving identities of Chinese (PRC) immigrants in New Zealand. *Journal of Population Studies, 33,* 61–102.

Ip, M., & Friesen, W. (2001). The new Chinese community in New Zealand: Local outcomes of transnationalism. *Asian and Pacific Migration Journal, 10*(2), 213–240.

Kasper, W. (1990). *Populate or Languish? Rethinking New Zealand's Immigration Policy.* Wellington: New Zealand Business Roundtable.

Li, W. W. (2011). Filial piety, parental piety and community piety: Changing cultural practices of elder support among Chinese migrant families in New Zealand. *The Journal of Multicultural Society, 2*(1), 1–30.

Lin, K., Yin, D., & Loubere, N. (2014). Social support and the 'left behind' elderly in rural China: A case study. *Journal of Community Health, 39*(4), 674–681.

Liu, L. (2016). Intergenerational dimensions of transnational Chinese migrant families in New Zealand. *Journal of Chinese Overseas, 12*(2), 216–250.

Liu, X. F., & Norcliffe, G. (1996). Closed windows, open doors: Geopolitics and post-1949 mainland Chinese immigration to Canada. *Canadian Geographer, 40*(4), 306–319.

Luo, K., Guo, F., & Huang, P. (2003). China: Government policies and emerging trends of reversal of the brain drain. In R. Iredale, F. Guo, & S. Rozario (Eds.), *Return Migration in the Asia Pacific* (pp. 88–111). Cheltenham, UK: Edward Elgar Publishing Limited.

Mckinnon, M. (1996). *Immigrants and Citizens: New Zealanders and Asian Immigration in Historical Context.* Wellington: Institute of Policy Studies.

McMillan, K., Trlin, A., Spoonley, P., & Watts, N. (2005). Immigration, nationalism, and citizenship debates in the 1990s. *New Zealand and International Migration: A Digest and Bibliography*, (4), 70–85.

Miller, P. W. (1986). Immigrant unemployment in the first year of Australian labour market activity. *The Economic Record, 62*(1), 82–87.

New Zealand Immigration Services. (1995). *A Review of NZ Immigration Policy: The "Targeted" Immigration Streams; A Briefing Paper for Minister, November 1994.* Wellington: New Zealand Immigration Service.

Ngai, J., Sneader, K., & Zecha, C. M. (2016). China's One Belt, One Road: Will it reshape global trade? *Mckinsey & Company.* Retrieved June 13, 2017 from www.mckinsey.com/global-themes/china/chinas-one-belt-one-road-will-it-reshape-global-trade

Office of the Minister of Immigration, N. Z. (2016). *New Zealand Residence Programme Cabinet Paper (October 2016).* Wellington: Ministry of Business, Innovation & Employment.

Ong, A. (1992). Limits to cultural accumulations: Chinese capitalists on the American Pacific rim. *Annals New York Academy of Sciences, 645,* 125–143.

Phillips, T. (2017). World's biggest building project amis to make China great again. *The Guardian News and Media.* Retrieved June 13, 2017 from www.theguardian.com/world/2017/may/12/chinese-president-belt-and-road-initiative

Poot, J. (1992). International migration in the New Zealand economy of the 1980s. In A. Trlin & P. Spoonley (Eds.), *New Zealand and International Migration: A Digest and Bibliography, Number 2* (pp. 29–47). Palmerston North: Department of Sociology, Massey University.

Poot, J. (1993). Adaptation of migrants in the New Zealand labor market. *International Migration Review, 27*(1), 121–139.

Qiao, J. (2013). Reinventing China's health system. In G. Wang & Y. Zheng (Eds.), *China: Development and Governance* (pp. 333–341). Singapore: World Scientific.

Robinson, D. (2013). Migration policy under the coalition government. *People Place and Policy Online, 7*(2), 73–81.

Simon-Kumar, R. (2015). Neoliberalism and the new race politics of migration policy: Changing profiles of the desirable migrant in New Zealand. *Journal of Ethnic and Migration Studies, 41*(7), 1172–1191.

Skeldon, R. (1996). Migration from China. *Journal of International Affairs, 49*(2), 434–455.

Skeldon, R. (2004). *China: From Exceptional Case to Global Participants.* Retrieved August 6, 2009 from www.migrationinformation.org/Profiles/display.cfm?ID=219

Spoonley, P., & Trlin, A. (2004). *Immigration, Immigrants and the Media: Making Sense of Multicultural New Zealand.* New Settlers Programme Occasional Publication No. 9. Palmerston North: Massey University.

Statistics New Zealand. (2014). 2013 *Census Ethnic Group Profiles: Chinese.* Retrieved June 29, 2017 from www.stats.govt.nz/Census/2013-census/profile-and-summary-reports/ethnic-profiles.aspx?request_value=24737&tabname=Education

Trlin, A. (1992). Change and continuity: New Zealand's Immigration policy in the late 1980s. In A. Trlin & P. Spoonley (Eds.), *New Zealand and International Migration: A Digest and Bibliography, Number 2* (Vol. 2, pp. 1–28). Palmerston North: Department of Sociology, Massey University.

Trlin, A. (1997). For the promotion of economic growth and prosperity: New Zealand's immigration policy, 1991–1995. In A. Trlin & P. Spoonley (Eds.), *New*

Zealand and International Migration: A Digest and Bibliography, Number 3 (pp. 1–27). Palmerston North: Department of Sociology, Massey University.

Trlin, A., & Kang, J. (1992). The business immigration policy and the characteristics of approved Hong Kong and Taiwanese applicants. In A. Trlin., & P. Spoonley (Eds.), *New Zealand and International Migration: A Digest and Bibliography, Number 2* (pp. 48–64): Department of Sociology, Massey University.

Waldinger, R. (1990). *Ethnic Entrepreneurs: Immigrant Business in Industrial Societies.* Newbury Park: Sage Publications.

Winkelmann, L., & Winkelmann, R. (1998). *Immigrants in New Zealand: A Study of Their Labour Market Outcomes* (Occasional Paper 1998/1). Wellington: Department of Labour, New Zealand.

Woodhouse, M. (2016). *NZRP Changes to Strike the Right Balance.*

Xiang, B. (2003). Emigration from China: A sending country perspective. *International Migration, 41*(3), 21–48.

Zeng, M., & Williamson, P. J. (2003). The hidden dragons. *Harvard Business Review, 81,* 1–10.

Zhang, Y. (2013). Meeting the ageing challenge: China's social care policy for the elderly. In G. Wang & Y. Zheng (Eds.), *China: Development and Governance* (pp. 343–349). Singapore: World Scientific.

Zolberg, A. R. (1989). The next waves: Migration theory for a changing world. *International Migration Review, 23,* 403–430.

3 Re-grounding "transnationalism" in theories and practices

Since the main focus of this research is the transnational character of the new PRC migrants, the primary theory employed to lay out the theoretical groundwork for the work was transnationalism, especially transnationalism in migration studies. The study of transnational migration stems from the interrogation of traditional international migration scholarship and the academic debates involving migration and globalisation (Bailey, 2001, p. 8; Faist, 2004; Kivisto, 2001). The reality that increasing numbers of migrants maintain contact and involvement with their origin nations and locales and also engage in cross-border activities has brought about serious questions regarding the processes, causes, and consequences of these new patterns of migratory movements. Previous scholarship in migration study has often viewed migration as a linear process or series of processes. It can be a permanent uprooting followed by assimilation into a new society or a temporary sojourn followed by a permanent return to the homeland or circulatory movement between a fixed home base and a temporary destination in which an unequal commitment to two places is maintained (Heisler, 2008). Heisler (2008) also suggests that there are two primary study focuses in the previous scholarship of migration study. The first has been a focus on the causes behind migration, and the second was migrant adaptation and settlement issues and the impact of migration on the immigrant-receiving countries. These two focuses have remained perpetual themes in migration study and indeed extensively examined.

Both the push-and-pull and the centre-periphery models are often used to chart the reasons for migration. The former simply concentrates on internal factors in the migrants' receiving and sending countries that together conspire to promote emigration. The latter views migration flow between emigration and immigration countries as a structural dependence that exists between the core and the periphery regions in a capitalist world economy. Namely, emigration countries are post-colonial regions that are economically less developed and a politically penetrated periphery, while the immigration countries are in a higher position in the politico-economic world hierarchy. This structural dependence between emigration and immigration countries is the primary cause of migration from the developing world to the economically more developed world (Faist, 2000b).

While previous migration scholarship paid attention to analysing the causes of migration, research priorities were also given to the post-migration processes and the patterns of migrant adaptation and integration, or sometimes even exclusion from their host society (Heisler, 2008; Vertovec, 2001b).The assimilation perspective[1] was regarded in the past and is still regarded to some extent as a useful concept that offers possible ways to understand and describe the migrant adaptation and integration process and the settlement outcome (Alba & Nee, 2003; Gans, 1999; Glick-Schiller, Basch, & Blanc-Szanton, 1992).

However, the current migration processes commonly associated with globalisation have brought into serious question the previous models and theories used to examine the movement of people. The main problem associated with the traditional models and theories of migration is the lack of a global perspective that can fully explain the complexity of the current situation and changed processes of migration. For example, the centre-periphery model that implies an enduring trajectory of migration from global South to North is insufficient to explain the recent return migration process from the economically well-developed countries to the economically developing countries, such as China and India. Traditional neoclassical economics and the new economics of migration that simply view migration as a flow and an outcome of individuals and families' conscious consideration of their economic well-being (Massey et al., 1997; Massey et al., 1993; Massey, Goldring, & Durand, 1994) is insufficient for a comprehensive understanding of the variety of migration rationale beyond economic motivations. Although the "world system theory"[2] moves beyond the examination of migration within a structured framework that emphasises micro-level economies as the main motivation of migration, its essential view of migration as labour transfer between different geographic regions that perform unequal functions in a global division of labour (Massey, Arango et al., 1994; Massey et al., 1993) carries certain limitations, because other important aspects, such as social, political, cultural, and historical factors that are actually associated with migration are ignored (Glick-Schiller et al., 1992). The theory of circular migration emphasises the importance of dual home bases (i.e. the homeland and immigrant-receiving countries) within the migrants' movement circle (Hugo, 2003; Vertovec, 2008), which is highly relevant to our understanding of the movement pattern of recent Chinese migrants. However, other movement patterns that are beyond this homeland-receiving country circle are largely left out.

Theories that particularly focus on the post-migration processes of adaptation also seem to be largely out-of-date. For example, assimilation theory that relies on the ideology of hegemony and emphasises the efforts migrants made to integrate into the host society seems hardly convincing today when exploring current migrants' frequent commuting behaviours that look highly likely to be an alternative strategy of adaptation. Another main limitation of the traditional models and theories comes from the way migration study has been built. Early social science, the cradle of migration study, has been dominated by static models for a long time wherein society and culture were viewed as bounded units within nation-states and territories to set the backdrop of viewing migration as only a fixed and closed process (Bailey, 2001; Glick-Schiller et al., 1992).

The inadequacy of such theories and models in examining current international migration has stimulated increasingly diverse debate on the topic of migration. This debate is often paralleled by a discussion of globalisation, partly because the increasing occurrence of transnational activity among many migrants is facilitated by the process of globalisation. It is also an outcome of the increasing availability and affordability of transportation, changed border configurations and international relations, and the development and increased use of new information technologies. These debates have forced migration researchers to reconsider the ways they examine international migration and rethinking the basic concepts closely associated with international migration, such as citizenship, race, class, and ethnicity. Migration is increasingly perceived as a fluid and dynamic process of movement. In this sense, migration is neither a process of uprooting and leaving the homeland permanently nor a process of sojourning with constant longing and expectation of an eventual return to the homeland. Rather, based on an on-going connection between the homeland and the immigration destination country, it is an open process in which migrants never completely leave their homeland nor totally stay at a new destination. It is a process with the potential for continuous movement ahead.

The rest of this chapter is divided into two parts. The first will briefly discuss the original theoretical articulation of the framework of transnational migration, further conceptual refinement and development, and recent developments in transnational migration studies. Particular research areas that closely relate to my research topic are identified and discussed. The second part of this chapter will discuss how relevant the theory of transnationalism in migration studies is for this book project and focus on the research methodology which was informed by the theories employed in this research.

Theoretical articulation of transnational migration and its conceptual refinement and development

Original theoretical articulation of transnational migration

Some of the first efforts that were made to conceptualise transnationalism in migration studies were by American anthropologists, Nina Glick-Schiller, Linda Basch, and Cristina Blanc-Szanton, in the early 1990s. Their primary aim in conceptualising transnational migration was to chart a new research paradigm "in which global economic processes, and the continuing contradictory persistence of nation-states can be linked to migrants' social relationships, political actions, loyalties, beliefs, and identities" (Glick-Schiller et al., 1992, p. 8). This theoretical conceptualisation was based on empirical case studies of increased cross-border activities of contemporary migrants from Haiti, the Eastern Caribbean, and the

Philippines living in New York. In this work, the authors defined transnationalism as follows:

> The processes by which immigrants forge and sustain multi-stranded social relations that link together their societies of origin and settlement. We call these processes transnationalism to emphasize that many immigrants today build social fields that cross geographic, cultural and political borders.
>
> (Basch, Glick-Schiller, & Blanc, 1994, p. 7)

The term "transnationalism" is often used interchangeably with the phrase "transnational migration" in migration studies to emphasise migrants' on-going and simultaneous embeddings in more than one society. Migrants who build social relationships across geographic, cultural and political borders, develop and retain multiple relations that span borders, and practice constant geographic mobility were defined as transnational migrants (Glick-Schiller et al., 1992; Glick Schiller, Basch, & Blanc-Szanton, 1995).

The theoretical point that Glick-Schiller and co-authors made suggests that the traditional theoretical frameworks for analysing migration were not up to the task of analysing the multi-faceted situation of contemporary migration. The transnational approach derives from a recognition that the constant flow of people back and forth cannot be captured accurately by the term "migrants", which traditionally evokes the meaning that migrants are people who uproot and move themselves to their country of destination and then settle there permanently. Other categories/terms are also used to identify different patterns of migration, such as "return migrants", "temporary migrants", "sojourners", or "diaspora", but are still not adequate to provide a holistic view of the contemporary situation of migrants. Glick-Schiller (1997) in her later work makes this point more explicitly by saying that scholars should be "discard[ing] previous categorizations of return, circulatory, or permanent immigration" (p. 158). Bailey supports the idea of changing the typologies for categorising migrants. He argues that the traditional classification of migration types, defined by using national borders as the paradigm of analysis in which individual migrants and groups are viewed as "retain[ing] fixed and monogamous connections to the territory of one nation-state or another, either the host or the origin", is highly problematic (Bailey, 2001, p. 415). The reality usually undermines the generalisability of using national borders as the defining basis for portraying the true picture of current migration.

To chart a new research paradigm, Glick-Schiller and co-authors introduced two key conceptual points. The first is that the study of migrants and migration in the social sciences must unwind from its traditional focus on the nation-state as the key container of social action. They advocated discarding the analysis of migration within nation states and situating contemporary migration in a global context "by recognizing that the world is currently bound together by a global capitalist system" (Glick-Schiller et al., 1992, p. 8). The second key conceptual point the authors made is that within the framework of transnational migration there is a need to rethink certain long-accepted understandings of class, race, nationalism, and ethnicity. What Glick-Schiller and co-authors suggest is that if migration is conceptualised in a new way as transnationalism indicates, concepts such as race, class, ethnicity, and nationalism that are immediately associated with migration have to be viewed in an alternative way (Glick-Schiller et al., 1992). Fundamentally, race, class, nationalism, and ethnicity in a transnationalism framework need to be more flexible to take into account the new multiple forms of identification that transnationals and transnational migrants potentially possess and apply.

Apart from these two key conceptual points is another important premise to understand regarding the conceptualisation of transnationalism. That premise is that transnationalism is grounded in the daily lives, activities, and social relationships of individual migrants (Glick-Schiller et al., 1992). In other words, transnationalism is a grassroots activity. This idea was further developed and conceptualised by other scholars as transnationalism "from below" or "grassroots transnationalism" (Portes, Guarnizo, & Landolt, 1999). This concept suggests that transnational migration and movement does not originate and is not initiated by actions or policies of governments, national or local. Rather, it is an individualised process and solidly grounded in personal and family decisions (Portes et al., 1999; Smith, 1992, 1994). The concept is a complementary one to the concept of transnationalism "from above" that is regularly manifested by multinational corporations, media, governments, and other macro-level structures and processes. These structures and processes transcend two or more societies controlled by powerful elites who seek economic, political, or social dominance in the world (Guarnizo, 1997; Guarnizo & Smith, 1998; Mahler, 2003). In terms of this project, a good grasp of the differences between the concepts of transnationalism "from below" and transnationalism "from above" is important, since migration, especially voluntary migration, is essentially an individual choice or a decision made by an individual family, but at the same time also closely related to government policies in both the immigration sending and the immigration receiving countries.

The original idea of transnationalism proposed several reasons for transnational migration. The first rationale is deeply rooted in "a global restructuring of capital based on changing forms of capital accumulation" (Glick-Schiller, Basch, & Blanc-Szanton, 1995, p. 50) and economic dislocations in both the Third World and the industrialised nations. This imbalance of capital distribution stimulates an increased immigration volume but simultaneously makes it difficult for migrants to construct "a secure terrain of settlement" (Glick-Schiller et al., 1992, p. 9). Under such circumstances, migrants construct a transnational existence as a survival strategy. The second rationale follows the first. Rapid economic, cultural, and labour exchanges can heighten the exclusion of new immigrants from the host populations or in some cases even from the host institutions. Concerns about labour market competition and economic well-being can be racialised and linked to immigration-related issues, and immigrants often become the scapegoat for any tightening of labour markets. Thus, racial discrimination and hostile attitudes toward migrants can result in the non-permanent residence of migrants in immigration receiving countries and even contribute to a permanent departure of migrants to seek opportunities either in the homeland or elsewhere. The last rationale refers to the fact that national building projects of both the home and the host society still try to cultivate national and political loyalties among immigrants, which has a significant impact on migrant maintenance of a connection to both societies (Glick Schiller et al., 1995).

Still another widely recognised reason frequently mentioned by scholars is the availability of technological advances in long-distance transport and communications, such as jet air transport, long-distance telephone, facsimile communication, and the Internet. These provide a technological basis for the emergence of transnationalism. With these facilitating factors, the space and cost of transnational transportation and communication have shrunk. Thus, the frequency and scope of transnational activities of contemporary migrants more easily accelerates and in recent years, expanded to an unprecedented level (Bailey, 2001; Portes, 1999; Portes et al., 1999; Vertovec, 1999).

Conceptual refinement and development

The works most responsible for contributing to the further development of the theoretical conceptualisation of transnational migration are by Portes, Vertovec, and Faist (Faist, 2000a, 2000b, 2004; Portes, 1999; Portes et al., 1999; Vertovec, 1999, 2001a, 2001b). Broadly speaking, the research proposed to refine and develop a theoretical conceptualisation of transnational migration is mainly devoted to four aspects. The first would define the analytical scope; the second, delimit the phenomenon; the third, address the significance of transnational migration; and the last, approach transnational migration by challenging current social theory, especially the "nation-state container" theory. In the following, I will briefly discuss these aspects.

Portes el al. (1999) point out that transnational migration study was highly fragmented by saying that "narratives presented in existing studies, for example, often use disparate units of analysis (that is, individuals, groups, organizations, local states) and mix diverse levels of abstraction" (p. 218). The authors suggest that the concept of transnationalism must be turned into "a clearly defined and measurable object of research" (Portes et al., 1999, p. 218). By inheriting the concept of transnationalism "from below", Portes et al. (1999) are particularly interested in "bottom-up" transnational activities and define individuals and their support networks as the proper unit of analysis. A structured working typology grounded within the framework of transnationalism "from below" and "from above" as economic, political, and socio-cultural categories, is also proposed (Portes et al., 1999). From the authors' point of view, that categorisation falls appropriately within the definition of both transnationalism "from below" and transnationalism "from above". Such an approach is used to define the analytical unit and to categorise different types of transnationalism, even if it is largely based on methodological convenience (Kivisto, 2001), at least provides a platform to use to organise the chaotic empirical studies on transnational migration.

For purposes of providing further clarity about what transnationalism refers to in migration studies, Portes and co-authors realised the importance of delimiting the scope of "transnational migration". They attempted to delimit the use of transnationalism to those migration-related activities that involve a "significant proportion of persons in the relevant universe" and "require regular and sustained social contacts over time across national borders for their implementation" (Portes et al., 1999, p. 219). The authors particularly stressed that occasional contacts, trips, and activities across national borders for members of an expatriate community are not sufficiently distinct enough to justify as being transnational migration or to form an empirical basis for a new area of investigation. The true transnational migration phenomenon should be characterised by a "high intensity of exchanges, new modes of transacting, and the multiplication of activities that require cross-border travel and contacts on a sustained basis" (Portes et al., 1999, p. 219). Such a point of view implies that not all recent migrants are actual transnationals.

Portes (1999, 2001) also attempts to identify the necessary preconditions that can extend the transnational phenomenon to the current intensive level. He particularly asserted that people with greater economic resources and human capital are more likely to forge transnational linkages (Portes, 1999, 2001). Other important forces that can shape individual migrants' movement choices include the migration incentive for the first movement, the maintenance of social networks with the homeland, and whether homeland issues remain salient for immigrants (Portes, 1999, 2001). Vertovec (2001b) concurs with these points and then adds a more macro factor that also contributes to the formation of transnational linkages, namely, the shifting economic and political circumstances in both sending and receiving countries, which may have a significant influence on shaping migrant desire to be involved in economic and political activities across borders.

In addressing the significance of transnationalism, Portes compared transnationalism to the traditional theory of assimilation. In some of the literature, Portes et al. (1999) viewed transnationalism as "an alternative adaptation path for immigrants" (p. 228). Elsewhere, Portes (1999) perceives transnationalism "as an effective antidote to the tendency towards downward assimilation" (p. 471). Regardless of the nuance, the point Portes and co-authors intend to make is that involvement in those transnational activities does not contradict the successful integration into a host society; rather, they facilitate successful adaptation by providing economic security and geographic mobility for immigrants through non-conventional pathways. The conventional path for economic success and climbing to a higher social status largely relies on the degree and speed of migrant acculturation and integration into the mainstream society of the host country. However, the non-conventional path is cultivating strong social networks across national borders to create a transnational social field in which economic security can be achieved, followed by a gradual lift in social status in the immigration host country (Portes et al., 1999).

Economic wellbeing is perceived as crucial for immigrants, because it is an infra-structural and material basis for immigrants who intend to climb the social ladder. Nonini and Ong's (1997) work on Chinese transnationalism supports Portes's point by perceiving Chinese transnationalism as a process as well as a strategy of capital accumulation, and such strategies are integral part of the transnational process and in turn are affected by them. As well as addressing the economic aspect of transnationalism, Portes (1999) also sees transnationalism as a way for immigrants to reinforce their self-confidence and re-affirm their collective worth by locating their original cultural anchors; thus, it offers a level of confidence, so immigrants can overcome the difficulties of adaptation to a certain degree.

Another significant wave of theoretical development in transnational migra-tion studies was to conceptualise transnational migration by challenging social theory and reformulating the notions of space and social structure (Levitt & Glick-Schiller, 2004). This development explicitly challenges the "nation-state container" theory that limits the research entity to migration studies within national borders, thus, missing out on the movement flow between nations and the cross-border engagements of migrants. Two widely used concepts that aim to re-conceptualise the meaning of transnationalism are then "transnational social fields" and "transnational social spaces".

The use of "transnational social fields" was initiated by several scholars (Glick-Schiller et al., 1992; Goldring, 1998; Levitt, 2001; Portes et al., 1999), but without a detailed articulation of what that concept really means (Kivisto, 2001). When Glick-Schiller (2004) later revisited the idea of transnationalism, she sug-gested that "transnational social fields" is an unbounded terrain in which the practices and interpersonal relationships of the transnational migrants span spe-cific geographic, cultural, and political borders. Others have suggested that trans-nationalism changes people's relations to space, particularly by creating "social fields" that connect and position some of the actors in more than one location (Goldring, 1998; Levitt, 2001). Levitt (2001) then suggests a key point that "transnational social fields . . . often form from connections between multiple localities" (p. 197), within which lie all aspects of social life that migration engen-ders, including economic relations and social, religious, and political connections between "here" and "there". Portes frequently used the notion of "transna-tional social fields" in his discussion and examination of transnational communi-ties (Portes, 1996a, 1996b, 1998). Recently, Levitt and Glick-Schiller (2007) strongly suggested that within the transnational migration research, social field "as a set of multiple interlocking networks of social relationships through which ideas, practices, and resources are unequally exchanged, organized, and trans-formed" became "a powerful tool for conceptualizing the potential array of social relations linking those who move and those who stay behind" (p. 188).

The concept of "transnational social spaces" also applies to the transnational approach for investigating international migration by moving beyond "the con-tainer theory of society" (Beck, 2000). This is a boundary-breaking process in which two or sometimes more nation-states that are closely linked together become a singular new social space (Faist, 2000a; Pries, 2001). Compared with the concept of "transnational social fields", the geographic metaphoric use of the concept of space, which was stimulated by studies of social practice and relationships among migrant communities spread across multiple localities (Castells, 1996; Vertovec, 2001b), was theoretically conceptualised in a more systematic way. When Thomas Faist, a political scientist, first introduced this concept, he clearly defined it as "combinations of ties, positions in networks and organizations, and networks of organisations that reach across the borders of multiple states" (Faist, 2000a, p. 191). He privileged social relations and institutions, defining these spaces as "characterised by a high density of interstitial ties on informal or formal, that is to say institutional levels" (Faist, 2000a, p. 190). Influenced by the theoretical perspective of the Swedish school of time-geographers (Kivisto, 2001), Faist's use of the term "space" was not equivalent to "place", which usually denotes physical localities. His emphasis on the term "space" was both symbolic and social, and different from physical places (Faist, 2000b).

In the transnational social spaces, not only are people, goods, and information circulated, but also ideas, symbols, and material culture (Faist, 2000b). Faist (2000a) emphasised that trust and reciprocity are crucial in the sustainability of transnational networks, and Kivisto (2001) explained that reciprocity and trust play an important role "in combating economic risk" and "serve to underpin and make instrumental transactions" (p. 568). Three types of transnational social spaces are identified using a structural approach: transnational reciprocity in small groups, namely, kinship groups; transnational exchange in circuits; and solidarity within transnational communities. The basis for the formulation of each type of transnational social space has its own characteristic,[3] and such a categorisation of three types of "transnational social spaces" indeed indicates three different units of analysis – ranging from a more individual-level analysis to a more community-level analysis (Faist, 2000a). Thus, the concept of "transnational social space" is well framed both theoretically and methodologically.

Faist identified the factors that contribute to the formation of transnational social spaces as economic, political, cultural, and technological (Faist, 2000a). Economically, transnational business networks established by migrants in the emigration country (e.g. lower production cost) can stimulate the existence of sustainable transnational linkages across borders. Obstacles of economic integration encountered by many immigrants, especially first-generation immigrants in the immigration-receiving country, also contribute significantly to the creation of transnational social spaces. Many migrants choose to conduct cross-border businesses or conduct businesses offshore where the social and business networks they are more familiar with become a strategy to overcome economic difficulty or maintain economic wellbeing. In this sense, transnationalism is treated as an additional/optional trajectory of immigrant adaptation. Culturally and socially, the lack of cultural belonging to the mainstream society or social discrimination towards immigrants is suggested as being extremely conductive to the formation of transnational social spaces, within which immigrants can generate a culturally comfortable zone for themselves by keeping physically or virtually constant contact with their original culture. Politically, liberal democracies and the multicultural claim of nations provide wider opportunities for immigrants to maintain their cultural distinctiveness and contacts with their countries of origin. Technologically, the development of communication technology and improvement in means of long-distance travel has accelerated the emergence of transnational social spaces (Faist, 2000a).

It should also be acknowledged that the most advanced aspect of "transnational social field" and "transnational social space" is the explicit challenge of the "nation-state container" theory that tends to treat the nation-state as the norm and its boundaries as a given unit in social analysis (Levitt & Glick-Schiller, 2007). Earlier social theory applied to migration study was the assimilation theory where immigration adaptation within nation-states was considered a normal process and one not significantly influenced by border-crossing transactions. However, the increasingly large-scale cross-border activities that contemporary migrants engage in provide strong evidence that those traditional theories do not relate well to the contemporary reality.

Re-grounding transnationalism in migration studies

Further development in transnational migration studies has been characterised by more detailed empirical work and more thoughtful conceptualisation. Greater efforts that have been put forward in the further development of the concept can be summarised as follows: 1) development of new research approaches; 2) more micro-level empirical studies of transnational practices of migrants, leading to an empirical and theoretical re-grounding of the field; 3) expanded studies on the consideration of broader effects that transnational activities of migrants have on the broader context of particular localities. The following text discusses the three aspects and particularly focuses on the research areas most relevant to my research topic.

Developing new research approaches

A great contribution to developing a new research approach for transnational migration studies took place in the field of anthropology and in particular with the work of George Marcus (1995) and Hannerz (1998). George Marcus's (1995) work on multi-sited ethnography and his argument that transnational research techniques need to involve more than one site provides enormous inspiration for further transnational migration scholarship. Marcus (1995) presented seven propositions for transnational research: follow the people; follow the thing; follow the metaphor; follow the plot, story, or allegory; follow the life or biography; follow the conflict; or engage in "strategically situated (single-site) ethnography" capable of grasping a multi-sited context (p. 110). He particularly indicated that migration studies that focus on mobile and contingently settled populations across borders "are perhaps the most common contemporary research genre of this basic mode of multi-sited ethnography" (Marcus, 1995, p. 106). Hannerz (1998) advocated further, stating that the research should be "not merely multi-local, but also trans-local" (p. 247). These approaches do not simply suggest conducting research, such as interviews or observations, in different places. Instead, the authors suggest that by shifting the research focus from a single site to more sites, any links and ruptures between or across places can be unfolded more easily.

This multi-sited ethnographic approach has inspired many transnational researchers in a range of disciplines. Closely related to Chinese migration studies, one example is a study on returnee Hong Kong immigrants from Canada (Ley & Kobayashi, 2005). The authors employed a multi-sited ethnographical approach to conduct interviews with those returnees and illustrate the back and forth movements between the immigration-receiving and the immigration-sending countries. As the authors recognised, a multi-site ethnographic approach

> rounded out transnational experiences and strategies across the life cycle. . . . As the participants[they] lived across two territories linked by dense electronic messaging and frequent travel, stretching relationships and resources across space, so our field research needed to range between the two sites that comprised their blended social field.
>
> (Ley & Kobayashi, 2005, p. 123)

Efforts to develop appropriate transnational research strategies have considered focusing more on empirical research on the "local" specificity of various socio-spatial transformations. Guarnizo and Smith (1998) suggest that traditional methods for studying migrant populations, such as ethnography, life histories, and historical case studies, must be contextualised into a "transnational socio-economic and political transformation" (p. 24). In other words, the authors propose that both macro- and micro-determinants of transnational activities and practices should be integrated into the full analysis.

Such development of new research approaches toward transnational migration studies provided a methodological guide for my own research project. As I will discuss in detail in the second section of this chapter, this project adopts a multi-sited ethnographic framework for the research topic.

Micro-level empirical studies of the migrant transnational practices

In the recent development of transnational migration studies, there have been a large number of detailed micro-studies of various contemporary manifestations of transnational migration and the associated issues of ethnic identities and conflicting allegiances. These studies provide empirically rich data and evidence of the scale and determinants of transnational activities pursued by many migrants and resulted in an empirical re-grounding and subsequently, some thoughtful conceptualisation of what transnational migration really means.

There has been a large body of research that tries to explain the variations in transnational practices across migrant groups. Some studies have focused on certain migrant groups' economic and political engagement with both the sending and the receiving countries (Guarnizo, Portes, & Haller, 2003; Portes, Haller, & Guarnizo, 2002; Smith, 1998; Wong, 2004). For example, Mexican migrants in the US who keep sending regular remittances back to their villages are a typical example of the transnational economic activities some migrants engage in regularly (Conway & Cohen, 1998). Similar transnational economic activity of remitting money back to the homeland also takes place in many Pacific island countries (Brown, 1994, 1995; Connell & Brown, 1995). Guarnizo et al.'s (2003) study shows the scope, extent, and social determinants for Colombian, Dominican, and Salvadoran migrants' transnational political engagement between their homelands and the US. There are particular studies too that focus on the actual social organisations built by transnational migrants (Caglar, 2006; Goldring, 1999, 2002) and the religious practices among certain transnational migrant groups (Levitt, 2003c, 2004, 2007).

More recently, research interest in the use of information technologies to communicate both across and within territorial borders is increasingly prevalent. Following the discussion that relatively affordable transportation and communication have facilitated a much greater level of interaction across borders (Levitt, 2001; Shield, 1996; Vertovec, 2004a), further research has focused on the use of advanced technologies, such as the Internet, among transnational migrant groups to establish social networks, sustain ethnic identity, and share common interests (Adams & Ghose, 2004; Parham, 2004; Zhou, Chen, & Cai, 2006). Specifically in dealing with Chinese migrants, Zhou et al.'s (2006) research on Chinese-language media in the US and Canada points out that the transnational identity of the Chinese-language press in those regions is facilitated by advanced technology, such as the Internet. The online Chinese media affects the Chinese transnational migrant community in many ways, not the least of which is creating a transnational public sphere in which Chineseness is constantly reinforced by promoting direct ties with the mainland of China. Reasoning along the same lines, Glick-Schiller and Fouron (1998) researched the identity politics of Haitian immigrants in the US and revealed that the identity formation of immigrants from Haiti closely relates to the ties with their homeland and the public identity of Haitian transnational communities in the US.

These studies strengthened my own intellectual understanding of the topic of transnational migration in ways of providing empirical evidence for why transnationalism occurs, how transnational networks are established in certain migrant communities, and what kind of significance transnationalism has for individual migrants' worldviews and life perspectives. These studies emphasise that the process of globalisation, initially motivated "from above" – that is, by multinational corporations and organisations – is now also pursued "from below". In particular, some of these studies support the importance of studying transnational migrant identity formation to understand grassroots transnational migratory experiences. Therefore, study of transnational migrant identity is an area identified as well worth further investigation.

In terms of the most relevant research focuses and aspects as both relate to my research, I reviewed five areas of the literature that were particularly informative:

1) studies of migrants' transnational movement trajectories and patterns; 2) studies of transnational families; 3) studies that use a transnational approach to re-formulate the meaning of "return migration"; 4) studies of transnationalism of the second-generation of migrants; and 5) studies of migrants' emotional experiences of transnational migration. The following context provides an in-depth discussion of these five areas of study.

TRANSNATIONAL MIGRATORY TRAJECTORIES AND PATTERNS OF MOVEMENT

This group examines the transnational trajectories and patterns of particular transnational migrant groups (Guarnizo, 1997; Hugo, 2006; Ley & Kobayashi, 2005; Xiang, 2004). For example, Xiang's (2004) research on Indian information technology (IT) professional transnational migration strategies and trajectories indicates that Singapore and Malaysia serve as a first strategic gateway for many Indian IT professionals to utilise on their route to their preferable destination – the US in terms of obtaining work experience in English-speaking countries. Australia or Canada serves as their second strategic gateway in terms of obtaining permanent residency in those countries. Permanent residential status from Australia or Canada can facilitate their entrance into the US and let them accumulate valuable work experience in English-speaking countries. They then move to the US to gain better employment opportunities (Xiang, 2004). Through such exhibition of these strategic transnational movements, Xiang (2004) suggests that the transnational characteristics of the migration patterns and career development of Indian IT workers clearly reflects the different positions of numerous nations in the global economy, "which is largely a legacy of the established relationship between the core, the semi-periphery and the periphery" (p. 162).

Hugo's research on young Australian expatriates illustrates their desire to leave Australia and go overseas to find opportunities for further career development. However, as these individuals establish their own immediate families and have children, there is an urge to go back to Australia for their children's education (Hugo, 2006). Ley and Kobayashi's (2005) study on returnee Hong Kong migrants to Canada reveals that the different stages of one's life cycle will determine the strategic movement trajectories from one site to another across the Pacific. These studies show that a switch in migratory strategy from an economic pole to a quality-of-life pole takes place to best suit one's needs at different life stages. These studies also provide a comprehensive explanation of transnational migratory trajectories that certain migrant groups create.

TRANSNATIONAL FAMILIES

The recent emergence of a large body of literature that concentrates on the study of transnational families (Garcia, 2006; Ley & Waters, 2004; Lima, 2001; Waters, 2002, 2005; Yeoh, Huang, & Lam, 2005) is one aspect of the literature most relevant to my own research project, since my research considers families to be the units of investigation. The work by Lima (2001) on Mexican families in the US defines transnational families as

> dispersed across international borders, and their members tend to spend periods of time in one or the other country and for a variety of reasons. . . . Their geographical location is fluid. They come and go on vacation and may stay for periods that are not previously determined. They may have properties and businesses – sometimes on both sides of the border – and, more important, they develop their work trajectories and projects in each of the two countries.
>
> (p. 178)

Based on case studies, Lima states that transnational families are a fundamental element of transnational social spaces within which migration and transnational movement decisions on when, where, and who within the family should migrate or move are strategically made in a broader family context. In a number of studies, scholars use the term "astronauting" (Hugo, 2003; Ip, 2006) or "astronaut"[4] (Lam, 1994; Skeldon, 1994b) to describe the deliberate strategy that some Asian migrant families take to maintain family ties in Asia as well as in their new home on the Pacific Rim. Such a family strategy is the subject of considerable discussion in the contemporary Asian immigration literature. Often, the strategies are perceived as a means deliberately taken by some immigrant families to achieve economic survival during immigration adaptation or to adjust to the different opportunities in their host and former source countries and produce better family outcomes. In the New Zealand context, there are several research efforts that concentrate on examining the characteristics of new Chinese transnational families and the transnational strategies of the Hong Kong and Taiwan immigrant groups (Beal, 2001; Ho, 2002; Ho, Ip, & Bedford, 2001). Elsewhere, for example in Australia and Canada, similar studies were also conducted (Chiang, Hibbins, & Chui, 2006; Pe-Pua, Mitchell, Iredale, & Castles, 1996; Waters, 2002, 2003, 2005).

Another aspect of research on transnational migration and consideration of family is the effects of family networks on individual migrants. A study on social capital and international migration emphasises that family networks are an important source of social capital that potentially and powerfully affect migration decision-making (Palloni, Massey, Ceballos, Espinosa, & Spittel, 2001). Nonini and Ong's (1997) work on Chinese transnationalism, however, takes a quite different point of view and grounds Chinese transnationalism as "a culturally distinctive domain within the strategies of accumulation of the new capitalism" (p. 4). The authors point out that family networks are often used flexibly as a channel of capital accumulation among Chinese transnationals under the conditions of late capitalism (Nonini & Ong, 1997). Research on the Pacific transnational communities shows a similar trend. For example, Marcus's early research on the Tongan migrant community supports the notion of "transnational corporations of kin" and shows "[the] international scale of family operations, still tied to kin at home . . . would equal or exceed in value the Tongan national product" (Marcus, 1981, p. 60). Other research shows that the potential for capital accumulation via migration and the remittances from expatriate Tongans are an important financial resource to Tongan families, and for the greater Tongan polity and economy (Lee, 2003, 2004, 2006).

Recently, studies on Asian transnational families have gone further to recognise the impact of the changing dynamics in transnational families on their decisions for further movement. The Journal of *International Migration* published a special issue in 2008 focusing on examining and illustrating the changing family strategies of Asian transnational families for immigration and re-location. In the introductory article titled "Asian Transnational Families in Transition: The Liminality of Simultaneity", Huang and co-authors propose that the transnational strategies undertaken by some transnational migrant families may change over time in response to a changing family structure, family life cycle changes, changes in family members' individual aspirations, or changes in the broader socio-economic and political context (Huang, Yeoh, & Lam, 2008). One paper in this special issue focuses on Asian transnational families in the case of New Zealand and in particular reveals that "astronauting" is only a temporary strategy undertaken by some migrant families for their short-term goals. As the young people in these families grow up and the family structure changes, families re-strategise their approaches to best suit the new circumstances. It may be that the younger members re-locate back to their former homeland where the economy is expanding faster to seek better career development opportunities, while the "astronaut parents" may re-join their spouses either in the origin country or the destination location. As a whole, the decision-making of different family members is done with an overall consideration of the entire family's collective well-being (Ho & Bedford, 2008).

These solid empirical studies provide thoughtful conceptualisation of transnational migration studies. They recognise the importance of family in migration decision-making, while also valuing the broader geo-political and economic forces that prompt the transnational migration of families. More importantly, these studies take a dynamic view of transnational migration. Early transnational migration studies were often pre-occupied with just snapshots of migrant short-term transnational strategies, but overlooked the full picture of transnational migration. The recent studies on transnational migrant families look at transnational migration as an on-going and dynamic process in which the migration trajectories are contingent, and often depend on one's or one's family's changing needs at different stages of life.

RETURN MIGRATION WITHIN THE FRAMEWORK OF TRANSNATIONALISM

Recently, studies on return migration have increasingly become framed by the theory of transnational migration (Guarnizo, 1997; King & Newbold, 2008; Ley & Kobayashi, 2005; Moore, 2003; Salaff, 2008; Tollefsen & Lindgren, 2006). This way of looking at return migration as part of the dynamic process of on-going migratory movement offers a distinctive contrast to the previous approaches to return migration that invoke instead a sense of finality that completes the circle movement of ocean crossing. Over the past two decades, return migration, especially voluntary return migration from immigration destination countries to the sending countries, has attracted considerable research interest among those in migration studies. In the context of voluntary return migration, one widely researched topic is the reasons why immigrants decide to return to their homeland. This topic is especially important among immigration policy makers since return migration may be strongly related to certain unsuccessful aspects of immigration policy. This topic also leads to further categorisation of the different kinds of return movements.

The traditional meaning of return migration emphasises the assimilation narrative and tends to obscure the significance of the return trip "home". The early work implied that either unsuccessful or successful migrants would be the ones to return to the sending country (Cerase, 1974; Wyman, 1993). Unsuccessful migrants returned to the homeland because at least their motherland could offer them a comfortable zone with familiar surroundings, language, and social networks when they did not achieve their initial goal for migration in the host society. This return is referred in the field as the "return of failure" in Cerase's work that categorises the different reasons for return (Cerase, 1974, p. 247). In contrast, successful migrants return with honour after they succeed and obtain considerable economic, social, or human capital. This return is referred to as a "return of innovation" (Cerase, 1974, p. 258). Lastly, some studies view return migration as a long-term plan and one that is only undertaken at retirement (Byron & Condon, 1996).

There are others who take a more structural approach to categorise the reasons for return. Rogers categorises the reasons of return as both individual and social. Changes in the homeland or in the receiving country and a recruitment project that targets overseas immigrants to draw them back to their countries of origin are seen as social reasons; while patriotism, disappointment over not achieving one's goals in the host society, and family consideration are accounted as individual reasons (Rogers, 1984). King (2000) categorises the reasons for return into four categories: social, economic, political, and family oriented. More recently, consideration of the wider social meaning for return migration, especially the economic and political effects for the sending countries has emerged as a new research focus (Cassarino, 2004; Oxfeld & Long, 2004; Wang, Wong, & Sun, 2006; Zweig, 2006).

Another distinctive theoretical approach developed and used widely by return migration scholars is the diaspora approach. This approach reconstructs return migration as a discourse whereby return is driven by a natural homing instinct, that is referred to as an "imagined return" or the "myth of return" (Muggeridge & Dona, 2006; Ni Laoire, 2008; Oxfeld & Long, 2004). It suggests that many migrants spend their whole lives as expatriates of their country of destinations but always imagine returning. Although they may never return, imagining that return to the homeland frames their lives. More recently, the explanation of return migration has been portrayed as a so-called brain exchange, further complicating the earlier emphasis on a brain drain from developing countries to the countries in the global North. In developing countries like China and India, emergent high-technology industry has led to return migration by those immigrants who moved to Western nations, but who now see career and entrepreneurial opportunities in their countries of origin (Iredale, Guo, & Rozario, 2002; Wang et al., 2006; Zweig, 1997).

However, the transnational approach conceptualises return migration quite differently. Researchers who adopt a transnational approach toward studying return migration recognise that traditional explanations of return migration as a linear process in which a temporary sojourning experience is followed by a permanent return "home" is not in many cases the true reality of contemporary returning migration. For many migrants, return is not their final adjustment; rather, it is another temporary stage in their continuing journey with future movements that lie ahead (Ley & Kobayashi, 2005; Zulueta, 2008). Zulueta (2008) refers to return as transitory in which that return is not a one-way process implying a means to an end. Ley and Kobayashi discuss the strategy of "double return" among many Hong Kong immigrants to Canada, first from Canada to Hong Kong for work and career development, and then the prospect of a later return to Canada for their children's education or retirement. The authors further suggest that "return migration is not a sufficient or the most precise description to use to explain the current hyper-mobility of transnational citizen living" (Ley & Kobayashi, 2005, p. 123).

Applying the framework of transnational migration, now researchers recognise that the great transnational mobility that many migrants possess brings a new twist to the concept of return migration. Return migration is no longer a simple, one-way reverse migration of people who left home countries and now are moving back to their place of birth (Gmelch, 1980). Some argue that the term "return migration" is indeed theoretically problem (Skeldon, 1994a; Xiang, 2008), and others argue that return migration is only a part of the transnational movement circle (King & Newbold, 2008; Ley & Kobayashi, 2005; Plaza, 2008).

TRANSNATIONALISM OF SECOND-GENERATION OF MIGRANTS

Apart from research that has focused on the transnational engagement of first-generation migrants, certain recent studies have turned their focus on the transnational involvement of the second generation of migrants. These studies particularly investigate how transnational the second generation of migrants actually are and what kinds of activities they do engage in (Alba & Nee, 2003; Foner, 2002; Fouron & Glick-Schiller, 2002; Kasinitz, Waters, Mollenkopf, & Anil, 2002; Lee, 2008; Levitt, 2002, 2003a; Perlmann, 2002; Portes & Rumbaut, 2005; Rumbaut, 2002; Smith, 2002; Somerville, 2008; Waters, 2004). Research on these questions, even though not directly relevant to my research on first-generation migrants, as Kivisto (2001) pointed out, does enhance the extent to which transnationalism is useful as a theoretical perspective. These detailed empirical studies counter the classic approach toward researching transnational migration, which largely has focused on first-generation migrants. It questions whether transnational migration is an ephemeral first-generation phenomenon or simply an enduring feature that persists across multiple migrant generations. Levitt and Glick-Schiller (2007) commented that these studies in many ways are a continuation of the on-going debate on immigrant integration.

Elsewhere, Levitt argues that if transnationalism is defined in a limited way, such as the length of time one spends in the homeland, frequency of taking homeland trips, remittances, engagement with homeland politics, or the use of homeland media, the transnational engagement of the second generation can be viewed as fairly limited (Levitt, 2009). She and Glick-Schiller further argue that if transnationalism is defined in such a limited way, many transnational social connections and capabilities that relate to migration and are possible without geographic and physical movement will be missing from the analysis. These social connections are important to the extent that the new second generation is reared in a transnational social environment. The authors suggest that any exploration of the extent to which the second generation engages in transnational practices can be divided into two levels. One is called the "way of being", and the other is called the "way of belonging". The former refers to those actual social relations and practices in which individuals engage, whereas the latter refers more to emotional connections to the homeland through memory, nostalgia, or imagination (Levitt & Glick-Schiller, 2004).

Some studies have attempted to tackle the issues by focusing on a close examination of the second generation's conceptualisation of "home" in relation to identity formation. The notion of "emotional transnationalism" or "symbolic transnationalism" that addresses life experiences and feelings when moving between places are widely used in these studies (Espiritu, 2003; Mitchell, 1997; Viruell-Fuentes, 2006; Wolf, 1997, 2002). For example, a study on second-generation Miami youth found that those who experienced "selective acculturation" were more likely to be interested in the parental home and its traditions, thus invoking the homeland as a transnational "way of belonging" (Haller & Landolt, 2005). Based on a study on Filipino second generation youth, it was suggested that immigrant parents are more actively engaged in maintaining relationships with the Philippines than are their children, but their children actually maintain ties "at the level of emotions, ideologies and conflicting cultural codes" (Wolf, 1997, p. 459). More recent studies stress that transnational engagement among the second generation can ebb and flow over the course of life and generations (Espiritu & Tran, 2002; Somerville, 2008). Whether the second generation ultimately forges a cross-border connection also depends on those individuals' aspirations at different stages of life, the strength of the transnational family networks to which these young people belong, and the extent to which the youth are brought up in transnational spaces (Levitt, 2002, 2009; Pries, 2004; Raj, 2000).

STUDYING THE EMOTIONAL EXPERIENCES OF TRANSNATIONALITY:
"HOME", IDENTITY, AND BELONGING

Continuing on with the topic of "emotional transnationalism", studies on migrant emotions when moving between places is a recently emerging focus within transnational migration research. Wolf (2002) uses the term "emotional transnationalism" to explain the negotiation process undertaken by second-generation Filipinos in terms of belonging (p. 285). Skrbis (2008), in her discussion on transnational families, calls this "bringing emotions in[to] transnational migration studies" (p. 235) and argues against "sociologies without emotions" (Barbalet, 1998, p. 13), and in particular advocates for the inseparability of emotions from the understanding of transnational families.

With a strong affirmation of the status of emotion in the research on transnational migration, a large amount of research in recent years has particularly dealt with migrant emotions during migratory movements. The works includes an analysis of the feeling of hope in migration (Mar, 2005; Wise, 2005), a sense of belonging (Nyiri, 2001; Westwood & Phizacklea, 2000), emotional struggle, emotional longing and missing, emotional journey (Baldassar, 2008; Gu, 2007; Ryan, 2008), feelings associated with migratory return (McKay, 2005), and even how emotion can condition the actual timing of emigration (Fitzgerald, 2008). Among these works on transnational emotions, explanation of "home" and its relevance to identity formation and a sense of belonging for migrants becomes a central point in the discussion (Ahmed, 1999; Ahmed, Castaneda, Fortier, & Sheller, 2003; Basu, 2004; Butcher, 2002, 2003; Pratt, 2004; Skrbis, 2008; Wiles, 2008). In these works, the discussion on the notion of "home" is injected into the exploration of transnational migrant identity and belonging and raises the study of transnational identity and migration to a new level. This aspect of that study is important because identity formation is actually a social indicator that can suggest ways in which people experience their migratory journeys and conceive their future movement intention.

Ahmed (1999) uses the notion of what "home" means to discuss the competing emotions that migrants feel as they move between places and illustrates the relationship between transnational journey, identity, belonging, and "home":

> The journey between homes provides the subject with the contour of a space of belonging, but a space which expresses the very logic of an interval, the passing through of the subject between apparently fixed moments of departure and arrival.
>
> (p. 330)

Basu (2004) agrees, saying that "the notion of 'home' is a powerful motif in the contemporary popular and academic project to (re)locate identity in a globalised world of movement" (p. 27). Similarly, Rapport and Dawson (1998b). suggest that "home" is "a useful analytical construct: as a means of encapsulating and linking and also transcending traditional classifications [of identity]" (p. 4).

"Home" is also a slippery concept. Traditionally, "home" is conceptualised as the stable centre of one's universe, a safe place to leave and return to, a principal focus of control and concern, a pattern of regular doing, furnishing, and appurtenances, indeed a physical space in which certain communitarian practices where realised, or a spiritual and psychological attachment to a place (Berger, 1984; Douglas, 1991; Tuan, 1971). In the realm of everyday understanding, "home" can be a place where children are or will be reared, a place of origin, a place of belonging, a place to relax or anchor one's fatigued mind, or a place to return to (Bowlby, Gregory, & McKie, 1997). In the context of transnational migration, the meaning of "home" becomes more complex and multi-dimensional. The traditional conceptualisation of "home" has also been challenged in the transnational era, given that a conventional "home" is disrupted because of transnational movements. Rapport and Dawson point out that any traditional conceptualisation of "home" "provides little conceptual purchase on a world of contemporary movement" (Rapport & Dawson, 1998b). Basu (2004) suggests that in many cases "home" is given substance and materialised in homeland – "a capacious concept and all that it connotes is given material forms" (p. 28).

Differing from Basu (2004) who conceptualised "home" as a material form, Mallett (2004) says that home can also be immaterial: "Home is place but it is also a space inhabited by family, people, things and belongings – a familiar, if not comfortable space where particular activities and relationships are lived" (p. 63). In Ahmed and co-authors' work, "home" is even conceived as part of the continuous, always changing, practices of "uprooting/regrounding" enacted by migration (Ahmed et al., 2003). Pratt (2004) calls the transnational feelings he investigated "gleaning the home" and speaks of the importance of home-making during migratory movements (p. 121). All these works denote a meaning that home is more than just a physical location; it is a place or space full of emotional attachment and feelings. In this sense, "home" gives context to time and space and embodies both anticipation and memory, or as Rapport and Dawson (1998b) argue, "home" brings together memory and longing, the ideational, the affective and the physical, the spatial and the temporal, the local and the global, the positively evaluated and the negative" (p. 9).

For transnational migrants, the migration journey involves "a splitting of home as place of origin and home as the sensory world of everyday experience" (Ahmed, 1999, p. 341). For some, "home" may evoke an emotional link to where they are originally from or maybe that nostalgia that often relates to a longing for their national home (Hage, 1997; Wiles, 2008). For others, "home" becomes "a mythic place of desire in the diasporic imagination" (Brah, 1996, p. 192). The concept has also been associated with ideas of old and traditional or treated as an on-going process in which "human beings continue to make themselves at home" (Rapport & Dawson, 1998a, p. 33).

As people grow up or move between places, their sense of belonging to their initial "home" may change, and they attach new feelings of "home" to different situations and spaces. This description suggests a strong sense that one's self discovery of "home" relates to personal identity (Lewin, 2001; Valentine, 2001).

Jackson and Penrose (1993) insightfully point out that searching for "homeness" and familiar places is much more dominant within immigrant societies. Valentine (2001) suggests that "home" can be experienced differently by each individual migrant. Wiles (2008) argues that ideas of home, whether constructed individually or collectively, are the indicators of migrant lives, because "home" embraces socially and culturally constructed meanings that may provide a true sense of belonging, identity, and security.

Taking all of the ideas discussed here, particularly the suggestion that "home" is an important aspect of understanding the hybrid process of identity formation and sense of belonging that migrants have (Rapport & Dawson, 1998b), the examination or analysis of "home" significantly embeds in this research. This approach dwells on the diversity of emotional experiences that occur in the course of migratory movements and focuses on analysing the competing emotions over the notion of "home" that associates with identity and one's sense of belonging. An investigation of the conceptualisation of "home" may provide a useful entry point for a discussion of sense of belonging, identity, and even transnational experiences of the researched cohorts. It is hoped that with a deeper understanding of the conceptualisation of "home" for Chinese transnationals, their transnational journeys and experiences can be unfolded in a fresh way.

Exploring the wider effects of transnational activities

The recent development of transnational migration studies pays more attention to the consideration of the impact and influence that transnational practices and activities have on broader contexts, such as their influence on the reconfiguration of cross-border connections or global influences that increased cross-border activities might have (Guarnizo & Smith, 1998; Vertovec, 2004b). Vertovec (2004b) states that transnational practices of migrants may contribute significantly to the on-going processes of structural transformation. He clarifies that viewpoint by suggesting three different "modes of transformation":

> 1) perceptual transformation affecting what can be described as migrants' orientational "bifocality" in the sociocultural domain; 2) conceptual transformation of meanings within a notional triad of "identities-border-orders" in the political domain; 3) institutional transformation affecting forms of financial transfer, public-private relationships, and local development in the economic domain.
>
> (p. 971)

In this regard, Vertovec (2004b) argues that transnational migration studies should also be concerned about the kinds of societal changes that are stimulated by the cross-border connections that migrants establish and maintain. Drawing ideas from Vertovec and other scholars, the following context provides a brief summary for each category.

First, some studies examine the changing world views of individual migrants. That research suggests that transnational migrants are at the forefront of new global subjectivities because of their association with more than one territorial area. For example, Guarnizo (1997) developed the idea of "transnational habitus" – "a particular set of dualistic dispositions . . . which has spread people's lives across national borders and becomes a second nature. [It] incorporates the social position of the migrant and the context in which transmigration occurs" (Guarnizo, 1997, p. 311). Mahler (1998) discussed the bi-focality of migrants' daily routines and habits. Such an argument highlights a personal transformation of migrants that derives from their transnational migration processes – a dual orientation to "here" and "there" that transnational migrants do experience every day. Such a transformation will become, if it is not the norm of migration narrative, at least "the predominant form of migrant belonging" (Castells, 2002, p. 1158). During this process, migrants are conscious of their world orientation which is in more than one locality. Such consciousness has the potential to influence the migrant family life course, strategies, sense of self, collective belonging, and the approach toward adaptation.

Transformation that results from migrant transnationalism can also take place in the political domain. There is a large body of recent literature that considers this aspect. Generally, these studies suggest that migrant transnationalism, as one part of the processes and outcomes associated with globalisation that emphasises deterritorialisation, challenges the nation-state ideals of identities, borders, and order in both the sending and the receiving countries (Fitzgerald, 2000; Vertovec, 2004b). Vertovec (2004b) proposed a framework – "identities-borders-orders" – for considering the political challenges the nation-state faces that are brought about by transnational migrants. This framework proposes that these three conceptual domains mutually influence each other, and therefore, they must be assessed in light of the others. Heisler (2001) suggests that migration "at least in some host societies . . . disturbs the sense of boundedness" (p. 229) because it is a process that "tends to attenuate territorial sovereignty, monolithic order, and identity solidarity" (p. 237). In this way, migration, especially transnational migration, erodes the power of the nation-state "by compounding identities, ignoring borders, and overruling orders" (Vertovec, 2004b, p. 979). Vertovec (2004b) thus argues:

> The political dimensions of migrant transnationalism are deeply embedded in particular kinds of structural change currently underway and which can be seen particularly to put to the test longstanding ideals of identities-borders-orders. These especially involve migrants' practices around dual citizenship/nationality and homeland political affiliation.
>
> (p. 980)

Since citizenship and nationality has been historically closely linked with the evolution of politics of nation/state and involves political issues that especially consider the rights of voting and the impact on countries' politics (Faist, 2000a), both become a more sensational issue when considered with migration. From a national perspective, citizenship is a mechanism of immigrant integration because it may mean the embracement by immigrants of domestic political participation. However, when this issue begins to involve a dual orientation, a particular concern and suspicion is raised in both the immigrant sending and immigrant receiving countries. Contemporarily then, although attitudes and policies toward dual citizenship are increasingly liberalising in many immigrant-receiving countries (Joppke, 1999), there is still a reluctance to give immigrants' the entitlement of citizenship in some countries, because dual citizenship institutionalises migrants' transnational ties, and offers legal status to transnational migrants, so that they are able to reside in or be absent from two or more nations and fully enjoy the legal rights of these nations simultaneously (Faist, 2000a).

The political rationale behind this issue is that dual citizenship runs counter to the fundamental assimilation theories. In Faist's (2000a) words, "dual state membership hinders immigrant adaptation in the country of immigration, encourages populism on the part of the majority groups" (p. 202). Concerns also have been raised regarding immigrant loyalty toward the immigrant-receiving countries, which can potentially be divided or diluted because of immigrants' political affiliation with their homeland (Brown, 2002; Spoonley, Bedford, & Macpherson, 2003; Werbner, 2000). Kastoryano (2002) argues that allowing dual citizenship probably presents "a confusion between rights and identity, culture and politics, states and nations" (p. 160). Ip and co-authors suggests that legal citizenship does not necessarily mean full incorporation into the host society or cultural identification with the host country (Ip, Inglis, & Wu, 1997). All these aspects contradict the original expectations of immigrant-receiving countries in terms of allowing citizenship for immigrants as an affirmation of their full sense of commitment and incorporation into the host societies.

For immigrant sending countries, dual citizenship is largely excluded from the national project, because domestic politicians see more disadvantages than advantages in allowing this (Østergaard-Nielsen, 2003). They particularly do not welcome dual citizenship because they recognise that any voting on domestic politics from diasporic communities usually includes too much oppositional influence. Some immigrant-sending countries in the West, such as Italy and Greece, have developed policies to grant dual nationality to their expatriates for decades (Brown, 2002). However, in many immigrant-sending countries in the Asian region, it is only a comparatively recent development that some have started to introduce certain policies toward their expatriates, including providing special ministries or government offices devoted to overseas nationals, special investment opportunities, privileged professional development opportunities and resettlement offers, special voting rights, and even offers of dual citizenship.

For example, China used to pursue extremely restricted border control but then officially started to implement its own "Green Card" system in August 2004. That policy allows foreigners, including Chinese with foreign passport, to apply for permanent residence in China. The Chinese "Green Card" gives its holders Chinese citizen privileges. The Shanghai municipal government is a pioneer in offering this benefit to highly skilled returnee Chinese expats. People who hold the "Green Card" enjoy expatriate expert status in terms of salary and related benefits (Ip, 2006). The Chinese government also has developed several programmes to encourage and support high-level scholars and professionals to come back to China to work (Wang et al., 2006). The effects of such a liberal policy towards expatriates in some immigrant-sending countries, as Levitt believes are the "re-inventing the role of states outside of territorial boundaries and in this way reconfiguring traditional understanding of sovereignty, nation, and citizenship" (Levitt, 2003b, p. 606).

Elsewhere, scholars have developed the idea of citizenship as "a negotiated relationship. Subject to change, it is acted upon collectively, or among individuals existing within social, political, and economic relations of collective conflict" on global as well as national levels (Stasiulis & Bakan, 1997, p. 113). Ong's early work that proposes the notion of "flexible citizenship" (Ong, 1993, 1999) coincides with this idea. In Ong's study of the construction of what citizenship means for overseas Hong Kong Chinese, she argues that the search for citizenship by overseas Chinese directly links to the diverse strategies in place to accumulate financial capital flexibly and evade political costs as minority entrepreneurs in Western countries. This incident suggests that "the citizenship concept should be examined in the context of the global economy and the range of meanings it can have for different groups of people" (Ong, 1993, p. 771). Her conclusion is that citizenship in the profound sense of having a duty toward, or identification with, a particular nation-state for overseas Chinese is minimal and an obvious subversion of what citizenship means traditionally (Ong, 1993).

These diverse forms of research on the political transformation that migrant transnationalism produces remind us that transnational migration studies should consider not only the practices of transnational migrants, but also the impact of their lives on others and their role in changing local, national, and global relations.

The last mode of transformation in Vertovec's summary examines economic transformation, particularly the re-institutionalising of development through remittances. Vertovec (2004b) identifies transnational economic activities as transnational ethnic entrepreneurship, facilitation of international trade, and business based in migrant-sending countries but reaching out to customers in the diasporic populations. In terms of direct economic benefits and value, remittances have the most significant transformational impact, especially on the migrant-sending countries. According to many empirical studies, especially those in Latin America and Pacific the impact of remittances on the migrant-sending countries is generally positive (Collins, 2006; Orozco, 2000, 2002; Portes & Landolt, 2000; Rogers, 2001; Rouse, 1992). As Vertovec (2004b) suggests, it does not matter that the remittances are sent privately or are channelled collectively, they "can transform the nature and pace of local development in migrant sending areas by, among other things, constructing infrastructures, providing equipment, and offering finance for enterprise" (p. 991). Much of the remittance sent serves as basic subsistence for food, or provision of education that would not otherwise be available. This money includes both personal remittance to relatives and families as well as those funds sent by hometown associations or channelled into sending countries by government organisations to support the development of infrastructure in the migrants' home countries. While such fund transfers can have generally positive effects, it is also suggested that they may also be exacerbating inequalities in immigrant-sending countries (Vertovec, 2004b).

However, when emphasising the economic transformation of migrant transnationalism, caution should be given to the impact of regional differences. The research discussed here largely draws from studies conducted in Latin America where social and political crisis and instability have occurred since the 1980s (Korczenwicz & Smith, 1996). The regional context of this research, however, is the Asia Pacific Rim, which presents a different picture. Since the economic performance in many East Asian nations over the last two decades appears as success stories, the economic transformation of migrant transnationalism in this region may have a striking divergence when compared with conclusions drawn from research conducted on the economic transformation of migrant transnationalism in Latin America. Through observation, remittances from Western immigration countries to East Asia are not a usual practice among recent Asian migrants, especially Chinese migrants. Sometimes, remittances may even reverse its flow direction as from immigration-receiving countries to immigration-sending countries. This manifestation is one of many caused by the regional differences of migrant transnationalism, and researchers should be cautious about research suggestions abstracted from different studies, especially studies that occur in different regional, national, and cultural contexts.

The discussions in this section provide an in-depth review of the recent development of research methodology and empirical research, as well as a further conceptualisation pertaining to transnational migration. This detailed empirical effort manifests where and how transnationalism occurs, what effects it has on the people situated in the transnational social space, and to what extent transnationalism exists in certain transnational migrant communities. These empirical studies strengthen the field of transnational migration studies by providing empirical evidence of migrant transnational practices and employing creative research methodology to do the research; more importantly, these studies lead to more thoughtful and reasonable conceptualisations. Unlike the early theoretical conceptualisation of transnationalism as a novel phenomenon, increasingly, transnationalism is recognised as a novel research perspective, a series of grassroots activities adopted by some migrants. More importantly, it has been recognised that transnationalism not only has a significant impact on individual migrants, but also has macro-social consequences.

For this book project, the theories on transnational migration studies provide a solid and relevant theoretical underpinning that permits the building of a theoretical framework to conceptualise the transnational activities in which PRC migrants engage. As a theoretical base, transnational migration is useful because it reveals the presence of cross-border activities while still being attendant to the continued significance of the role of the nation-state. The review of the early transnational literature on the articulation of transnational migration and its conceptual refinement allows this project to grasp the basic concepts around the theories of transnational migration and its development systematically. The in-depth review of recent empirical studies on transnational migration, especially the newly emerged field of study of "emotional transtionalism" deepens and broadens my research perspective. In this regard, I link transnational migration to citizenship, especially dual citizenship, identity formation, perceptions of "home" and identity, and return migration; and all of those are treated as a synthesis in this literature review as well as in my project.

Development of the research framework and methodology

Drawing on the relevant themes raised above, this section outlines the methodology and methods used to collect empirical data and to analyse the different types of data. In broad terms, this project adopts a multi-method research design[5] that involves using both qualitative and quantitative research components towards a research project. Methods employed in this research are considered orthodox methods, such as in-depth interviews, a questionnaire survey, and second-hand statistic data analysis, all widely used in social sciences, anthropology, and human geography (Crang, 2002; Crick & Geddes, 1998; Flick, 2002; Fontana & Frey, 1994; Hay, 2005; Hughes & Sharrock, 2007; Robson, 2002; Schweizer, 1998; Trift, 2000). The use of both qualitative and quantitative methods for this project is "likely to result in complementary strengths and non-overlapping weaknesses" (Johnson & Onwuegbuzie, 2004, p. 18).

In-depth interviews: enriching understanding of the research topic

In transnationalism, some discussion has occurred regarding the significance of what George Marcus calls "multi-sited ethnography" (Marcus, 1995). He suggests that researchers need to shift their ethnographic practice from the focus on a single encounter site to research that traces "cultural formation across and within multiple sites of activity" (Marcus, 1995, p. 96). In the study of transnational migration in particular, there has been a tendency to speak of "multi-sited" fieldwork. As Hannerz (1998) points out, "the practice of ethnography may have to be distributed over several places" (p. 248).

These points of view all suggest that a shift in focus for any research conducted with transnational actors should interrogate the links and connections between the places where individual people and groups are deeply influenced. By realising the necessity of involving voices from various types of Chinese transnational migrants, it was decided to conduct the qualitative interviews in multiple sites, including China, New Zealand, and Australia.

Interviews with return Chinese migrants were considered first because of the theoretical considerations regarding return migration and transnational migration studies. First, the theoretical articulation of transnational migration stems from the recognition of migrants' on-going engagement in more than one society, especially their countries of origin and their countries of adoption (Glick-Schiller et al., 1992; Glick Schiller et al., 1995). Second, as mentioned before, studies on return migration are increasingly framed under the theory of transnationalism (King & Newbold, 2008). Based on these theoretical considerations, PRC return migrants were conceptualised as part of the Chinese transnational migration flow, and interviews with PRC return migrants was considered one important source of the qualitative data for the project.

Interviews with those returning migrants were paralleled with interviews conducted in Auckland with those Chinese return migrants' immediate family members who stayed or at least spend the majority of their time in New Zealand. The group of Auckland interviewees is very diverse in their patterns of transnationality and indeed includes four sub-groups: 1) some return Chinese migrants' family members who settle in New Zealand or at least spend the majority of their time in New Zealand; 2) some Chinese who commute between New Zealand and China; 3) some Chinese who had already have concrete plans to go to Australia; and 4) some Chinese whose immediate family member(s) moved to a third destination. Regardless of this diversity, the common nature these four sub-groups share is that all keep on-going contacts across borders, especially contacts with the homeland – China, and their first immigration destination country – New Zealand. As mentioned already, when studying Chinese transnational migration, the homeland and the immigration destination are not isolated sites; rather, they are inter-related locations because many Chinese maintain on-going contacts between the two sites. Therefore, while interviews with returned Chinese migrants conducted in China are one of the central elements of this project, interviews conducted in Auckland with those who are residing in New Zealand are equally important.

The interviews were also expanded to Chinese migrants who have obtained New Zealand permanent residence or citizenship, but currently living in Australia. To illustrate the character of transnationality and multi-locational movement of PRC migrants, Australia was chosen as a third ethnographic fieldwork site. However, it should be noted that in reality, the multi-locational movements of PRC migrants do not just take place between New Zealand and Australia; rather, the movements happen between New Zealand and many other countries. Here in this project, Australia was only taken as one example to show PRC migrant transnational mobility because of its geographic convenience for conducting interviews. The choice of Australia as another research site is also based on the fact that Australia and New Zealand were opened to new Chinese migration around the same time (i.e. 1980s). These two countries also share a long-standing migratory connection historically. In the late 1990s, this long-standing connection intensified with the "back-door" migration discussed in Chapter 2. Many new Chinese migrants actively participated in this significant migration flow.

The traditional ethnographic and phenomenological approaches were the rationale and philosophical orientation underlying the qualitative part of this research project. It was my hope that the phenomenological research, which centres on uncovering the necessary structural invariants of human experience or certain social phenomenon through efficient understanding of "the inherent logic of that experience or social phenomenon" (Dukes, 1984, p. 199), can allow me to explore the complexity of the mobility and the decision-making of PRC migrants during transnational movement. The ethnographic approach employed in this research will enable me to understand PRC transnational migrants within their own context; namely, through fieldwork and engagement with the Chinese transnational community in the places they actually live and have activities. Thus the broader economic, political, social, and personal circumstances related to this community would be uncovered. The qualitative findings are discussed in both Chapter 4 and Chapter 5.

The online quantitative questionnaire survey: validating findings from ethnography

In the research design, the qualitative part of this research is parallel with an online questionnaire survey that sought gather quantitative data to chart the overall movement patterns of PRC Chinese migrants. The quantitative results from the survey are discussed in Chapter 6 and Chapter 7 and can make meaningful connections between the transnational behaviours of PRC migrants and some associated forces.

Translocality became a distinctive feature of this research, not only for the qualitative ethnographic fieldwork but also for the quantitative online survey. This means that a physical and geographic translocality was embedded in the ethnographic fieldwork because the fieldwork interviews were re-designed to be multi-sited (i.e. Beijing, Shanghai, Auckland, Melbourne, and Sydney). Meanwhile, this research is virtually trans-locational because the quantitative online survey also targets Chinese with New Zealand permanent residence or citizenship in China, New Zealand, other countries, or commuting between locations.

In general, the in-depth interviews and online questionnaire survey for this research took place concurrently throughout the discourse on conducting this project. There was no choice in terms of priority between the two methods of data collection in terms of time order. However, in terms of formulation of the online survey questionnaire, the finalisation of the survey questionnaire took place after I completed the interview fieldwork in China. The insights obtained from these interviews contributed significantly to the development and final formulation of a well-structured survey questionnaire. For example, the interviews in China revealed that although the returning Chinese migrants went back to China and had prolonged stays there, there was a continuous transnational intention within this group, as manifested by many who planned to go back to New Zealand or move to a third destination. To test how widespread transnational intention is among PRC migrants, the online survey was set up to clarify and extend the qualitative interview findings. For example, for interviewees who currently reside in New Zealand, even though they now are staying in New Zealand, their transnational intention may still be present. That intention will be particularly informative to indicate the possible future transnational movement of this group.

Second-hand statistic data analysis: quantifying Chinese return migration and "trans-Tasman" migration

Since "return migration" and "trans-Tasman" migration are significant manifestation of PRC migrants' transnational mobility (Liu, 2009, 2011), it is important to examine the volume of these two type of transnational migration in a quantitative sense. To achieve this, New Zealand's permanent and long-term travel (PLT) data collected by INZ was retrieved and analysed. The focus of this analysis is to compare the volume, pattern, and timing of "trans-Tasman" migration and return migration to China and their associated reasons and social implications. The analysis results of "trans-Tasman" migration are presented in Chapter 6 together with the results of the online quantitative survey. Results of return migration to China are presented in Chapter 7. The analysis compares return migration of PRC Chinese migrants with return migration of New Zealand's other four major immigrant groups from the Asia-Pacific region (i.e. South Korea, Taiwan, India, and Pacific Island region). The distinct feature of return migration patterns of the PRC migrants can be only revealed through such a comparison.

Notes

1 The assimilation theory pioneered by the members of the Chicago School of Sociology in the 1920s and 1930s postulates that the assimilation of immigrants is an eventual outcome of immigration and a process in which immigrants break off all homeland social relations and cultural ties and take full acceptance of the mainstream culture and become totally incorporated with the economic, cultural, and political life of the immigration host society.

2 The "world system theory" was developed by sociologist Immanuel Wallerstein in 1976. This theory generally sees migration as a natural consequence of economic globalisation and market penetration across national boundaries. The penetration of capitalist economic relations into peripheral, non-capitalist societies creates a mobile population that is prone to migrate abroad. As capitalism has expanded outward from its core mainly in Western Europe, North America, and Oceania, ever-larger portions of the globe and growing shares of the human population have been incorporated into the world market economy. Increased labour demand in the capitalised sectors inevitably generates a large-scale international labour transfer from non-capitalised sectors.

3 Transnational kinship groups are formed by those who uphold the same social norm of equivalence, and whose transnational ties are sustained by a personal reciprocity in which one receives from others while others may require something in return in the meantime. Remittance is a typical example among transnational kinship groups. Transnational circuits require an instrumental reciprocity/exchange and are characterised by "a constant circulation of goods, people, and information transversing the borders of emigration and immigration states" (Faist, 2000b, p. 206). Transnational communities are based upon a solidarity within which members share collective identity and are connected by "dense and strong social and symbolic ties over time and across space to patterns of networks and circuits in two

countries" (Faist, 2000b, p. 207). Such a connection requires not only personal intimacy and emotional depth, but also moral commitment, social cohesion, continuity in time, and "a common repertoire of symbolic and collective representations" (Faist, 2000b, p 208).

4 "Astronaut" is a widely used term in any studies on Asian migrant families. It refers to those Asian migrants who commute or circulate over long distances with a place of residence in immigration-receiving countries, but then place their businesses and professional lives in Asian locations, usually their place of origin. They technically "settle" in immigration destination countries, but then continue to work in the Asian region.

5 It is a research design for a single research project that attempts to involve both qualitative and quantitative sub-projects each of which is relatively complete on its own. They are then used together towards answering research questions. The results from both qualitative and quantitative sub-projects are used deliberately to triangulate the advantages and disadvantages derived from both methods.

References

Adams, P. C., & Ghose, R. (2004). India.com: The construction of a space between. *Progress in Human Geography, 27*(4), 414–437.

Ahmed, S. (1999). Home and away: Narratives of migration and estrangement. *International Journal of Cultural Studies, 2*(3), 329–347.

Ahmed, S., Castaneda, C., Fortier, A. M., & Sheller, M. (2003). Introduction: Uprootings/regroundings: Questions of home and migration. In S. Ahmed, C. Castaneda, A. M. Fortier, & M. Sheller (Eds.), *Uprootings/Regroundings: Questions of Home and Migration* (pp. 1–19). Oxford: Berg.

Alba, R., & Nee, V. (2003). *Remaking the American Mainstream: Assimilation and Contemporary Immigration*. Cambridge: Harvard University Press.

Bailey, A. J. (2001). Turning transnational: Notes on the theorisation of international migration. *International Journal of Population Geography, 7*, 413–428.

Baldassar, L. (2008). Missing kin and longing to be together: Emotions and the construction of co-presence in transnational relationships. *Journal of Intercultural Studies, 29*(3), 247–266.

Barbalet, J. (1998). *Emotions, Social Theory, and Social Structure*. Cambridge: Cambridge University Press.

Basch, L., Glick-Schiller, N., & Blanc, C. S. (1994). Transnational projects: A new perspective. In L. Basch, N. Glick-Schiller, & C. S. Blanc (Eds.), *Nations Unbound: Transnational Projects, Postcolonial Predicaments, and Deterritorialized Nation-States* (pp. 1–20). Basel, Switzerland: Gordon and Breach Publishers.

Basu, P. (2004). My own island home: The Orkney coming. *Journal of Material Culture, 9*(1), 27–42.

Beal, T. (2001). Taiwanese business migration to Australia and New Zealand. In M. Ip (Ed.), *Re-Examining Chinese Transnationalism in Australia-New Zealand* (pp. 25–44). Canberra: CSCSD, Australia National University.

Beck, U. (2000). The cosmopolitan perspective: Sociology in the second age of modernity. *British Journal of Sociology, 51*(1), 79–107.

Berger, J. (1984). *And Our Faces, My Heart, Brief as Photos*. London: Writers and Readers.

Bowlby, S., Gregory, S., & McKie, L. (1997). 'Doing home': Patriarchy, caring and space. *Women's Studies International Forum, 20*(3), 343–350.

Brah, A. (1996). *Cartographies of Diaspora: Contesting Identities*. London: Routledge.

Brown, G. (2002). Political bigamy? Dual citizenship in Australia's migrant communities. *People and Place, 10*(1), 71–78.

Brown, R. (1994). Migrants' remittances, savings and investment in the South Pacific. *International Labour Review, 133*(3), 347–367.

Brown, R. (1995). Hidden foreign exchange flows: Estimating unofficial remittances to Tonga and Western Samoa. *Asian and Pacific Migration Journal, 4*(1), 35–54.

Butcher, A. (2002, 22–24 November). *Whose Home?* Symposium conducted at the meeting of the Social Anthropologists Conference, Auckland.

Butcher, A. (2003). *No Place Like Home? The Experiences of South-East Asian International Students in New Zealand and Their Re-Entry Into Their Countries of Origin* (PhD). Massey University, Albany, New Zealand.

Byron, M., & Condon, S. (1996). A comparative study of Caribbean return migration from Britain and France: Towards a context-dependent explanation. *Transactions of the Institute of British Geographers, 21*, 91–104.

Caglar, A. (2006). Hometown associations, the rescaling of state spatiality and migrant grassroots transnationalism. *Global Networks, 6*(1), 1–22.

Cassarino, J. P. (2004). Theorising return migration: The conceptual approach to return migrants revisited. *International Journal on Multicultural Societies, 6*(2), 253–279.

Castells, M. (1996). *The Rise of the Network Society*. Oxford: Blackwell.

Castells, M. (2002). Migration and community formation under conditions of globalization. *International Migration Review, 36*(4), 1143–1168.

Cerase, F. (1974). Expectations and reality: A case study of return migration from the United States to Southern Italy. *International Migration Review, 8*, 245–262.

Chiang, L. N., Hibbins, R., & Chui, W. H. (2006). Immigrant Taiwanese women in the process of adapting to life in Australia: Case studies from transnational households. In D. Ip, R. Hibbins., & W. H. Chui (Eds.), *Experiences of Transnational Chinese Migrants in the Asia-Pacific* (pp. 69–86). New York: Nova Science Publishers.

Collins, F. L. (2006). *Learning to Cross Borders: Everyday Urban Encounters Between South Korea and Auckland*. University of Auckland, Auckland.

Connell, J., & Brown, R. (1995). Migration and remittances in the South Pacific: Towards new perspective. *Asian and Pacific Migration Journal, 4*(1), 1–33.

Conway, D., & Cohen, J. H. (1998). Consequences of migration and remittances for Mexican transnational communities. *Economic Geography, 74*(1), 26–44.

Crang, M. (2002). Qualitative methods: The new orthodoxy? *Progress in Human Geography, 26*(5), 647–655.

Crick, M., & Geddes, B. (1998). Introduction. In M. Crick & B. Geddes (Eds.), *Research Methods in the Field: Eleven Anthropological Accounts* (pp. 1–15). Geelong, VIC: Deakin University Press.

Douglas, M. (1991). The idea of home: A kind of space. *Social Research, 58*(1), 287–307.

Dukes, S. (1984). Phenomenological methodology in the Human Sciences. *Journal of Religion and Health, 23*(3), 197–203.

Espiritu, Y. L. (2003). *Home Bound: Filipino Across Cultures, Communities, and Countries*. Berkeley: University of California Press.

Espiritu, Y. L., & Tran, T. (2002). Vietnamese Americans and transnationalsim. In P. Levitt & M. C. Waters (Eds.), *The Changing Face of Home: The Transnational Lives of the Second Generation* (pp. 367–398). New York: Russell Sage Foundation.

Faist, T. (2000a). Transnationalization in international migration: Implications for the study of citizenship and culture. *Ethnic and Racial Studies, 23*(2), 189–222.

Faist, T. (2000b). *The Volume and Dynamics of International Migration.* Oxford, UK: Oxford University Press.

Faist, T. (2004). The transnational turn in migration research: Perspectives for the study of politics and policy. In M. P. Frykman (Ed.), *Transnational Spaces: Disciplinary Perspectives* (pp. 11–45). Malmo: Prinfo Team Offset & Media.

Fitzgerald, D. (2000). *Negotiating Extra-Territorial Citizenship: Mexican Migration and the Transnational Politics of Community.* La Jolla, CA: Centre for Comparative Immigration Studies.

Fitzgerald, P. (2008). Exploring transnational and diasporic families through the Irish emigration database. *Journal of Intercultural Studies, 29*(3), 267–281.

Flick, U. (2002). Qualitative research – state of the art. *Social Science Information, 41*(1), 5–24.

Foner, N. (2002). Second-generation transnationalism, then and now. In P. Levitt & M. C. Waters (Eds.), *The Changing Face of Home: The Transnational Lives of the Second Generation* (pp. 242–254). New York: Russell Sage Foundation.

Fontana, A., & Frey, J. H. (1994). Interviewing: The Art of Science. In N. Denzin & Y. Lincoln (Eds.), *Handbook of Qualitative Research* (pp. 361–376). London: Sage.

Fouron, G., & Glick-Schiller, N. (2002). The generation of identity: Redefining the second generation within a transnational social field. In P. Levitt & M. C. Waters (Eds.), *The Changing Face of Home: The Transnational Lives of the Second Generation* (pp. 168–208). New York: Russell Sage Foundation.

Gans, H. J. (1999). Towards a reconciliation of 'assimilation' and 'pluralism': The interplay of acculturation and ethnic retention. In C. Hirschman, P. Kasinitz, & J. DeWind (Eds.), *The Handbook of International Migration: The American Experience* (pp. 161–171). New York: Russell Sage Foundation.

Garcia, D. (2006). Mixed marriages and transnational families in the intercultural context: A case study of African-Spanish couples in Catalonia. *Journal of Ethnic and Migration Studies, 32,* 403–433.

Glick-Schiller, N. (1997). The situation of transnational studies. *Identities, 4*(2), 155–166.

Glick-Schiller, N. (2004). Transnationality. In D. Nugent & J. Vincent (Eds.), *A Companion to the Anthropology of Politics* (pp. 448–467). Malden, MA: Blackwell Publishing.

Glick-Schiller, N., Basch, L., & Blanc-Szanton, C. (Eds.). (1992). *Towards A Transnational Perspective on Migration: Race, Class, Ethnicity, and Nationalism Reconsidered.* New York: The New York Academy of Sciences.

Glick-Schiller, N., Basch, L., & Blanc-Szanton, C. S. (1995). From immigrant to transmigrant: Theorizing transnational migration. *Anthropology Quarterly, 68*(1), 48–63.

Glick-Schiller, N., & Fouron, G. (1998). Transnational lives and national identities: The identity politics of Haitian immigrants. In M. P. Smith & L. E. Guarnizo (Eds.), *Transnationalism From Below* (pp. 130–161). New Brunswich, U. S. A.: Transaction Publishers.

Gmelch, G. (1980). Return migration. *Annual Review of Anthropology, 9*(135–159).

Goldring, L. (1998). The power of status in transnational social fields. In M. P. Smith & L. E. Guarnizo (Eds.), *Transnationalism From Below* (pp. 165–195). New Brunswick, U. S. A.: Transaction Publishers.

Goldring, L. (1999). Power and status in transnational social spaces. In L. Pries (Ed.), *Migration and Transnational Social Spaces* (pp. 162–186). Aldershot: Ashgate Publishing Ltd.

Goldring, L. (2002). The Mexican state and transmigrant organizations: Negotiating the boundaries of membership and participation. *Latin American Research Review*, *37*(3), 55–99.

Gu, C. (2007, 11 August). *Transnational Struggles at Home: Taiwanese Immigrant Women's Family Relations and Mental Distress*. Presented at the meeting of the Annual Meetings of the American Sociological Association, New York. Retrieved from www.allacademic.com/meta/p183813_index.html

Guarnizo, L. E. (1997). The emergence of a transnational social formation and the mirage of return migration among Dominican Transmigrants. *Identities: Global Studies in Culture and Power*, *4*(2), 281–322.

Guarnizo, L. E., Portes, A., & Haller, W. (2003). Assimilation and transnationalism: Determinants of transnational political action among contemporary migrants. *The American Journal of Sociology*, *108*(6), 1211–1248.

Guarnizo, L. E., & Smith, M. P. (1998). The locations of transnationalism. In M. P. Smith., & L. E. Guarnizo (Eds.), *Transnationalism From Below* (pp. 3–34). New Brunswick: Transaction Publishers.

Hage, G. (1997). At home in the entrails of the west: Multiculturalism, 'ethnic food' and migrant home-building. In H. Grace, G. Hage, L. Johnson, J. Langsworth, & M. Symonds (Eds.), *Home/World: Space, Community and Marginality in Sydney's West* (pp. 99–153). Annandale: Pluto Press.

Haller, W., & Landolt, P. (2005). The transnational dimensions of identity formation: Adult children of immigrants in Miami. *Ethnic and Racial Studies*, *28*, 1182–1214.

Hannerz, U. (1998). Transnational research. In H. R. Bernard (Ed.), *Handbook of Methods in Cultural Anthropology* (pp. 235–256). Walnut Creek, CA: Altamira Press.

Hay, I. (2005). *Qualitative Research Methods in Human Geography*. South Melbourne, VIC & New York: Oxford University Press.

Heisler, B. S. (2008). The sociology of immigration: From assimilation to segmented integration, from the American experience to the global arena. In C. B. Brettell & J. F. Hollifield (Eds.), *Migration Theory: Talking Across Disciplines* (pp. 83–111). New York: Routledge.

Heisler, M. O. (2001). Now and then, here and there: Migration and the transformation of identities, borders and orders. In M. Albert, D. Jacobson, & Y. Lapid (Eds.), *Identities, Borders, Orders: Rethinking International Relations Theory* (pp. 225–248). Minneapolis: University of Minnesota Press.

Ho, E. (2002). Multi-local residence, transnational networks: Chinese 'astronaut' families in New Zealand. *Asian and Pacific Migration Journal*, *11*(1), 145–164.

Ho, E., & Bedford, R. (2008). Asian transnational families in New Zealand: Dynamics and challenges. *International Migration*, *46*(4), 41–62.

Ho, E., Ip, M., & Bedford, R. (2001). Transnational Hong Kong Chinese families in the 1990s. *New Zealand Journal of Geography*, 24–30.

Huang, S., Yeoh, B. S. A., & Lam, T. (2008). Asian transnational families in transition: The liminality of simultaneity. *International Migration*, *46*(4), 3–13.

Hughes, J. A., & Sharrock, W. W. (2007). *Theory and Methods in Sociology: An Introduction to Sociological Thinking and Practice*. Basingstoke, New York: Palgrave Macmillan.

Hugo, G. (2003). Asian migration to Australia. *Scottish Geographical Journal, 119*(3), 247–264.

Hugo, G. (2006). An Australian diaspora? *International Migration, 44*(1), 105–133.

Ip, D., Inglis, C., & Wu, C. T. (1997). Concepts of citizenship and identity among recent Asian immigrants in Australia. *Asian and Pacific Migration Journal, 6*(3–4), 363–384.

Ip, M. (2006). Returnees and transnationals: Evolving identities of Chinese (PRC) immigrants in New Zealand. *Journal of Population Studies, 33*, 61–102.

Iredale, R., Guo, F., & Rozario, S. (2002). Introduction. In R. Iredale, F. Guo., & S. Rozario (Eds.), *Return Skilled and Business Migration and Social Transformation* (pp. 1–19). Wollongong, Australia: Centre for Asia Pacific Social Transformation Studies, University of Wollongong.

Jackson, P., & Penrose, J. (1993). Introduction: Place 'race' and nation. In P. Jackson & J. Penrose (Eds.), *Constructions of Race, Place and Nation* (pp. 1–23). London: UCL Press.

Johnson, R. B., & Onwuegbuzie, J. O. (2004). Mixed methods research: A research paradigm whose time has come. *Educational Researcher, 33*(7), 14–26.

Joppke, C. (1999). How immigration is changing citizenship: A comparative view. *Ethnic and Racial Studies, 22*(4), 629–652.

Kasinitz, P., Waters, M. C., Mollenkopf, J. H., & Anil, M. (2002). Transnationalism and the children of immigrants in contemporary New York. In P. Levitt & M. C. Waters (Eds.), *The Changing Face of Home: The Transnational Lives of the Second Generation* (pp. 96–122). New York: Russell Sage Foundation.

Kastoryano, R. (2002). Turken mit Deutschem pass: Sociological and political aspects of dual nationality in Germany. In R. Hansen & P. Weil (Eds.), *Dual Nationality, Social Rights and Federal Citizenship in the U.S. and Europe* (pp. 158–175). Oxford: Berghahn.

King, K., & Newbold, K. (2008). Return immigration: The chronic migration of Canadian immigrants, 1991, 1996 and 2001. *Population, Space and Place, 14*(2), 85–100.

King, R. (2000). Generalizations from the history of return migration. In B. Ghosh (Ed.), *Return Migration: Journey of Hope or Despair?* (pp. 7–56). Geneva, Switzerland: International Organization for Migration and the United Nations.

Kivisto, P. (2001). Theorising transnational immigration: A critical review of current efforts. *Ethnic and Racial Studies, 24*, 549–577.

Korczenwicz, R. P., & Smith, W. C. (1996). A great transformation? In R. P. Korczenwicz & W. C. Smith (Eds.), *Latin America in the World Economy* (pp. 1–31). Westport, Conn: Greenwood Press.

Lam, L. (1994). Searching for a safe haven: The migration and settlement of Hong Kong Chinese immigrants in Toronto. In R. Skeldon (Ed.), *Reluctant Exiles? Migration From Hong Kong and the New Overseas Chinese* (pp. 163–179). Hong Kong: Hong Kong University Press.

Lee, H. (2003). *Tongans Overseas: Between two Shores.* Honolulu: University of Hawai'i Press.

Lee, H. (2004). Second generation Tongan transnationalism: Hope for the future? *Asia Pacific Viewpoint, 45*(2), 235–254.

Lee, H. (2006). 'Tonga only wants our money': The children of Tongan migrants. In S. Firth (Ed.), *Globalisation and Governance in the Pacific Islands: State, Society and Governance in Melanesia* (pp. 121–136). Canberra: Australia National University Press.

Lee, H. (Ed.). (2008). *Ties to the Homeland: Second Generation Transnationalism.* Newcastle Cambridge Scholars.

Levitt, P. (2001). Transnational migration: Taking stock and future directions. *Global Networks, 1*(3), 195–216.

Levitt, P. (2002). The ties that change: Relations to the ancestral home over the life cycle. In P. Levitt & M. C. Waters (Eds.), *The Changing Face of Home: The Transnational Lives of the Second Generation* (pp. 123–144). New York: Russell Sage Foundation.

Levitt, P. (2003a). Keeping feet in both worlds: Transnational practices and immigrant incorporation. In E. C. Joppke & E. Morawska (Eds.), *Integrating Immigrants in Liberal Nation-States: From Post-Nationals to Transnational* (pp. 177–194). London: Palgrave Macmillan.

Levitt, P. (2003b). Transnational migration and the redefinition of the state: Variations and explanations. *Ethnic and Racial Studies, 26*(4), 587–611.

Levitt, P. (2003c). You know, Abraham really was the first immigrant: Religion and transnational migration. *International Migration Review, 37*(3), 847–873.

Levitt, P. (2004). Redefining the boundaries of belonging: The institutional character of transnational religious life. *Sociology of Religion, 65*(1), 1–18.

Levitt, P. (2007). *God Needs No Passport: How Immigrants are Changing the American Religious Landscape.* New York: The New Press.

Levitt, P. (2009). Roots and routes: Understanding the lives of the second generation transnationally. *Journal of Ethnic and Migration Studies, 35*(7), 1225–1242.

Levitt, P., & Glick-Schiller, N. (2004). Conceptualizing simultaneity: A transnational social field perspective on society. *International Migration Review, 38*(3), 1002–1039.

Levitt, P., & Glick-Schiller, N. (2007). Conceptualizing simultaneity: A transnational social field perspective on society. In A. Portes & J. DeWind (Eds.), *Rethinking Migration: New Theoretical and Empirical Perspectives* (pp. 181–218). New York: Berghabn Books.

Lewin, F. A. (2001). The meaning of home among elderly immigrants: Directions for future research and theoretical development. *Housing Studies, 16,* 353–370.

Ley, D., & Kobayashi, A. (2005). Back to Hong Kong: Return migration or transnational sojourn? *Global Networks, 5*(2), 111–127.

Ley, D., & Waters, J. (2004). Transnational migration and the geographical imperative. In P. Jackson, P. Crang, & C. Dwyer (Eds.), *Transnational Spaces* (pp. 104–121). London: Routledge.

Lima, F. H. (2001). Transnational families: Institutions of transnational social space. In L. Pries (Ed.), *New Transnational Social Spaces: International Migration and Transnational Companies in the Eearly Twenty-First Century* (pp. 77–93). London: Routledge.

Liu, L. (2009). Home is calling? Or home is on the move? Return Chinese immigrants of New Zealand as transnationals. *New Zealand Journal of Asian Studies, 11*(2), 164–171.

Liu, L. (2011). New Zealand case sstudy of PRC transnational migration: Returnees and trans-Tasman migrants. In M. Ip (Ed.), *Transmigration and the New Chinese: Theories and Practices From the New Zealand Experience* (pp. 57–101). Hong Kong: The Centre of Asian Studies of the University of Hong Kong.

Mahler, S. J. (1998). Theoretical and empirical contributions toward a research agenda for transnationalism. In M. P. Smith & L. E. Guarnizo (Eds.), *Transnationalism From Below* (pp. 64–100). New Brunswich, USA: Transaction Publishers.

Mahler, S. J. (2003). Theoretical and empirical contributions toward a research agenda for transnationalism. In M. P. Smith & L. E. Guarnizo (Eds.), *Transnationalism From Below* (pp. 64–100). New Brunswick, USA and London: Transaction Publishers.

Mallett, S. (2004). Understanding home: A critical review of the literature. *The Sociological Review*, 52(1), 62–89.

Mar, P. (2005). Unsettling potentialities: Topographies of hope in transnational migration. *Journal of Intercultural Studies*, 26(4), 361–378.

Marcus, G. E. (1981). Power on the extreme periphery: The perspective of Tongan elites in the modern world system. *Pacific Viewpoint*, 22(1), 48–64.

Marcus, G. E. (1995). Ethnography in/of the world system: The emergence of multi-sited ethnography. *Annual Review of Anthropology*, 24, 95–117.

Massey, D. S., Arango, J., Hugo, G., Kouaouci, A., Pellegrino, A., & Taylor, J. E. (1994). An evaluation of international migration theory: The North American case. *Population and Development Review*, 20(4), 699–750.

Massey, D. S., Arango, J., Hugo, G., Kouaouci, A., Pellegrino, A., & Taylor, J. E. (1997). Migration theory, ethnic mobilization and globalization. In M. Guibernau & J. Rex (Eds.), *The Ethnicity Reader: Nationalism, Multiculturalism and Migration* (pp. 257–269). London: Policy Press.

Massey, D. S., Arango, J., Hugo, G., Kouaouci, A., Taylor, J. E., & Pellegrino, A. (1993). Theories of international migration: A review and appraisal. *Population and Development Review*, 19, 431–466.

Massey, D. S., Goldring, L., & Durand, J. (1994). Continuities in transnational migration: An analysis of nineteen Mexican communities. *American Journal of Sociology*, 99, 1492–1533.

McKay, D. (2005). Migration and the sensuous geographies of re-emplacement in the Philippines. *Journal of Intercultural Studies*, 26(1–2), 75–91.

Mitchell, K. (1997). Transnational discourse: Bringing geography back in. *Antipode*, 29(2), 101–114.

Moore, G. (2003). Return migration of Vietnamese Aucklanders. *New Zealand Journal of History*, 37(2), 189–209.

Muggeridge, H., & Dona, G. (2006). Back home? Refugees/experiences of their first visit back to their country of origin. *Journal of Refugee Studies*, 19(4), 415–432.

Ni Laoire, C. (2008). 'Settling back'? A biographical and life-course perspective on Ireland's recent return migration. *Irish Geography*, 41, 195–210.

Nonini, D. M., & Ong, A. (1997). Introduction: Chinese transnationalism as an alternative modernity. In A. Ong & D. M. Noni (Eds.), *Ungrounded Empires: The Cultural Politics of Modern Chinese Transnationalism* (pp. 3–33). New York: Routledge.

Nyiri, P. (2001). Expatriating is patriotic? The discourse on 'new migrants' in the People's Republic of China and identity construction among recent migrants from the PRC. *Journal of Ethnic and Migration Studies*, 27(4), 635–653.

Ong, A. (1993). On the edge of empires: Flexible citizenship among Chinese in diaspora. *Positions*, 1(3), 745–778.

Ong, A. (1999). *Flexible Citizenship: The Cultural Logics of Transnationality*. Durham, NC Duke University Press.

Orozco, M. (2000). *Latin Hometown Associations as Agents of Development in Latin America*. Washington, DC: Inter-American Dialogue.

Orozco, M. (2002). *Attracting Remittances: Market, Money and Reduced Costs*. Washington, DC: Multilateral Investment Fund of the Inter-American Development Bank.

Østergaard-Nielsen, E. (2003). *Transnational Politics: Turks and Kurds in Germany* London: Routledge.

Oxfeld, E., & Long, L. D. (2004). Introduction: An ethnography of return. In L. D. Long & E. Oxfeld (Eds.), *Coming Home? Refugees, Migrants, and Those Who Stayed Behind* (pp. 1–15). Philadelphia: University of Pennsylvania Press.

Palloni, A., Massey, D. S., Ceballos, M., Espinosa, K., & Spittel, M. (2001). Social capital and international migration: A test using information on family networks. *The American Journal of Sociology, 106*(5), 1262–1298.

Parham, A. A. (2004). Diasporam community and communication: Internet use in transnational Haiti. *Global Networks, 4*(2), 199–217.

Pe-Pua, R., Mitchell, C., Iredale, R., & Castles, S. (1996). *Astronaut Families and Parachute Children: The Cycle of Migration Between Hong Kong and Australia.* Wollongong, Australia: Centre for Multicultural Studies, University of Wollongong.

Perlmann, J. (2002). Second-generation Transnationalism. In P. Levitt & M. C. Waters (Eds.), *The Changing Face of Home: The Transnational Lives of the Second Generation* (pp. 216–220). New York: Russell Sage Foundation.

Plaza, D. (2008). Transnational return migration to the English-speaking Caribbean. *Revue Européenne des Migrations Internationales, 24*(1), 115–137.

Portes, A. (1996a). Global villagers: The rise of transnational communities. *American Prospect, 25,* 74–77.

Portes, A. (1996b). Transnational communities: Their emergence and significance in the contemporary world-system. In R. P. Korczenwicz & W. P. Smith (Eds.), *Latin America in the World-Economy* (pp. 151–168). Westport, Conn: Greenwood Press.

Portes, A. (1998). Divergent destinies: Immigration, the second generation, and the rise of transnational communities. In P. H. Schuck & R. Munz (Eds.), *Paths to Inclusion: The Integration of Migrants in the United States and Germany* (pp. 33–57). New York: Berghahn Books.

Portes, A. (1999). Conclusion: Towards a new world – the origins and effects of transnational activities. *Ethnic and Racial Studies, 22,* 463–476.

Portes, A. (2001). Introduction: The debates and significance of immigrant transnationalism. *Global Networks, 1*(3), 181–194.

Portes, A., Guarnizo, L. E., & Landolt, P. (1999). The study of transnationalism: Pitfalls and promise of an emergent research field. *Ethnic and Racial Studies, 22*(2), 217–237.

Portes, A., Haller, W., & Guarnizo, L. E. (2002). Transnational entrepreneurs: The emergence and determinants of an alternative form of immigrant economic adaptation. *American Sociological Review, 67,* 278–298.

Portes, A., & Landolt, P. (2000). Social capital: Promise and pitfalls of its role in development. *Journal of Latin American Studies, 32*(2), 529–547.

Portes, A., & Rumbaut, R. G. (2005). Introduction: The second generation and the children of immigrants longitudinal study. *Ethnic and Racial Studies, 28*(6), 983–999.

Pratt, G. (2004). *Working Feminism.* Philadelphia: Temple University Press.

Pries, L. (2001). The approach of transnational social spaces: Responding to new configurations of the social and the spatial. In L. Pries (Ed.), *New Tranasnational Social Spaces* (pp. 3–33). London: Routledge.

Pries, L. (2004). Determining the causes and durability of transnational labour migration between Mexico and the United States: Some empirical findings. *International Migration, 42*(2), 3–39.

Raj, D. S. (2000). 'Who the hell do you think you are?' Promoting religious identity among young Hindus in Britain. *Ethnic and Racial Studies, 23*(3), 535–558.

Rapport, N., & Dawson, A. (1998a). Home and movement: A polemic. In N. Rapport & A. Dawson (Eds.), *Migrants of Identity: Perceptions of Home in a World of Movement* (pp. 19–38). Oxford: Berg Press.

Rapport, N., & Dawson, A. (1998b). The topic and the book. In N. Rapport & A. Dawson (Eds.), *Migrants of Identity: Perceptions of Home in a World of Movement* (pp. 3–18). Oxford: Berg Press.

Robson, C. (2002). *Real World Research: A Resource for Social Scientists and Practitioner – Researchers*. Oxford, UK: Blackwell Publishers.

Rogers, A. (2001). Latin America: Migrants flow out, remittances flow in. *Trace, 14*. Retrieved from www.transcomm.ox.ac.uk/traces/iss14pg11.htm#latin

Rogers, R. (1984). Return migration in comparative perspective. In D. Kubat (Ed.), *The Politics of Return* (pp. 277–299). New York: Centre for Migration Studies.

Rouse, R. (1992). Making sense of settlement: Class transformation, cultural struggle, and transnationalism among Mexican migrants in the United States. In N. Glick-Schiller, L. Basch, & C. Szanton-Blanc (Eds.), *Towards a Transnational Perspective on Migration: Race, Class, Ethnicity, and Nationalism Reconsidered* (Vol. 645, pp. 25–52). New York: Annals of the New York Academy of Sciences.

Rumbaut, R. G. (2002). Severed or sustained attachments? Language, identity, and imagined communities in the post-immigrant generation. In P. Levitt & M. C. Waters (Eds.), *The Changing Face of Home: The Transnational Lives of the Second Generation* (pp. 43–95). New York: Russell Sage Foundation.

Ryan, L. (2008). Navigating the emotional terrain of families 'here' and 'there': Women, migration and the management of emotions. *Journal of Intercultural Studies, 29*(3), 299–313.

Salaff, J. W. (2008, 24–26 October). *Return Migration: The Role of Social Networks and Family Relations*. Symposium Conducted at the Meeting of the Conference on Globalisation and Chinese Culture: History and Challenges, Nanjing University, Nanjing, China.

Schweizer, T. (1998). Epistemology: The nature and validation of anthropological knowledge. In H. R. Bernard (Ed.), *Handbook of Methods in Cultural Anthropology* (pp. 39–87). Walnut Creek, California: A Division of Sage Publications, Inc.

Shield, R. (1996). *Culture of Internet: Virtual Spaces, Real Histories, Living Bodies*. London: Sage.

Skeldon, R. (1994a). Hong Kong in an international migration system. In R. Skeldon (Ed.), *Reluctant Exiles? Migration From Hong Kong and the New Overseas Chinese* (pp. 21–51). Hong Kong: Hong Kong University Press.

Skeldon, R. (1994b). Reluctant exiles or bold pioneers: An introduction to migration from Hong Kong. In R. Skeldon (Ed.), *Reluctant Exile? Migration From Hong Kong and the New Overseas Chinese* (pp. 3–18). Hong Kong: Hong Kong University Press.

Skrbis, Z. (2008). Transnational families: Theorising migration, emotions and belonging. *Journal of Intercultural Studies, 29*(3), 231–246.

Smith, M. P. (1992). Postmodernism, urban ethnography, and the new social space of ethnic identity. *Theory and Society, 21*, 493–531.

Smith, M. P. (1994). Can you imagine? Transnational migration and the Globalization of grassroots politics. *Social Text, 39*, 15–33.

Smith, R. (2002). Life course, generation and social location as factors shaping second-generation transnational life. In P. Levitt & M. C. Waters (Eds.), *The Changing Face of Home: The Transnational Lives of the Second Generation* (pp. 145–167). New York: Russell Sage Foundation.

Smith, R. C. (1998). Transnational localities: Community, technology and the politics of membership within the context of Mexico and U. S. Migration. In M. P. Smith & L. E. Guarnizo (Eds.), *Transnationalism From Below* (pp. 196–240). New Brunswich, U. S. A.: Transaction Publishers.

Somerville, K. (2008). Transnational belonging among second generation youth: Identity in a globalized world. *Journal of Social Sciences, Special Volume*, (10), 23–33.

Spoonley, P., Bedford, R., & Macpherson, C. (2003). Divided loyalties and fractured sovereignty: Transnationalism and the nation-state in Aotearoa/New Zealand. *Journal of Ethnic and Migration Studies, 29*(1), 27–46.

Stasiulis, D., & Bakan, A. B. (1997). Negotiating citizenship: The case of foreign domestic workers in Canada. *Feminist Review, 57*, 112–139.

Tollefsen, A., & Lindgren, U. (2006). Transnational citizens or circulating semi-proletarians? A study of migration circulation between Sweden and Asia, Latin America and Africa between 1968 and 2002. *Population, Space and Place, 12*, 517–527.

Trift, N. (2000). Dead or alive? In I. Cook, D. Crouch, S. Naylor, & J. Ryan (Eds.), *Cultural Turns/Geographical Turns: Perspectives on Cultural Geography* (pp. 1–6). Harlow, Essex: Prentice Hall.

Tuan, Y. F. (1971). Geography, phenomenology, and the study of human nature. *Canadian Geographer, 15*(3), 181–192.

Valentine, G. (2001). *Social Geographies: Space and Society.* New York: Prentice Hall.

Vertovec, S. (1999). Conceiving and researching transnationalism. *Ethnic and Racial Studies, 22*(2), 447–462.

Vertovec, S. (2001a). *Transnational Social Formations: Towards Conceptual Cross-Fertilization* (conference paper). Retrieved May 6, 2010, from Princeton University. www.transcomm.ox.ac.uk/working%20papers/Vertovec2.pdf

Vertovec, S. (2001b). Transnationalism and identity. *Journal of Ethnic and Migration Studies, 27*(4), 573–582.

Vertovec, S. (2004a). Cheap calls: The social glue of migrant transnationalism. *Global Networks, 4*(2), 219–224.

Vertovec, S. (2004b). Migrant transnationalism and modes of transformation. *International Migration Review, 38*(3), 970–1001.

Vertovec, S. (2008). Circular migration: The way forward in global policy? *Canadian Diversity, 6*(3), 36–40.

Viruell-Fuentes, E. A. (2006). 'My heart is always there': The transnational practices of first-generation Mexican immigrant and second-generation Mexican American women. *Identities: Global Studies in Culture and Power, 13*(3), 335–362.

Wang, C., Wong, S. L., & Sun, W. B. (2006). Haigui: A new area in China's policy toward the Chinese diaspora? *Journal of Chinese Overseas, 2*(2), 294–309.

Waters, J. (2002). Flexible families? 'Astronaut' households and the experience of lone mothers in Vancouver, British Columbia. *Social and Cultural Geography, 3*(2), 117–134.

Waters, J. (2003). Flexible citizens? Transnationalism and citizenship amongst economic immigrants in Vancouver. *Canadian Geographer, 47*, 219–234.

Waters, J. (2005). Transnational family strategies and education in the contemporary Chinese diaspora. *Global Networks*, 5, 359–377.

Waters, M. C. (2004). Worlds of the second generation. In P. Kasinitz, J. H. Mollenkopf, & M. C. Waters (Eds.), *Becoming New Yorkers: Ethnographies of the New Second Generation* (pp. 1–19). New York: Russell Sage Foundation.

Werbner, P. (2000). Divided loyalties, empowered citizenship? Muslims in Britain. *Citizenship Studies*, 4(3), 307–323.

Westwood, S., & Phizacklea, A. (2000). *Trans-Nationalism and the Politics of Belonging*. London: Routledge.

Wiles, J. (2008). Sense of home in a transnational social space: New Zealanders in London. *Global Networks*, 8(1), 116–137.

Wise, A. (2005). Hope and belonging in a multicultural suburb. *Journal of Intercultural Studies*, 26(1–2), 171–186.

Wolf, D. (1997). Family secrets: Transnational struggles among children of Filipino immigrants. *Sociological Perspectives*, 40(3), 457–483.

Wolf, D. (2002). There is no place like 'home': Emotional transnationalism and the struggles of second-generation Filipinos. In P. Levitt & M. C. Waters (Eds.), *The Changing Face of Home: The Transnational Lives of the Second Generation* (pp. 255–294). New York Russell Sage Foundation.

Wong, L. L. (2004). Taiwanese immigrant entrepreneurs in Canada and transnational social space. *International Migration*, 42(2), 113–152.

Wyman, M. (1993). *Round Trip to America: The Immigrants Return to Europe, 1880–1930*. New York: Cornell University Press.

Xiang, B. (2004). Indian information technology professionals' world system: The nation and the transnation in individuals' migration strategies. In B. S. A. Yeoh & K. Willis (Eds.), *State/Nationa/Transnation: Perspectives on Transnationalism in the Asia-Pacific* (pp. 161–178). London: Routlege.

Xiang, B. (2008, 31 July–1 August). Back in place? Return and a new order of mobility in Asia. *Asia Research Institute*. Symposium conducted at the meeting of the Return migration in Asia: Experiences, Ideologies and politics, National University of Singapore, Singapore.

Yeoh, B. S. A., Huang, S., & Lam, T. (2005). Transnationalizing the 'Asian' family: Imaginaries, intimacies and strategic intents. *Global Networks*, 5(4), 307–315.

Zhou, M., Chen, W., & Cai, G. (2006). Chinese-language media and immigrant life in the United States and Canada. In W. Sun (Ed.), *Media and the Chinese Diaspora: Community, Communications and Commerce* (pp. 42–74). New York: Routledge.

Zulueta, J. O. (2008, 31 July–1 August). 'Home' is where the heart is? The 'return' migration of Okinawan-Filipino to Okinawa. *Asia Research Institute*. Symposium conducted at the meeting of the Return Migration in Asia: Experiences, Ideologies & Politics, National University of Singapore.

Zweig, D. (1997). To return or not to return? Politics vs economics in China's brain drain. *Studies in Comparative International Development*, 32(1), 92–125.

Zweig, D. (2006). Competing for talent: China's strategies to reverse the brain drain. *International Labour Review*, 145, 65–89.

4 Changing family strategies and onward movements

Conceiving Chinese transnational migration in multi-sited ethnographies is a central element of this project. By following the migratory trajectories of those transnational PRC migrants, this ethnographic study posits a cohesive and interlocked relationship as seen in the first-hand interviews that resulted from investigations carried out in different geographic localities. Such an approach lets this research explore the complex connections these migrants as individuals and as families have established between New Zealand, China and third countries.

Based on in-depth interviews conducted in China, New Zealand, and Australia with PRC Chinese migrants who are New Zealand permanent residents or citizens, this chapter examines transnational PRC migrant motives for their initial immigration to New Zealand, the determining factors behind their choice of a transnational family lifestyle, their future movement intentions, transnational connections between their place of origin and immigration destination, and family dynamics and inter-generational issues in relation to transnational migration. These aspects are discussed within a relevant wider social-economic context. To facilitate and support the arguments, interviewee narratives are quoted with pseudonyms for the purpose of illustration and preserving anonymity.

This chapter is divided into seven sub-sections. The first briefly describes the research methods used to collect the qualitative data. The second discusses PRC Chinese migrants' initial motivations and reasons to immigrate to New Zealand. Findings from the ethnographic fieldwork conducted in China and in Australia stands separately in the third and fourth sub-sections. The fieldwork conducted in Auckland, New Zealand is embedded in those two sub-sections. There are factual and methodological reasons behind such organisation of the interview research materials. In the context of New Zealand, the migratory mobility of new Chinese migrants was commonly characterised as a "returnee" phenomenon to the homeland (Ip, 2006), or a process of step-migration to a third country, more specifically, a "back-door" migration trend using New Zealand as a "revolving door" to Australia (Rapson, 1998, p. 56). Therefore, the fieldwork is centred on the off-shore destinations of PRC migrants' transnational movements. However, the interviews conducted in Auckland, New Zealand targeted those "returnees" and "trans-Tasman" interviewees' on-shore family members, which aim to provide a family context to enhance the understanding of the transnational connections that many PRC immigrants established in their initial immigration destination country. It also provides further discussion on why many Chinese migrants returned to China and why many moved to Australia, rather than settling in New Zealand. Within those two sub-sections, a non-linear mode is used to examine the transnational mobility of those interviewees. Each individual transnational trajectory is examined by following the line of departure, arrival, departure again, relocation, and future intention. By using this mode, interviewee motives and reasons for their initial immigration to New Zealand, and later transnational movement are discussed. Findings from different ethnographic sites are compared, and convergences and divergences are addressed. To underscore the family importance in transnational migration, the fifth sub-section of this chapter provides a family case study to reveal the inter-generational dynamics in PRC migrants' transnational movements. The following sixth sub-section highlights the significance of social networks in the decision-making of re-location of the interviewees after they immigrated to New Zealand. In the last sub-section, some significant findings from the ethnographic fieldwork are summarised.

Multi-sited in-depth interviews – enriching understanding of the research topic

China, New Zealand, and Australia were the three ethnographic interview sites. This multiple-site research aims to target different groups of transnational Chinese migrants who have different transnational trajectories. Interviews in China targeted returned Chinese migrants who used to reside in New Zealand and have since returned to live and work in China. This group of interviewees is termed "returnees" in the research. The interviews conducted in Australia were done with Chinese migrants with New Zealand permanent residence or citizenship who moved across the Tasman Sea and now live and work in Australia for the long-term. Although some of them travel between China and Australia and also frequently travel to other countries, they regard Australia as their "home" base. This group of interviewees is termed "trans-Tasman" interviewees. The interviews in New Zealand collected voices of Chinese migrants currently residing in New Zealand, but keeping constant linkages/contacts with the homeland or other destinations where other family member(s) or other personal ties exist. Their migration trajectory shows no record of prolonged absences from New Zealand. This group of interviewees is called "settlers". Many of them have family members, who are "returnees", "trans-Tasman" interviewees, or "commuters", the last reference being to those who commute frequently between New Zealand and China.

It should be noted, however, that the categorisation of the interviewee groups (i.e., "returnees", "trans-Tasman" interviewees, "settlers", and "commuters") in this research is based on transnational migration trajectories and is only for labelling purposes and methodological convenience. Theoretically, transnational migrants should not be categorised in such fixed terms because further movement is contingent for these highly mobile migrants. Their transnational trajectories may change when their lives enter another stage. In other words, they may easily convert from one category to the other, depending on what particular life time they are situated in and what particular needs they have in the different stages of their life cycles.

As shown in Table 4.1, 47 PRC migrants were interviewed in total. Among these 47 interviewees, at the time of interview, 27 were "returnees" in China, 10 were "trans-Tasman" interviewees in Australia, 2 were "commuters" who travelled between China and New Zealand frequently, and 8 were "settlers" in New Zealand of which two were preparing to move to Australia. Overall, the 47 interviewees matched the profile of typical transnational migrants, possess great human, social, and financial capital (Ip, 2000; Portes, 1999, 2001). They were well educated, relatively young, bilingual, highly skilled, in early or mid-career, and have considerable earning capacity. Many hold high-paying professional jobs, while others own their own businesses. They arrived in New Zealand the first time between 1987 and 2005 with the majority arriving between 1996 and 2002. Among the 27 "returnees", only four had already decided to return to China prior to immigrating to New Zealand. Nearly half have acquired New Zealand citizenship. At the time of the interviews, all had returned and settled in China for at least one year. As for the two "commuters", both decided to keep their Chinese citizenship while being New Zealand permanent residents. As for the "settlers" and "trans-Tasman" interviewees, all have obtained New Zealand citizenship. Among the 10 "trans-Tasman" interviewees, five had acquired Australian citizenship, and the remainder were either in the process of applying or planning to apply for Australia citizenship. Their time of arrival in Australia was between 2000 and 2009.

The recruitment of interviewees was accomplished mainly via the New Zealand Embassy in Beijing, the New Zealand Consulate-General in Shanghai, Auckland

Table 4.1 Interviews conducted at three fieldwork sites and profiles of the three interview cohorts

Fieldwork site	Targeted Interviewee groups	Number of interviewees by Gender: (Male/Female)	Average age	Number of people with NZ bachelor's or higher degree	Number of people with NZ citizenship
China (Beijing, Shanghai)	A*	27 (13/14)	38	23	13
Auckland	B*, C* & E*	10 (3/7)	34	10	10
Australia (Melbourne & Sydney)	D*	10 (8/2)	40	7	10 (5 of whom also acquired Australia citizenship)

(Note*: A. "returnees"; B. "settlers"; C. "commuters"; D. "trans-Tasman" interviewees; E. immediate family members of "returnees" and "trans-Tasman" interviewees.)

University's alumni in Beijing, the Kiwi Club[1] in Shanghai, personal networking, and a snowballing technique. One effective way of recruiting interviewees was to follow up with some interviewee family members and ask them to introduce other family members to participate.

In-depth interviews were conducted face-to-face. Principally, the interviews were conducted with single individuals except on only two occasions where the interviewees wished to be interviewed with their spouses. The language used in the interviews was the interviewee's choice. In most interviews, Mandarin was used. There were some cases where interviewees replied in English to certain questions. Such manner of responding was respected. As for the interview venue, many interviews were conducted in interviewee households with tea or coffee served, some occurred in interviewee offices, and some happened in cafes, tea-houses, and restaurants. Each interview takes about one and half hours to finish. In general, the manner of conducting the interview was informal. It was rather an interesting conversation between friends based on mutual trust and took place in a leisurely environment. Interviewees were provided the freedom to ask any questions during the interviews.

In many cases, the interviews were followed by lunch or dinner with the interviewees, sometimes also including interviewees' colleagues, family members, or close friends in circumstances where both the interviewer and interviewee felt they could relate well with each other. Such social interactions with the interviewees was more beneficial than I expected, because these occasions provided me first-hand experience of the real life of my interviewees in the locations I was researching. It also served a very important complementary and contextualising role in research practice. Even though the observational information derived from these social interactions with the interviewees was not included in the concrete data serving the research objectives, it did explain, confirm, or even contest information gathered through the interviews and provided rich and highly illuminating social evidence of their lived experience. Hughes and Sharrock suggest that an interview is a social encounter between an interviewer and an interviewee and is rightly "governed by the proprieties of interpersonal relationship between people who do not know each other" (Hughes & Sharrock, 2007). In the case of this particular ethnographic fieldwork, I would say that the interviews were far beyond a simple one-off short conversation with interviewees; rather, each was an immersed social interaction that required active engagement and close involvement with each participant. This approach is what ethnographic research requires as well as what this particular research needed.

The Interview Questions (see Appendix 4) cover interviewees' demographic information, reasons for their initial immigration to New Zealand, driving forces behind their transnational trajectories, and their future movement intentions and motivations. These questions are used as the primary data source to construct this chapter. As mentioned, different types of interviewees were involved in this research, including "returnees", "settlers", "commuters", and "trans-Tasman" interviewees. The interview questions were universal to all types of interviewees, but especially tailored to suit the different positions of these participants. For example, if an interviewee was a "returnee", I would ask why he/she returned to China. If an interviewee was a "trans-Tasman" person, I would ask why he/she moved to Australia.

From China to New Zealand

- *New Zealand is a beautiful and peaceful country with fresh air and good natural environment. It is a perfect place for living or retirement. Here, Beijing, China, however, is an exciting place – fast development and a quick change of economic environment, as well as cruel competition. I feel that I am an active participant and creator of this city.*
- *New Zealand is a clean, green, and friendly country, but China is my home, and will always be my home. I love this country because love is what you cannot describe, but what you can feel.*
- *The thing over there I value the most is the democracy, liberty, freedom, and law-and-order. You can only find them in a Western society like New Zealand. China used to be poor and undeveloped, but now she is rising.*

These passages are taken from narratives of three "returnees", when they replied to my question of describing their impressions of China and New Zealand. Such sentiments were frequently repeated during the fieldwork. These narratives illustrate the attractiveness of New Zealand as a popular immigration destination country for many PRC Chinese migrants, as well as the "pull" factors exerted by China where deep emotional roots, a fast-growing economy, and greater opportunities for business and career development now lie. These three narratives are an entry point for understanding why many PRC Chinese migrants chose to return to their home country as well as to move to another destination. The ways in which "home" and "away", "here" and "there", are defined in the narratives are likely indications of the decision to return, further movements, or the dilemma of choosing to stay or to return. The peaceful, social, and positive natural environment in New Zealand and the bustling metropolitan atmosphere in urban China are different magnets, each affecting PRC migrant decision-making on movements.

These narratives also explain the important reasons for PRC immigrants to choose New Zealand. Discussing PRC Chinese migrants' initial motivations and reasons to step into their first immigration destination (i.e. New Zealand) is important to understand their transnational movements, since their initial motivations to immigrate to New Zealand had considerable influence on their immigration outcomes. The field of return migration studies has recognised that return is largely influenced by the initial motivations for migration as well as the duration of the stay abroad, particularly by the conditions under which the return does take place (Cassarino, 2008; Ghosh, 2000). Without addressing Chinese migrant initial motivations to move to New Zealand, a full understanding of their return to the homeland and their transnational migration cycle cannot be achieved. This research yields findings that are largely in line with the previous findings that few new Chinese migrants immigrated to New Zealand for economic reasons (Ho, 2003; Ho, Ip, & Bedford, 2001; Ip, 2000, 2003a; Ip & Friesen, 2001). Interview evidence of this research shows that economic well-being was not a major factor for PRC migrants to immigrate to New Zealand; rather, non-economic reasons appeared to be dominant among this migrant group. As discussed in Chapter 2, the attractions of New Zealand for PRC migrants were mainly a social and natural environment, a democratic political system, and an advanced education system. From a practical point of view, compared with other immigration countries like Canada, Australia, and the US, lower entry criteria and living costs also contribute to choosing New Zealand as an immigration destination country. Many interviewees revealed that New Zealand was not their first choice; instead, preferences were frequently given to the US, Canada, or Australia, although their final decision, for a practical consideration of a lower threshold, was New Zealand.

There is another crucial factor that propels PRC immigrants to come to New Zealand. It is New Zealand's strong historical linkage with Britain, giving the country an image of a Western society. This cultural factor is important to many PRC migrants. Quite often, interviewees stated their main reason for coming to New Zealand as "going to the outside world to have a look", "eye-opening experiences", or "getting a gilded wrapping to myself (镀金)". Here, "the outside world" and "eye-opening experiences" usually refer to experiencing life in developed Western countries, and "getting a gilded wrapping" means that an overseas experiences or an overseas degree can give one a valuable overseas credential and an international outlook. These will have considerable value in China's job market and provide the advantage of embracing a bright future that may not necessarily take place in the destination country.

The dimension discussed above is largely in line with what Ong suggested, namely, that there is a cultural notion behind the phenomenon of many Chinese going overseas in the contemporary era (Ong, 1999). That is a "cultural logic" where the West is often presented as a superior civilisation "in terms of capital development, secularisation of [the] cultural, and democratic state formation" (Ong, 1999). This opinion often promotes movement toward the West and constantly invokes a longing for Western experience among many Chinese. Emigrating to a Western country to obtain permanent residence or citizenship for many prospective PRC migrants means obtaining a safeguard for their future or a stepping ladder to climb to new financial and social heights. This attitude is built on historical and social reasons. China suffered defeats and humiliation from the Western powers during the nineteenth century and twentieth century and was a closed society until the late 1980s with a bleak economy and slow social development. Therefore, it is true to say that up to the beginning of the new millennium, immigrating to developed Western countries was perceived by the Chinese general public as an astute move towards personal advancement that could only be taken by those elites who possessed considerable human and financial capitals. Migration to the West was seen as a courageous step to escape from the bleak situation at home and pursue positive personal goals. These notions appeared pervasive among the "returnees" when they explained their reasons for immigrating to New Zealand initially.

- Michael stated, "Immigrating to a developed Western country, like New Zealand, for my generation was a prestigious thing to do, everybody envied me".
- John revealed, "I have been educated to go overseas to better myself since I was a little boy. At the time when I graduated from university, there was a wave that excellent young graduates all prepared to go the West. I was not qualified to go to US; therefore, I chose New Zealand".
- Paul explained, "I was not satisfied with the situation in China at that time, and also was not confident about the prospect of China. At that time, it seemed that China's political system was unstable and the government's determination to develop the economy was not apparently shown. New Zealand is a Western country and definitely one of my choices at that time".

However, going to the West for PRC migrants was just an immigration aspiration and a rather ambiguous and intangible one at that. In this sense, PRC Chinese migrants were quite different from Hong Kong and Taiwan Chinese migrants in terms of motivation and reasons for immigrating to New Zealand. The influx of new Chinese migrants from Hong Kong to New Zealand in the mid-1990s mainly associated with fears of the political uncertainty associated with Hong Kong's 1997 handover to the Chinese government (Ho, 2003). This fear intensified with the Tian'anmen Square Incident in 1989, which propelled an exodus of Hong Kong Chinese between the late 1980s and mid-1990s. The results of this exodus have been widely noticed in Canada, Australia, and New Zealand. Skeldon (2006) commented on the exodus of Hong Kong Chinese: "their sojourn overseas was aimed solely at fulfilling the residence requirements for a foreign passport, which was sought as an insurance policy against things going wrong after 1997" (p. 69). Migrants from Taiwan shared a similar fear of communist China, especially after Chinese missiles were launched across the Taiwan Strait. Some immigrated to New Zealand to protect their male children from compulsory military training (Boyer, 1996; Ip, 2003b). Apart from the political insecurity, pursuing better education opportunities for children and a relaxed lifestyle also contributed to the arrival of many Hong Kong and Taiwan migrants to New Zealand. It is fair to say then that their immigration goal was more specific and clearer.

In contrast, the goal for PRC new immigrants to New Zealand was generally ambiguous and not as specific as the Hong Kong and Taiwan immigrants. Like Ann said, "it was a little bit aimless for many PRC people to immigrate to New Zealand; it seemed that as long as they could leave China and enter a Western country, they would make the move". This trend can be partly verified by cases of "returnees" who landed in New Zealand for the first time as international students and then applied for residency on shore. A number of those interviewed revealed that they did not have a clear purpose for immigration; they came to New Zealand initially for education only. Then when they found they could score quite high in the point-based immigration system, applying for permanent residence became the next logical step in their overseas experience. Taking one interviewee as an example, Sarah explained her arrival in New Zealand "as purely for postgraduate education and as an investment in self-development", and her decision for immigration was "a norm of trajectory that many Chinese from China had experienced – studying, working and immigrating".

While the primary objectives of New Zealand's immigration policy after 1987 were economic factors, such as covering a labour force shortage and stimulating business, the new PRC migrants' initial motivation ran in a different direction. This was a topic of much policy and government debate and challenged the usual traditional assumption that migration is generally economically motivated. Of interest here is the issue of limited interest in economic integration into New Zealand among PRC migrants as their primary immigration motivation. Economic integration into a host society requires patience and time. The underlying rationale is that the more time and effort one spends on obtaining employment in the immigration host society, the more likely it will be that one can gain better labour market performance. A limited economic interest in immigrating to New Zealand among many PRC migrants may have pre-determined that their residence in New Zealand would not be long. The question that needs to be asked here is whether high absenteeism links to or is even caused by limited economic interest. If one's original intention was largely utilitarian, such as viewing New Zealand as a place for advanced education opportunities, eye-opening experiences, or collecting useful personal credentials, an immigrant might pack up and leave once he/she achieved those original goals. This is one indication that further movement of PRC migrants is highly possible and contingent. This aspect is further discussed in the following sections.

Returning to China: a calling from "home"?

The return journey taken by "returnees" is emotionally costly and involves critical decision-making and uproots a person once again to re-enter the homeland, and facing inevitable re-adjustments and re-integration issues. This research found that the factors behind PRC migrants' return to the homeland are multi-layered; there is no single reason for the decision to make that return journey. The factors that motivate returning are interwoven with macro forces and also personal and family reasons.

Macro-factors: the economic pull of China

The strength of the Chinese economy and the huge Chinese market were undoubtedly important factors that propelled some movement homeward. For example, Jeff, an insurance claim broker based in Shanghai, whose wife and children still live in Christchurch, mentioned,

> I really dislike being separated from my wife and children geographically, but if I drop my business in Shanghai and stay in New Zealand permanently, the quality of my family's lives would decline dramatically because of the lower income over there. Here in Shanghai, the bigger population means more clients and more money.

Even though Jeff was once employed by a New Zealand electronics company and had a stable income, it was not enough to sustain the lifestyle he wanted for his family.

The impact of China's booming economy adds more force to motives related to career-development opportunities and higher professional satisfaction. Given that many "returnees" received re-training and re-education in New Zealand, their overseas qualifications, work experience, and English language proficiency equipped them with the special skills and knowledge they needed to take on the opportunities and challenges offered by China's rapidly growing economy. When they competed in the China job market, they had an advantage over the locals. Almost all "returnees" emphasised that the immigration experience and their study in New Zealand gave them additional strength and advantage when embracing their new life and work in China. In this sense, the experience of immigrating to New Zealand was generally perceived as positive among those "returnees". Susan, a young mother who is currently working in an international-management-system corporation in Beijing, highlighted the immediate advantages of her New Zealand experience:

> If I didn't have my New Zealand qualification, I wouldn't have my current job. This is a multinational corporation which requires professionals to have specific skills. For example, I am a HR person. Theoretically, there are heaps of HR available, and it is easy to recruit them. However, it is difficult to find a HR person who specialises in accounting and also speaks fluent English.

Equipped with such human and cultural capital, as well as creative ideas gleaned from overseas, many of the "returnees" found it impossible to resist the higher professional satisfaction and career development opportunities now available in China. Michael, who returned to China in 2008 and is working as a finance analyst specialising in adventure investment analysis, mentioned that, compared with China, the job and entrepreneurial opportunities in New Zealand were relatively limited. When he immigrated to New Zealand in the mid-1990s, he had never expected China to become an economic giant within such a short period of time. Seeing China's booming economy, which provides more scope for his career development, he gave up his middle-income job in Auckland and took a position in a newly established local share company in China. He left his wife, who was doing her PhD, in New Zealand, so she could complete her studies. The decision was risky because the company he joined was a newly established one, but he has no regrets. He expressed his satisfaction over his current work situation in Beijing:

> The job is more interesting and exciting job compared with those I ever had in New Zealand. My specialised field is finance. Even though I was lucky compared with many Chinese immigrants because my last job in New Zealand was closely related to my special training, it was not challenging enough.

The decision to return was not easy for him and for his wife. It took him many years to make up his mind. As a finance analyst, he finally rationalised his decision of returning by using what he called a personal "cost-and-benefit analysis":

> Immigration to New Zealand cost us a lot. I'd like to use a "cost-and-benefit analysis" to answer your question about my returning decision. Yes, we have benefited from immigrating to New Zealand, such as the eye-opening experience, being in a country with a good natural environment and peaceful social environment, and gaining New Zealand qualifications. However, what we lost was much more than what we gained. If I did not immigrate to New Zealand, I believe that my career would be on another completely different trajectory. I would be a very successful entrepreneur in China, and I would have more money than what I have now. In New Zealand, what I have achieved is only an ordinary middle-class lifestyle. That is not what I want. You may say I am ambitious. To be honest, I am ambitious. Now my opportunity is coming, I have to return to China to take it and get back what I have lost. . . . My New Zealand boss was very reluctant to let me go, but he was not able to offer me what my current employer could offer.

While Michael's return was mainly driven by his career ambition, it was not only a monetary matter; it was also one of self-esteem:

> In relation to career development . . . if I had stayed in New Zealand, I would be a person who gives up all my dreams and just lived ordinary life. . . . I am a person who always has dreams and wants a successful career.

Personal and family reasons

The interviews conducted in China revealed a complex set of personal and family trajectories. For many of these "returnees", family responsibility, such as taking care of their aging parents, played an important role in their decision to return. A couple who had stayed in New Zealand for more than ten years suddenly decided to return to China, not only because of a great job offer for the husband from a multi-national company, but also because of his aging parents. Jack, the husband explained his return in a very touching way:

> Of course, the company I am now working for offers me a lot, not only the high salaries. I also have many opportunities to go overseas. I now travel between many European countries and China every week. I am sure that I have already achieved a very high economic and social status. But this is not all. The primary reason for us to return to Beijing was because my parents are aging. They really need me to be close to them, and I am truly happy to return for them. As their only son, what I really want to do for them is to take care of them on a daily basis when they are ill. When their time runs out, I can be with them at the end.

Jack's wife, Tina, made clear that this consideration for Jack's parents was actually incorporated into the whole family's movement plans. Tina's parents are still in Auckland with Tina's younger sister, so the younger sister can take care of them in Tina's absence.

> My parents immigrated to New Zealand under the family (parents) reunion category. They stayed with us in Auckland for several years. Later on, my younger sister came as well. She is working there now. It is fortunate that my sister is in Auckland. If she were not, I really could not have left my parents and come back to Beijing with my husband. My husband is the only son of his parents – you know, the "one-child" policy in China. My parents are lucky that they have two girls. My sister now takes the main responsibility for taking care of my parents in New Zealand, so I can be away.

Given the "one-child" policy in China that was introduced in 1978 and initially applied to first-born children in 1979, many new PRC Chinese migrants are the only children of their parents. Jack's case is one example and shows that return homeward movements are often necessitated by the fact that aging parents require long-term care for declining health. Filial piety could be an important pull factor in the decision to make the return journey.

Reunion with family back in China is also an important reason that draws many PRC migrants home. For example, there was Sandy, whose husband and son are all New Zealand permanent residents, but her husband and son have not been in New Zealand for very long. Sandy stayed in New Zealand for six years, so the whole family could qualify as permanent residents. In the meantime, her husband and son and she travelled between New Zealand and Beijing three or four times annually for family reunions in either Beijing or New Zealand. She also studied and obtained her MBA from a New Zealand university. After graduation, she found a job in a government organisation and worked there for more than a year. She returned to Beijing in 2008 because her family needed her:

> It is not good to be separated from my husband and son for a long time. . . . Now all of us have secured New Zealand residence as our back-up in the

future, and I got my MBA as well as work experience from a Western society. That is more than enough. It is time to be back.

As some other transnational Chinese migrants also did, an arrangement where some family members were located in China and others in New Zealand was put in place deliberately prior to immigration. Long-distance family separation was also dictated by the needs of different family members, needs that could not be accommodated within the same geographical space or abode. For her husband, a lawyer who can earn a very high income in Beijing, giving up his job to move to New Zealand with Sandy would not be a wise choice because his Chinese salary is the financial backbone of their family. Their son would receive a full Chinese education based on the plan and desire of his parents, so the task to fulfil the immigration requirement fell on Sandy's shoulders; in addition, she had better English language skills and did not need to work intensively to sustain the family's financial needs.

They deliberately maintained family ties in both China and New Zealand via the strategy of "astronauting". During the period of family separation, the family ties were not disrupted; instead, they were sustained by frequent commuting of all family members between the homeland and the immigration destination country. Moreover, there was likely a clear plan of reunion for a time in the near future. When the immediate goal of obtaining a New Zealand permanent Returning Resident's Visa (RRV)[2] was achieved, the family moved on to the next stage of their lives. Assessment of where they would spend the next stage of their lives was then made rationally and based on the different needs of each family member. Returning to China was definitely one among many choices.

In the case of Sandy, her return to China was solely family-driven. Her son still needed a few years to complete secondary school in China, and her husband had good earning power, with his career reaching its peak in China. For Sandy, her New Zealand qualification and work experience were useful by-products of the immigration process and definitely gave her advantages when competing in China's labour market. These reasons, coupled with the attraction of China's booming economy and the associated huge demand for skilled professionals, made them decide that "it is the right time to be back".

Unlike Sandy's choice, many families with school-age children still choose family separation, where the husband remains in China to work and the children and mother stay in New Zealand. This choice is mainly made because the children have become accustomed to New Zealand's educational system, and many are not willing to go back to schools in China, where the education system is rigidly restricted and involves tremendous stress and competition. Most Chinese parents also believe that the New Zealand education system is better than the one in China. For example, Stella, whose husband commutes between China and New Zealand at least three times a year, compromised her aspiration to return based on consideration for her two school-age children:

> Once [my 14-year-old daughter] got into the school here, she never wanted to go back to school in China. Children are very sensible, and they can

compare which one is better for them and which is not. Now it is impossible to take her back even if I wanted to return China with my husband. Her English is much better than her Chinese and, more importantly, she has her own friends in the school, church group, and music team. How can I take these things away from her?

Sometimes the decision to continue with a family situation of separation was deliberately made before applying for immigration just as Sandy's family did. However, in many cases, decisions were made after a difficult attempt to establish a business or find employment in New Zealand. Even though many PRC migrants' main reason for coming New Zealand was not economic well-being, the basic economic factor of a stable job with reasonable income to sustain the family was clearly an important consideration. When seeing that it is much harder to generate reasonable income in New Zealand, many family members, usually the men, went back to China to pick up their previous businesses, but travel frequently between China and New Zealand for family reunions.

The early literature on transnational migrant families often used the word "astronauting" to describe the frequent commuting behaviour of some Asian immigrants, especially the husband/father of the family (Ho, Bedford, & Goodwin, 1997; Pe-Pua, Mitchell, Iredale, & Castles, 1996; Skeldon, 1994; Waters, 2002). This phenomenon has been widely seen in media reports as an aberration of the traditional expectations of immigrants. However, the reality of transnational migration shows that in many cases "astronauting" is only part of a family's transnational trajectory and only denotes a strategy used to satisfy a migrant family's short-term needs. When the goal of a life stage is achieved, the strategy may change; re-arrangement or re-location may take place, and the re-location destination for the next stage of life will be assessed and determined based on the needs of the changing family structure. This pattern is discussed further in a later sub-section.

For some nuclear migrant families with single working adult and aging parents, their choice may be that the working adult goes back to China to enjoy the benefits provided by China's fast-growing economy, while the aging parents stay in New Zealand to enjoy their retirement in a natural and peaceful environment. It is obvious that within the family context, the decision to return or stay involves an overall consideration of how to balance the different needs of all the family members and how to achieve overall family well-being.

Other non-economic reasons: Chinese cultural milieu and emotional links to the homeland

For many "returnees", the desire to go back to old, comfortable surroundings also contributes to their return decision. Sandy elaborated on her reasons for return as follows: "To be honest, we can have more in China than in New Zealand, both materially and spiritually. But for me, the spiritual gain was more important. I have many friends in China, and my family and my parents". China's

cultural milieu was comfortable, familiar, and highly reassuring, offering a familiar language and social environment, which produced a high sense of security and
belonging. Paired with the Chinese cultural milieu, there is a feeling of alienation from the Kiwi circle and culture that underlies the final decision to return.
Nichole expressed her sense of frustration about trying to integrate into the Kiwi
culture:

> I am sure that I am a person who has integrated into the mainstream rela-
> tively well, at least compared with most new Chinese. My English is good
> enough to communicate at both social and professional levels. I can use a lot
> of slangs and make jokes when I speak in English. My boss, my colleagues,
> and my previous supervisors in university all like to talk to me. I also like the
> café and picnic culture. I truly appreciate and accept the Kiwi values. But are
> these all enough? This is a serious problem. As an immigrant, you are just
> another bloody Asian newcomer for the locals anyway.

Sunny referred to one of the reasons for her returning as "New Zealand is not
international enough". When the interviewer asked her to explain further, she said:

> I mean that New Zealand is not tolerant enough toward foreigners. On the
> institutional level, New Zealand does very well. There is almost no policy or
> regulation that imposes racial segregation and division. It is a country that
> is inclusive and open to minority immigrants. However, the locals here are
> another matter, especially the Maori. They feel that there are too many new
> immigrants. We Chinese are very sensitive to these issues. We can feel the
> suspiciousness some locals hold toward us.

Thus, while many PRC "returnees" are motivated primarily by China's economic
success, by the energetic pursuit of career development, and by personal and
family reasons, race relations in the host country also partially and significantly
contributed to the decision to return. When the macro- and micro-factors that
contribute to the cross-border movements of transnational migrants are considered all together, the social relationships and structure of the destination country
cannot be underestimated.

For some "returnees", the emotional link to China as their "home" also contributed to their return. Some interviews revealed how the emotional link with
China conditioned their decision to return. Sophia, who quit her job as a programme manager at a New Zealand university and is now working as a trade
development executive in Shanghai, mentioned that her emotional link with her
birthplace, Shanghai, was an important factor in her return. While the interview
with her reinforced the attractiveness of China as an economic powerhouse, she
particularly emphasised that "home is calling. Here is my home. Hamilton is my
home away from home. My real home is in Shanghai, China". For her, the idea
of returning to her hometown filled her with nostalgia. The interview with Lucy
revealed a similar tendency to perceive China as the home to which she can and

should return: "I am a Chinese, and China is my country. My home is here. Here is a place where I feel I belong. In New Zealand, even though they offered me citizenship, I could not find the feeling of being home".

These interview results also show that the emotional link to China as the "home" relates to the promotion of patriotism among many young Chinese migrants, and this patriotism is immediately related to China's rising international status and its growing profile as an emerging world power. As George explained, "China, my home, still has many things that are not very good, but I love her as I love my mother. I cannot refuse to go back to my mother. Now China is rising, I am really proud of it, and I hope that it will become stronger and stronger".

In summary, the majority of these "returnees" are highly educated, and a sizeable number have already obtained New Zealand qualifications and work experience. This research strongly suggests that when those immigrants made the move back to China, many did so not because of their failure to settle down in New Zealand; rather they moved because there are better opportunities in China. Equipped with English proficiency, New Zealand qualifications and professional skills, they are able to take advantage of those opportunities. The opportunity for professional advancement and to "play a bigger role" in China's market and economic development is the most important factor for many return migration decisions. Other factors beyond economic reasons, such as family consideration, patriotic pride, cultural alienation with the host society, and an emotional linkage with China, are equally important. The interviews conducted in China also found that the consideration of family members' different needs at their different life stages played a significant role in weighing returning to China and staying there.

Future movement intentions: a permanent settling back?

Given the pulling power exerted on the PRC migrants by the bigger China market, one important question related to return migration was whether there is an expiry date in their plan to make a return journey. To determine the motives and implications of return migration in a transnational context, these interviews asked about future movement plans of those "returnees".

Back to New Zealand for sure

Some "returnees" have definite plans to go back to New Zealand for their children's education. For example, Sandy explained her future plan: "I'll be with my son in Auckland for his high school education after he finishes his intermediate school in Beijing. Bilingualism is an advantage for his future. New Zealand's education will benefit him as well". Thus Sandy will renew the trans-Pacific migration cycle and register her son and herself for a return journey to their immigration destination country in the near future. The driving force behind this decision is education. As a young family with a school-age child, Sandy's family focus is on the child. Giving children a relatively liberal educational environment is often a priority in a family's future plans. This is not, however, the end of that journey. The subsequent movement plan in the future goes along with the nature of this migrant's shifting motivations at different stages of life. As Sandy explained:

> Once my son enters university, I can be free. I can totally focus on my own career. As a mother, my task has been accomplished. I want to go to Australia afterwards, and my husband can go there with me if he wants. My best friend owns a big trading company in Sydney, and he always asks me to go there to help with his business. I can also have the option of going back to China again.

This is a family whose social habitat is definitely transnational. Its remarkable family trajectory once again confirms the point that changing family structure and family dynamics underpins a family's transnational strategy, which in turn significantly influences the next location of each family member (Ho & Bedford, 2008; Yeoh, Huang, & Lam, 2005). The negotiation of any transnational trajectory is a skilful balancing act and dictated by the consideration of the needs of different family members at different life stages. In doing so, the needs of some family members can be accommodated within the same geographical locality, but some cannot. This results in various special arrangements like temporary split, dispersal, translocality, and convergence. Although the patterns are varied, in the end, only choices that maximise the benefits for a collective family well-being will be made.

While the education-driven return to New Zealand for children is pervasive, retirement is another significant event frequently associated with the decision to return to New Zealand. For many, retirement is that time when one moves away from bustling metropolitan urban centres to live in a quieter environment. Working in China will give retirees enough savings to sustain a comfortable lifestyle back in New Zealand. For example, Andrew saw his immediate future in China because his career is in China. However, his future plan for settlement is still in New Zealand: "New Zealand is good for long-term settlement. People enjoy the natural environment there, and so do I. I'll go back to New Zealand after retirement for sure". Retirement is a significant stage of one's life course that is often associated with the context of one's migration narrative. In Andrew's case, there is a direct link between retirement and returning to the immigration destination. Indeed, his current "settling back" to the homeland is a preparation stage for embarking on another return journey back to the immigration destination he left. Returning to the homeland where there is a fast-growing economy can maximise his earning power and let him realise the eventual circulatory route back to the immigration country, where the lifestyle and environment are what he really longs for.

This research also found that "returnees" ' further migration movement plans are usually based on a shift in their life stage, especially when life moves to the stage of having one's own family. Continuing with the case of Andrew, he is currently a single man, but his construction of his future movement plans goes hand in hand with the possibility of having his own family in the near future:

"If I get married and have children, perhaps I'll send my children to New Zealand when they reach school age. In that case, my wife-to-be will have to go to New Zealand with the children". Here "astronauting" is very likely to happen to meet the family's shifting needs during different life stages. Hugo's study of the "Australian Diaspora" highlights the tension between the Australian expatriates' desire to further their careers and maximise income overseas and the attractions of lifestyle advantages for the family in the homeland, Australia (Hugo, 2006). He finds that many migrants decide to return to Australia when they enter the early family formation stages of their life cycle, because it is important for many that their children spend part of their childhood in Australia. In the case of those "returnees", a similar decision-making process takes place. Like what Andrew planned, the wife and children of a family will return to the immigration destination country, or even the whole family might return. Young families prefer to have their children educated in New Zealand where a carefree and less pressurised childhood exists. This will define where these transnational actors will be for another period of time.

For some, returning to New Zealand means to go back "home" after their life savings have been secured by working in China. In Jeff's words, "I'll go back to New Zealand maybe after ten years. I'll give myself ten more years to make money in China. I hope that after ten years I have enough money to go back to my children and my wife. My home is in Christchurch because my wife and two children are there". In his statement, "going back home" means returning to the immigration destination where his family still is. Here the term "home" is once again incorporated into his immigration narrative, but it conveys markedly different meanings than the conventional meaning of "home" as immigrants' places of origin. Jeff's conceptualisation of "home" is a typical example of the way that many migrants conceive "home" to be where their families are.

Double-return journey and transnational family strategies

The education-led and retirement-led return to New Zealand is a strategy of double return, first from New Zealand to China for work and career development and then back to New Zealand for the children's education or their own retirement. Such findings echo the results of international research. Ley and Kobayashi's research on returnee Hong Kong immigrants who immigrated to Canada reveals the same trend of double-return (Ley & Kobayashi, 2005). They found that the transnational longing of skilled Hong Kong returnees led to a novel trajectory through a seamless social space that crosses oceans and national borders, passing from the native homeland as a workplace to their adopted residence for rest and retirement. During this transnational process, people will take different return trajectories. In the case of this research, some people regard returning to China as a completion of their immigration narrative, some regard returning to New Zealand as a final adjustment upon retirement, and some see returning to New Zealand as yet another temporary move with possible further movement still possible in the future. Indeed, among the different interview groups for this research, the intention to pursue further movement was the strongest among the "returnees". In addition, their intention to return to and to keep a close contact with New Zealand was also strong (this will be further discussed in the following sections). The interview results show that the mobility patterns of those "returnees" were far more complex and dynamic, and their choice of location or re-location was both wide and diverse. On the one hand, China rising was a strong pull factor that attracted many PRC migrants to return to China to live or work. On the other hand, the attraction of New Zealand, such as its peaceful social climate, good natural environment, and advanced education, will repeatedly draw some of these "returnees" back, leading a family to stretch across borders and scatter in different continents to be able to achieve different personal goals and their family's collective well-being.

Attraction may also be from a third country where better life and opportunities might lie, leading people to end up somewhere else that are other than one's place of origin and first immigration destination. These findings mean that the return to China for many "returnees" may not be permanent. Returning for many does not mean permanent re-settlement in the homeland; rather, it is only a part of their multiple and evolving transnational trajectories.

Quite often, returning to China is a transitional stage where they can work on the eventual route back to New Zealand or step up to a third destination where their ultimate goal lies.

For many "returnees", the transnational migration trajectories are open-ended. They may have forward planning in mind that may not necessarily involve returning to New Zealand. The choice of their future workplace very much depends on the global job market and its demand. However, like many new Chinese migrants, considerations related to the different, changing needs of their family members during their life stages play an equally important part in their decisions regarding further movement. There are two crucial considerations that influence one's decision for re-location and family arrangement. The first is the consideration of school-age children as discussed, and the second is aging parents.

Veronica, who is now working in a branch office of an international non-government organisation in Beijing, revealed her personal immigration narrative within her own family context where special consideration was given to how to arrange for her parents when she does take on a transnational lifestyle.

> I am an energetic young woman. After I have accumulated some work experience from this organisation in Beijing, I'll go to another country, maybe the US. The headquarters of this organisation is located in Washington. My next step really depends on where I will be needed, where I can earn more, and where I can have a better life.

She then immediately turned to a discussion about how to balance her transnational aspirations and her responsibility to take care of her parents who are now in New Zealand:

> At my age, I need a place full of excitement and energy. I enjoy the feeling of professional satisfaction and self-esteem. Natural environment is a minor

thing at my age. But for my parents, what they need is a safe, clean, and quiet place where they can enjoy the rest of their lives. Therefore, it's better for them to stay in New Zealand now.

Taking care of aging parents is not only a moral responsibility, but also a Chinese cultural tradition. Filial piety prescribes children's co-residing with their parents as a proof for demonstrating their commitment to provide care and support to their aging parents (Whyte & Ikels, 2004). This has played an important role in many cases where Chinese migrants brought their parent(s) to New Zealand under New Zealand's family reunion policy. Veronica is one of such example. It is fair to say that New Zealand's family reunion policy before 2016 policy change is comparatively generous for migrants to bring their parents to this country, at least before the 2016 policy change that closed up the Parent Category (see Chapter 2). Before the 2016 policy change, if a migrant who was 18 years of age or over, a New Zealand citizen or residents or Australian citizen, could provide evidences to show his/her capability of providing financial support to his/her parents, he/she could sponsor his/her parent(s) to come to New Zealand as permanent resident(s). The waiting time for those sponsored parents to be granted permanent residence in New Zealand under Tier 1 was particularly reasonable, about 18 to 24 months. Moreover, New Zealand's family reunion policy to sponsor parents' residence in this country before 2016 policy change was especially Chinese-friendly by default because the "one-child" policy in China made many Chinese migrant families could easily demonstrate their family's centre of gravity was in New Zealand and thus satisfy the "centre of gravity" principle (DeShaw, 2006).

While to bring parents to New Zealand was comparatively easy, what is not easy however for Chinese migrants is to find a realistic and feasible way to solve the conflict between their responsibility of co-residence with parents in terms of care provision and the pursuit of their transnational ambitions. As shown in the case of Veronica and her family, when Veronica took into account being separated from her parents in New Zealand, her balancing skill was tested and contested. She actually employed a space-time assessment approach to try to solve the conflict between her own transnational ambition and the care giving for her parents. There were two evaluations that can take place within the family context. The first is that the younger generation needs to be in a place where economic opportunities are, and the second is that the older generation should stay in the immigration destination country to enjoy a relaxing and peaceful retirement lifestyle. Apart from these two considerations, another dilemma that many other Chinese migrant families face is that when those adult migrant children are on their move to leave New Zealand towards homeland or a third destination, where their parents should go is a difficult decision to make.

Ideally for many parents, they want to be with their children. If their children go back to China, it is a relatively easy scenario for adult migrant children to deal with because there would be no significant re-settlement issues in the homeland where the surroundings and language are highly familiar. For some parents who are still not qualified for the two-year residence condition to be issued permanent

Returning Resident's Visa, they have to stay in New Zealand and are not able to follow their children to go back to China. They have to face many difficulties when they try to settle in a new and unfamiliar environment without the assistance of their children. They have to face problems of housing, language barriers, access to health care, and access to social services. Even everyday tasks, such as banking, transportation, and shopping, can be formidable ordeals (Li, 2011). If their children head to another destination, arrangement for the parents becomes intractable. Migration requirements for parents' entry into a third destination make their co-residence with their children in a third destination highly impossible. Thus, family separation and disruptive family life become inevitable. If the parents stay in New Zealand and their children move to another country, they can benefit from this country's lifestyle and good natural environment. However, the cost has been mentioned above, including the stress from family separation, disruptive family lifestyle, and many other problems associated with elderly people's adaptation of a new environment.

As Veronica continued the discussion of her family plan for the near future, the family arrangement for her parents was clearly a very challenging task. Veronica stated,

> As a family, we should be together in the end, especially when my parents are more aging. Now they are okay to manage themselves, but how about 10 years later if their health situation deteriorates? This is a big problem for a family like mine. I am the only child. I must finally figure out a way to be together with my parents. I guess that I have to compromise my own aspirations on a certain level for them. Where I will go will be restricted somehow to those places where immigration law would allow the entry of my parents. I must find a way to bring them with me. We also have the option of having me return to New Zealand.

As can be seen here, transnationalism creates a travel plan for back and forth between each single social field. When one's social field enlarges, there is a dispersal of family members on different continents with parents, siblings, and children scattered in different places that best suit their present life stage. This movement in the transnational framework is definitely not a one-way movement, but neither is it two-way movement. For many, it is only a step within a circular cycle that follows its own logic of arrival, departure, and further movement. These transnational trajectories are thus defined by different family structures and changing dynamics. Sometimes they can intersect, and sometimes they can converge; but in essence, they do remain temporary and divergent.

A voyage to Australia

The transnational mobility of PRC migrants has been seen clearly through interviews conducted in China with "returnees" and their related family members. The trend in mobility of PRC migrants is also characterised by re-location to a third country. Possibly motivated by similar economic and career-advancement pulls, there is no fundamental difference between "step-migration" to a third destination and returning to the homeland. Both stem from migrants' aspiration to seek better opportunities to maximise their social, human, and financial capital on a full scale to achieve a better long-term migration outcome. The difference is that this mobility can manifest in various forms. Apart from "return migration", in which those migrants choose to re-locate to the homeland, the mobility of re-locating to a third destination often takes place across the Tasman Sea in the case of New Zealand, often termed "back-door" migration, referring to migrants who use New Zealand as a "revolving door" to enter Australia (Rapson, 1998, p. 56). In this sense, I posit that Australia is only one of many examples of PRC migrants' diverse choices to re-locate to a third destination. This section focuses on the interviews conducted in Australia with those "trans-Tasman" interviewees and illustrates the on-going migratory mobility that many PRC immigrants possess.

In terms of their initial motivation to immigrate to New Zealand, the "trans-Tasman" interviewees share some similarities with "returnees"; that is, they had no strong economic incentive to just settle down in New Zealand. Even though their motives for immigrating to New Zealand were primarily not economic, to secure employment with reasonable income in the new land they chose was their preferable status. When they could not meet their basic economic needs, they would choose to leave and head somewhere else where the employment and business opportunities were more abundant. Stepping into Australia is a typical example of those transnational PRC migrants' decision to further move and pursue economic and social goals. Indeed, the onward movements of highly mobile PRC migrants do take place worldwide, depending on where opportunities are and how social networks are stretched.

Local-born New Zealanders are actually taking part in similar movements across the Tasman Sea. There is a net migration flow from New Zealand to Australia every year since many local-born New Zealanders move to Australia for better job prospects and income, a process termed as the "brain drain" by the New Zealand news media. This movement is associated with the desire of young people to gain overseas experience (termed OE in New Zealand society). The PRC migrant group is no exception; many of them move to Australia like local-born New Zealanders, taking advantage of the convenient travel between these two countries in terms of the short geographical distance; the existence of a long-standing agreement on free bilateral international migration; the strong historical, cultural, and contemporary economic and social linkages; and perhaps a similar social structure and integrated labour market.

Moving to Australia: the final destination?

Economic attractions of Australia

Similar to the economic factors that "returnees" consider in their decision to return to China, the interviews conducted in Australia found that concerns about employment and career development opportunities played a vital role in the decision to move to Australia. Some "trans-Tasman" interviewees revealed their concerns about a sense of uncertainty and insecurity for their future employment prospects in New Zealand, and their views directly contributed to their decision to move to Australia. In the words of Joe,

> There was no other reason for me to come to Australia except for employment opportunity. I couldn't find a job in New Zealand that matched my expectations, education, and academic background. I got my Master's degree in Food Science from the University of Auckland. I hoped that at least I could find a position like lab technician. I got a contract job from New Zealand Crown Research Institute, but they asked me to wash glass test tubes and bottles in the lab. For me, it was a joke and a waste of my time and talent. Australia is much better. At least I can find real work and do things that match my professional training. I always work as a lab technician or analyst, and my income increased significantly after arrived in Australia, as well as our quality of life. We could afford a house and cars. This is obvious evidence that the decision to move to Australia was right.

The problem of employment and New Zealand's weak job market is a clear contrast to the Australian situation. For many, the pursuit of career development opportunities and higher income motivated crossing the Tasman Sea. For example, Lawrence, a branch manager at an immigration agency, moved to Australia in 2004 after he worked at an immigration consultancy agency in Auckland for about two years. His departure was almost accidental when he found that expanding that immigration consultancy service to Australia was highly feasible and profitable:

> The market in Australia is bigger, which is good for business development. Comparatively, New Zealand is a small country, and its market is small. Information circulated there is not the most up-to-date. I didn't plan to move to Australia when I landed in New Zealand. Later on, I started to work in that immigration consultation company and gradually found that the market for immigration consultation business in Australia was much bigger than that in New Zealand. That is why I left. It is my idea to set up a branch office in Sydney, and my business partner in New Zealand fully supports me.

In this sense, the trans-Tasman movement for many PRC migrants is essentially no different from that of local-born New Zealanders who seek better employment opportunities across the ocean. For many young New Zealanders, Australia remains a favourable destination in terms of advancing a career. For those who are struggling to find employment at home, the Australian labour market is an alternative well worth exploring. Such a pursuit of economic advancement is also markedly similar to the aspirations of some "returnees" who are pursuing economic benefits in China's booming economy. The similarities found in the two sets of interviews show one trend. Those people who are young, well educated, bilingual, and in the early stage of their careers, and who have a high earning potential are very likely to engage in transnational migration. They undertake it strategically to capitalise on their assets and maximise their opportunities for economic and social advancement.

Pursuing education opportunities for children

Another key driver of trans-Tasman movement is education for children. Since the Chinese tradition believes that the higher the education, the better the job opportunities and the future, Chinese parents place great importance and attention on their children's education (Ho & Bedford, 2008). To ensure that their children will have a good future, many Chinese migrants from the PRC went to New Zealand to take advantage of its advanced educational system. Driven by that same motivation, many PRC migrants moved on to Australia from New Zealand because they believed that the educational system in Australia was even better than that in New Zealand. For example, James emphasised that his move to Australia was made solely for his children's education:

> I am a freelance translator, and my professional networks are mainly in Europe and North America. The contacts between me and my clients are on-line, actually the physical location is not a problem for myself, but it does matter for my daughters. We came to Australia only because of the education for our children. I always felt that the education perspective in New Zealand is over-relaxed, just like its lifestyle. Kiwi parents sit back and never push their children to learn more. There is no academic pressure on children. It is not good. Sometimes children need pressure to become better. We compared the curriculum of New Zealand and Australia, as well as the course books for the same degree, and the difference is obvious. The New Zealand course book is much simpler than the Australian one. If children are educated like this, they won't be competitive enough when they face their future. For example, in New Zealand, the teacher said to my older daughter, "It would be enough for you to read these two books for today, and you don't need more". In Australia, the teacher said to her, "I'll give you the sixth book if you can finish reading these five". This is very encouraging, and I believe that it is good. New Zealand's education does not encourage young children to climb higher.

Pitt, another interviewee, repeated a similar point of view and mentioned in particular that the tertiary education in Australia can provide wider opportunities than that in New Zealand: "In general, I don't think that New Zealand's education is worse than that of Australia, but in terms of the scholarship opportunity, Australia is definitely superior and can offer more".

The logic of trans-Tasman movement

Apart from the reasons cited above, there is another interesting reason behind trans-Tasman re-location. The interviews conducted in Australia provided no strong evidence that, for many PRC migrants, moving to Australia was something they deliberately decided on prior to immigrating to New Zealand; but it is true that, after settling down in New Zealand for a while, many did move to Australia. In the words of David, "Many people moved to Australia, and my family is just one part of that flow. We were heavily influenced by others. After my best friend in New Zealand headed up there, we finally made the decision to leave". Some interviewees referred to their move to Australia simply as "for the better":

> I believe that immigration is all about getting better and going to a better place to work or live. People immigrate to places where there are more opportunities or places where there are more benefit to their families. It is basic human nature that people want to get better.

Regardless of whether it is true that Australia is superior to New Zealand in terms of job opportunities or education, it is quite understandable that migrants re-emigrate to a third destination in pursuit of the better collective welfare of their families. However, what has not been addressed sufficiently is whether "step-migration" from New Zealand to Australia is an enduring feature, and whether it is driven by deliberate strategic planning or by a pervasively perceived image that moving to Australia is simply the preferable thing to do.

It should be noted that New Zealand and Australia have enjoyed a special close relationship for a long time in terms of bilateral international migration, similar cultural values derived from similar colonial roots, close economic ties, and a high degree of labour market integration (Bedford, Ho, & Lidgard, 2000). Trans-Tasman migration is a prominent phenomenon that occurs between these two countries, but it is also a common action often taken by citizens of both countries. Even though this movement is essentially international, in another sense it is more likely to be regarded by most as internal migration (Birrell & Rapson, 2001). Based on the Trans-Tasman Travel Arrangement, New Zealand and Australia have pursued less restrictive immigration controls between each other, and migration flows between the two countries has been less regulated for a long time. It is not until recent years that control of migration has become more restrictive, especially on the Australia side.

The debate over trans-Tasman migration has suggested that far more New Zealanders are choosing to move across the Tasman Sea to live in Australia than Australians moving in the opposite direction. Additionally, a sizeable number of those New Zealanders are non-New Zealand-born (Bedford, Ho, & Hugo, 2003; Bedford et al., 2000; Hugo, 2004). Australia, as a much bigger country than New Zealand, has a more vibrant market and better employment and business opportunities. Apart from these economic attractions, a similar social structure and cultural values of the two countries might also make re-settlement much easier than in other destinations. All of these elements propel local-born young New Zealanders to move to Australia and also attract New Zealand citizens who are recent immigrants and born overseas. In this regard, it is fair to say that there is no difference in the trans-Tasman movement between local-born New Zealanders and new immigrants born outside of New Zealand. The macro-eco-political factors within New Zealand and Australia actually encourage both local-born New Zealanders and new migrants to undertake similar mobility patterns.

However, the trans-Tasman movement of New Zealand citizens born outside of New Zealand, especially those born in Asia, has attracted criticism and suspicion in both New Zealand and Australia. In New Zealand, this movement has been criticised as disloyal (Spoonley, Bedford, & Macpherson, 2003); and in Australia, it has been mentioned that new Asian migrants use New Zealand as a "revolving door" to step into Australia (Rapson, 1998, p. 56). Their presence in Australia also has attracted much more media hype and a policy debate as it is regarded as "back-door" migration (Bedford et al., 2003). The 2001 immigration policy change in Australia introduced stricter controls over access to welfare provisions by New Zealand citizens who arrived in Australia under policies other than Australia's own immigration programme. This policy change made New Zealand citizens who arrived in Australia, but not under Australia's immigration programme, ineligible for most social security support for a period of time and effectively reduced the influx of New Zealand citizens into Australia, including those born in Asia (Bedford, Ho, & Lidgard, 2005).

The interviews for this research project conducted in Australia revealed that many PRC migrants moved to Australia simply because "Australia would soon close its door" to New Zealand citizens. Several "trans-Tasman" interviewees moved to Australia just before enforcement of the new policy. They realised they had to rush into Australia before the policy came into force, as in Peter's words,

> One of my friends told me that Australia would close its door to migrants from New Zealand; therefore, we arrived at Australia in a hurry. I had to apply for a New Zealand passport before I came here as well because it is a necessary landing condition to reside in Australia. We thought that we wouldn't have another chance to come here so easily.

Indeed, statistics show that the number of New Zealanders who entered Australia in 2000, when there was advanced warning of a possible policy change, was particularly high (Bedford et al., 2003). Bedford et al. (2003) point out that this influx of New Zealanders into Australia represents a response to advanced warning of the policy change. Although the policy change cannot stop the migration flow into Australia from New Zealand, before the enforcement of the new policy in Australia, there was, however, a rush to enter this preferable immigration. Otherwise, latter acquisition of Australian permanent residence or citizenship would become a much longer and more complex application process. Seeing opportunities in their closest neighbour country, Australia, many PRC migrants made another migratory trip to that destination. However, this trip may not be the final one of their on-going migration journey. As I will illustrate in the next section, their re-location to Australia is essentially a continuation or extension of their first migratory step from China to New Zealand.

Mobility patterns of "trans-Tasman" interviewees

Compared to the complex dynamics of "returnee" personal and family trajectories, the "trans-Tasman" interviewees in Australia revealed a much simpler and more stable mobility pattern. First, unlike the "returnee" group, whose migration narrative is much more open-ended, the migration narrative of many "trans-Tasman" interviewees included a sense of finality about their ocean crossing. Many "trans-Tasman" interviewees revealed that long-term residence in Australia was the most realistic choice for them at this stage of their lives, especially for the whole family. As many interviewees revealed, better employment prospects, a more stable income, and successful settlement of the whole family are the main reasons they stay in Australia and do not undertake further movements. Nick questioned the plan of further movement: "Why would we move again? We have already settled here pretty well. We purchased a house and have a stable income to pay the mortgage, so why not stay? Our life here is damn good. There is no need to move". Nick's perspective illustrates how the immigrant intention to take up long-term residence in an immigration destination largely depends on how well immigrant families do settle in. If an immigration destination cannot address their economic well-being, they will consider other options, whether it is to return to the homeland or step further on to a third destination.

Even though the "trans-Tasman" interviewees generally showed the intention of long-term settlement in Australia, this finding does not mean that the group is no longer mobile. They still have great flexibility in terms of visa-free international travel because of their legal status as holders of Australian or New Zealand passports. As a result, temporary and short-term re-location among "trans-Tasman" interviewees can take place frequently. Very often, a temporary re-location or frequent commuting between countries is work related, and the whole family is not involved. For them, Australia is still the "home" base where those family members who do take short-term re-location out of Australia eventually come back to enjoy. For example, Tony, as one person at the top management level in an Australia-based multi-national company, is currently travelling to Asia frequently and is highly likely to be transferred to China in the near future for work, but he still firmly sees the long-term residence base for his family still in Australia:

> As the only person who has a Chinese background and is on the top management level in the company, I'll definitely be the director of the Chinese branch office if this company will set up an office in China. If this happens, I'll go back to China to work, but my family will stay. Now I am the director who is in charge of the Asian market for this company. I am always out of Australia and travelling between here and Asia. But my life focus is still here because my family is here.

As can be seen, the possibility for Tony to return China to work temporarily in the next five years is considered likely, within which a bi-national residence of the family could take place and family members could be separated physically as a result of his career path. In this sense, where one's life focus and residential base is contributes directly to the fact that moving to Australia for many "trans-Tasman" interviewees is more likely to be a finished set. The interviews conducted in Australia revealed that the current location of the family and successful settlement of the whole family is the core consideration for not having further family movement.

Second, the "trans-Tasman" interviewees are different from the "returnees" who have a great interest in returning to and/or keeping close connections with New Zealand. They were less enthusiastic about doing so. The "trans-Tasman" interviewee connection with their first immigration destination country is rather loose, and returning to New Zealand is less likely in the future. Most of the ten "trans-Tasman" interviewees explicitly said they would not go back to New Zealand, other than for a holiday, and only one interviewee thought there was a possibility of returning to New Zealand for retirement. The underlying reasons for the difference between these two interviewee groups in terms of their willingness to return to New Zealand suggest that the settlement outcome is better in Australia than in New Zealand, and a strong homeland attraction may be a distraction that makes the desire to maintain contact with the first immigration destination less intense.

In contrast to the lower interest in keeping close contact with New Zealand, the "trans-Tasman" interviewees show much more interest in connections with their homeland, China. The strong attraction to the homeland is largely economic, but it can also be emotional and/or family-related. The potential for business success in China adds one more layer to the mobility patterns of "trans-Tasman" interviewees that could result in another re-location or more frequent travel between Oceania and East Asia. Interviews with many young "trans-Tasman" interviewees in their thirties revealed that they are highly interested in developing close ties with China for future business development. Lawrence, an owner of an immigration consultation agency, was very optimistic about the possibility of expanding his business to China:

> The market there is very big. For business people like me, China is definitely a good place to expand business. I am now working towards setting up a branch office in Beijing in the next two years. If this plan goes smoothly, I'll travel between China and Australia frequently. If the business in China is really profitable, I'll probably hand the Australian part of my business to someone I trust, while I will go back to China for a while to take care of that part of the business.

The business connections with China for some "trans-Tasman" interviewees can take various forms. Some run business importing goods from China, some possess shares in Chinese companies they previously ran before immigration, some operate their businesses in Australia, using profits generated from the Chinese share market, and some juggle between their Australian full-time jobs and their own companies in China jointly owned by trustful business partners. Such business connections with China potentially contribute to the complexity of the contemporary transnational migration circulation. Again, for many, returning to the homeland is temporary. It's only for accumulating sufficient financial capital and is followed by a return to Australia for longer-term residence. Bi-national residence is also an option for some if it is economically viable.

Apart from those with concrete business connections with China, these interviews reveal that there is a generally positive perspective towards China's potential employment market, which would be a potential driving force for some "trans-Tasman" interviewees to relocate to the homeland temporarily. Joe, a lab technician and analyst who has a middle-class job and income in Australia, still expects that better opportunities exist in China. In his words, "If better opportunities occur, I'll go back to China for a while just for my economic well-being". Unlike those who proactively engage in transnational business activities and their associated cross-border movements, Joe's prospects for going back to China are more like a longing to be transferred to the homeland to work where the booming economy is.

Indeed, such a desire to relocate to the homeland for a while was pervasive among the "trans-Tasman" interviewees. In some cases, it is not driven by just an economic perspective; instead, it is an intertwining of factors and forces that relate to each individual and each family. Similar to the "returnees", some "trans-Tasman" interviewees intend to return to China to take care of their aging parents. Sometimes it is an imagined return, which is then driven by an emotional longing for the homeland as one's "home". For example, Frances revealed his deep desire to return to China as a returning to his "home":

> I really feel that I belong to China, although I have been overseas for more than 13 years. China is my home, and I really miss her. I miss her not because I miss someone or certain places there. It is perhaps a nostalgic feeling about the country of my birth. It is a place I truly want to return to in my dreams.

A case study: multi-generational migrant families across borders

As hypothesised and showed before, consideration of other family members plays a significant role in influencing individuals' as well as whole families' transnational migratory trajectories, this section draws out a family case from the qualitative interview to illustrate the variety of mobility patterns followed by different generations of family members, and how family members might influence each another at different point of their life cycles. The author has followed up this family's migratory trajectories for about seven years (from 2008 to 2015) and interviewed different family members at different places and times.

Diana, the mum and the principal applicant of immigration to New Zealand, arrived in Auckland for the first time in 2004, together with her husband and her son, who was ten years old at the time. Her husband is a company director owning a very profitable business in Shanghai. He came to Auckland the first time with the intention of going back to China to work. After everything was settled, he returned to China as planned. The first interview was with Diana in 2008. At the time, her son was studying at high school. With her husband's financial support from Shanghai, Diana had an easy life in New Zealand. Unlike many other Chinese migrants who struggle to find employment, she could live comfortably without worrying about job and income. Her life was taken up with looking after her son. She and her son traveled between New Zealand and China every school holiday, while her husband visited his New Zealand home regularly. In Diana's original words,

> Such family arrangement is the only choice for us. My life focus is on my son, and he still needs me. But for my husband, his life focus is to earn money to support us. He has to do business in Shanghai, and his professional network is over there. Opportunities in China are abundant. We have never thought of starting a business in New Zealand. Such a pattern of temporary family separation at this stage was decided upon even before we arrived in Auckland.

A year later, when I interviewed her husband in China, his words confirmed what Diana had said about the family plan, but revealed more perspectives in terms of the family's changing future plan. He stated,

> My son has three years to go to finish his high school. We will make a different arrangement after he gets into university. The time for him to start his tertiary education is probably the time for us to change family arrangements. Diana perhaps can spend more time with me in Shanghai because Ding [the son] will be well prepared for an independent life. If he goes to another country to pursue his tertiary education, the family probably will be in three different locations. But I guess, we fly, and fly often. I will still be mainly based in Shanghai, and Diana will spend some time with me but also in Auckland. She can go to where Ding is for short visits whenever needed. If I have time, I can go with her.

A few years later, in 2013, I interviewed their son (Ding) when he was back in Auckland from Sydney for his university break. He explained,

> I really like to study and live in another new country and I can deal with it because I am growing and becoming independent. I am just following the plan and flow. Mum and dad are supportive. After my mum was stuck with me [in Auckland] for quite a bit time, now she can do things she really wants. She is much happier now because she can be with dad in Shanghai for a much longer time than in previous years. If she misses me, she just flies. She now travels a lot not only to Sydney, Auckland, and Shanghai but to anywhere that is on her wish list. She has the artistic and traveler spirits. She is fulfilling her life, I guess.

What has been witnessed here is that once the life needs of the children change, the family priority changes, resulting in new patterns of mobility. In this case, once Ding becomes independent, looking after him is no longer Diana's first priority, and she can pursue her life with a sense of self-worth as an individual while at the same time enjoying family life as a caring mother and wife.

Interestingly, when I asked Ding about his future plan over the next five years, he insisted that he would go back to China to inherit his dad's business after graduating: "This is my pathway. I must go back to China to have my dad's business. He will get old one day, and it is a big business, and I am the son and the only child in the family. China is a great place to do business, isn't it? If I don't take over the business, who else?" I then asked about his plans for the next 15 years, and the reply was vague but implied a subtle sense of privilege regarding geographical mobility: "I really cannot foresee where I would be after 15 years. But as you know well about my family, I have options: the business in China, and also I can go back to New Zealand freely whenever I want to". What is revealed here is a clear example of the typical transnational disposition of a 1.5 generation migrant child. The families have all maintained the family home in their country of origin, facilitating easy and flexible multi-locality arrangements. These 1.5 generation migrant children are growing up in a social milieu in which such patterns are the norm and in which the dominant discourse regarding New Zealand is that it is a beautiful place to live but not to work (Bartley, 2010). For them, physical boundaries between different countries are only symbolic. This transnational normality is naturally unsettling and is as a response to the desire to fulfill both economic, cultural, and lifestyle aspirations in terms of experiencing the best the world can offer.

In 2015, I met Diana again in Auckland and was updated about the current situation of this family. Diana's mother, who is over 75, is now visiting and staying in Auckland with her. Over the past couple of years, her mother has spent about two months each summer (December to February) in Auckland with Diana. The two women then travel back to Shanghai for Chinese New Year, when Ding takes some time out of his study break in Australia to join in this family reunion. Once the New Year holiday ends, Diana spends a couple of months with her husband in China and then goes to various places as a tourist. She is very interested in visual arts and theater performance and works part-time directing and organising theater performances in Shanghai and Auckland.

Unlike in the previous interviews with Diana, from which the elderly parent factor was mostly absent, this factor has become very important in her current personal narratives. She explained,

> My dad passed away three years ago, and I need to make more time with mum. I need to take care of her and give her more company. I have an older sister and brother and they are in China; so it is not easy to sponsor my mum to emigrate to New Zealand. I have already submitted an application for her, and the process and waiting time is long. Luckily, I can afford to bring her to Auckland regularly. Here it is quiet, and the environment is great for her health. She also likes to spend time with me in Auckland.

This narrative shows how intergenerational relations and the changing life needs of different generations impact on or constrain people's mobility patterns. Often, the existing literature argues that children in migrant families wield a great amount of power in deciding other family members' transnational trajectory (Council, 2014; Ho & Bedford, 2008). However, as shown in this case, the elderly generation of a migrant family also plays a vital role in affecting adult children's life trajectories and governing a family's overall migratory arrangements. This is very common in migrant families where the first-generation adult migrant is an only child, and is largely because of cultural factors, in particular filial piety. With China's continuing economic prosperity and the resulting empowerment of Chinese nationals, it is that many Chinese would be able to meet the financial criteria of sponsoring their elderly parents to immigrate to New Zealand before the policy of the Parent Category was changed in 2016. The high proportion of elderly parents in the overall Chinese migration flow is therefore unlikely to change substantially in the foreseeable future. In short, the family case presented above, together with other interviews, reflects migration and mobility patterns typical of the three-generation transnational Chinese family. While the family migration trajectory is, for the most part, planned and executed neatly and strategically, as life evolves, the family focus shifts from the children to the elderly generation, and decision-making regarding location and re-location is continuously reviewed.

Parallel with this greater migrant mobility, together with its relevance to elderly parents, it is obvious that the younger generations in a migrant family, both the adult parents and their children, are more mobile. Driven by the different needs at different stages of people's lives, these family members extend their residence bases to a third country, so that family members end up located in two or three countries, in accordance with each individual's needs. This empowerment of migrant mobility frees up cross-border navigation for all generations, but it also poses challenges to migrant families. Adult migrants face increasing pressures in terms of caring for their elderly parents if they choose to live in a different country from their elderly parents (Liu, 2016).

The importance of social networks

The interviews also find that the interviewees' social networks have an important influence on their decisions on re-location. In many cases for "returnees", whether they re-settle in their homeland successfully and achieve their expectations is not based only on their human and financial capital, but also on how well they maintained their social and professional networks when absent from China. This aspect of Chinese return migration appears to be especially important. Social networks or relationships in the Chinese language are usually called *Guanxi*关系, although recently a more fashionable name is *renmai*人脉. The concept is embedded in every aspect of every Chinese person's daily life and influenced the "returnees'" decisions to return and re-settle in many ways. Many interviewees indicated that their decision to re-locate was partly based on what was appropriate within the context of maintaining and developing their social networks in the homeland or in a third destination. For example, Andrew revealed,

> To be honest, I returned to China because of my current business partner. He is my former university classmate, and we kept contact with each other through the years. He called me one day and told me that opportunities in China now are enormous and to please come back and take the opportunity. Our business will go very well if we can work shoulder-by-shoulder. When I did some homework on his business proposal, I felt that it was feasible, so I bought the air ticket and thought "no matter what this business is like, I'll go back to have a look anyway". I didn't go back to New Zealand because his proposal worked.

This was not the only example that showed the importance of maintaining social networks across borders to facilitate successful re-location. Amy said,

> For immigrants like my age, it would be a rare case that people return to China with absolute uncertainty. I mean if there is no job for me or no likelihood of being employed, I wouldn't go back. Some people did return without any job offer. But from what I know, most of these people are young graduates. That's okay for them because they are young. But for people like me who are over 30 years, most already located a job or a business proposal before returning. This is the way we go.

When I suggested that it was difficult to locate a job in China without physical presence, her answer reflected how important it is to keep social networks in the homeland:

> My way is to contact my friends and people who I know in China and ask them to help me pay attention to job advertisements relevant to my profession or ask them to use their networks to recommend me to potential employers. They also helped me to distribute my CV to some head-hunting companies. They know what kind of position suits my profession as well as my expectation for salary.

Many studies have emphasised the importance of transnational social networks in understanding the patterns of interpersonal relationships during the transnational process and the specific context of transnational migrant experiences (Garcia, 2006; Glick Schiller, Basch, & Blanc-Szanton, 1992; Salaff, 2008). Glick-Schiller et al. (1992) posited that migration provides a channel for the bidirectional flow and circulation of material goods and ideas where social relations are embedded. Faist (2000) paid particular attention to explaining the importance of transnational business networks established on condition of reciprocity, exchange, and mutual benefits when investing economic capital across borders. In his view, transnational business networks can stimulate and solidify sustainable transnational links across borders; simultaneously, any obstacles to economic integration encountered by many transnational migrants during immigration and re-locating movements can be overcome or eased through their social and business networks. These can help facilitate the establishment of a successful business (Faist, 2000). The comments made by Nonini and Ong (1997) were more relevant to the context of Chinese transnational migration: "*Guanxi* relations [networking] among diaspora Chinese present a long-standing habitus whose very flexibilities have now been placed in the services of accumulation strategies under the novel conditions of late capitalism, and in the process are thereby being reworked themselves" (p. 21). Results from the qualitative interviews in this project show that all the established theories around transnational migration were indeed relevant.

The interviews revealed that the extent of PRC transnational migrant social and business networks as spread across borders was one of the key factors in successfully re-starting or developing a career, establishing a business, and re-settling a family in a re-located place. They also showed that transnational migratory movements occur not only because the transnational actors possess great human and financial capital that can forge transnational mobility, but also because these transnational movements are sustained and supported by social capital, namely the personal, social, and business networks existing across borders as well as transnational communication. This soft and social capital appears especially important for return migration to China, where "returnees" are already familiar with the homeland culture and have sufficient support from their personal social networks.

Summary

The ethnographic fieldwork revealed four striking findings. The first is that the transnational trajectories many PRC immigrants pursue are part of a continuous and on-going process. For many of them, there is no closure or finality. The research revealed a dynamic and unfinished set of personal and family trajectories, given the evidence that return migration or re-emigration to a third destination is not the end of the migration narrative of many PRC migrants but that an itinerary with further movement is possible or has even already been planned. Many PRC migrant families are very mobile, and many families extend their residence bases to a third country where family members may be bi- or tri-nationally located as best suits their needs.

The second important finding is that the factors and motivations behind PRC migrants' transnational movements are multi-dimensional; that is, more than one factor can lead to their cross-border movements. In addition to economic reasons, negative interactions with wider society and relationships with family members or close friends are also associated with the decision to move. Motivations for those PRC migrants to undertake transnational movements are interwoven with individual, family, and nation-state factors, as well as the dynamic geo-economic conditions of globalisation.

Third, considerations of family members' needs at different life stages are central to the decision to move. The locations of family members, especially older parents and school-age children, are heavily involved in the decision. The transnational migration strategies that many PRC migrants have adopted may shift with the changing circumstances of family members. Transnational movements are often undertaken as a collective family tactic in order to maximise opportunities and the family's collective well-being. The dynamic strategies behind transnational movement, as well as the movements themselves by PRC Chinese migrants, challenge the traditional way of seeing migration as an activity of permanent uprooting and seeking residence out of the place of origin. In the transnational era, migration has become difficult to define. Terms such as "return migration" and "step migration" become problematic, as these terms cannot really capture the multi-faceted contemporary situation of international migration. Migration now tends to be an on-going process, as Huang, Yeoh and Lam. (2008) suggested: "There is no predetermined script for migration. Migration trajectories are always contingent, often precarious and sometimes even volatile" (p. 9).

Lastly, paralleled with the family, personal, and economic consideration in deciding returning to China or stepping into a third destination, the social network is also a powerful pull to draw Chinese migrants to move out of New Zealand and determine where they have stayed or moved to.

Notes

1 The Kiwi Clubs in Beijing, Shanghai, and Hong Kong hold regular informal gatherings and welcome all Kiwis (New Zealanders). These gatherings are casual events that take place every month and are a good place to make friends or establish networks.
2 The first Returning Resident's Visa of New Zealand is issued to one at the time he/she is issued a residence visa or permit. It is valid for two years from the date the first residence permit is granted. After the first Returning Resident's Visa expires, one must apply for a second Returning Resident's Visa. The second or subsequent visa may be valid indefinitely (enabling multiple trips in and out of New Zealand indefinitely, commonly referred as permanent Returning Resident Visa) or may be valid for 12 months or 14 days. An indefinite visa is granted provided one was the principal applicant in the original residence application, or is included in the RRV application lodged by the original principal applicant, and one is able to meet the requirements that show commitment to New Zealand, e.g. spent most of your time in New Zealand. If one is unable to meet those requirements, he/she may be eligible for a 12 month or 14 day Returning Resident's Visa (for more details, please visit this official website: www.immigration.govt.nz/migrant/stream/alreadyinnz/residents/returningresidents/).

References

Bartley, A. J. (2010). 1.5 generation Asian migrants and intergenerational transnationalism: Thoughts and challenges from New Zealand. *International Migration*, *12*(4), 381–395.

Bedford, R., Ho, E., & Hugo, G. (2003). Trans-Tasman migration in context: Recent flows of new New Zealanders revisited. *People and Place*, *11*(4), 53–62.

Bedford, R., Ho, E., & Lidgard, J. (2000). *International Migration in New Zealand: Context, Components and Policy Issues* (Discussion Papers No. 37). Hamilton, New Zealand: Population Studies Centre, University of Waikato.

Bedford, R., Ho, E., & Lidgard, J. (2005). From Targets to outcomes: Immigration policy in New Zealand, 1996–2003. In A. Trlin, P. Spoonley, & N. Watts (Eds.), *New Zealand and International Migration: A Digest and Bibliography, Number 4* (Vol. 4, pp. 1–43). Palmerston North: Department of Sociology, Massey University.

Birrell, B., & Rapson, V. (2001). New Zealanders in Australia: The end of an era? *People and Place, 9*(1), 2–15.

Boyer, T. (1996). Problems in paradise: Taiwanese immigrants to Auckland, New Zealand. *Asia Pacific Viewpoints, 37*(1), 59–79.

Cassarino, J. P. (2008, 31 July–1 August). Rethinking conceptual approaches to return migrants: Reasons and proposals. *Asia Research Institute*. Symposium conducted at the meeting of the Return Migration in Asia: Experiences, Ideologies and Politics, National University of Singapore.

Council, A. I. (2014). *Basics of the United States Immigration Sytem*. Washington, DC: Immigration Policy Centre.

DeShaw, R. (2006). The history of family reunification in Canada and current policy. *Canadian Issues, 9*, 9–14.

Faist, T. (2000). Transnationalization in international migration: Implications for the study of citizenship and culture. *Ethnic and Racial Studies, 23*(2), 189–222.

Garcia, D. (2006). Mixed marriages and transnational families in the intercultural context: A case study of African-Spanish couples in Catalonia. *Journal of Ethnic and Migration Studies, 32*, 403–433.

Ghosh, B. (2000). Return migration: Reshaping policy approaches. In B. Ghose (Ed.), *Return Migration: Journey of Hope or Despair?* (pp. 181–226). Switzerland: United Nations Publication.

Glick Schiller, N., Basch, L., & Blanc-Szanton, C. (1992). Transnationalism: A new analytic framework for understanding migration: Race, Class, Ethnicity, and Nationalism Reconsidered. In N. Glick-Schiller, L. Basch, & C. Blanc-Szanton (Eds.), *Towards A Transnational Perspective on Migration* (Vol. 645, pp. 1–24). New York: The New York Academy of Sciences.

Ho, E. (2003). Reluctant exiles or roaming transnationals? The Hong Kong Chinese in New Zealand. In M. Ip (Ed.), *Unfolding History, Evolving Identity: The Chinese in New Zealand* (pp. 165–184). Auckland: Auckland University Press.

Ho, E., & Bedford, R. (2008). Asian transnational families in New Zealand: Dynamics and challenges. *International Migration, 46*(4), 41–62.

Ho, E., Bedford, R., & Goodwin, J. (1997). Astronaut families: A contemporary migration phenomenon. In W. Friesen, M. Ip, E. Ho, R. Bedford, & J. Goodwin (Eds.), *East Asian New Zealanders: Research on New Migrants, Aotearoa/New Zealand Migration Research Network Research Papers* (pp. 20–39). Palmerston North: Department of Sociology, Massey University.

Ho, E., Ip, M., & Bedford, R. (2001). Transnational Hong Kong Chinese families in the 1990s. *New Zealand Journal of Geography*, 24–30.

Huang, S., Yeoh, B. S. A., & Lam, T. (2008). Asian transnational families in transition: The liminality of simultaneity. *International Migration, 46*(4), 3–13.

Hughes, J. A., & Sharrock, W. W. (2007). *Theory and Methods in Sociology: An Introduction to Sociological Thinking and Practice*. Basingstoke & New York: Palgrave Macmillan.

Hugo, G. (2004). Future immigration policy development in Australia and New Zealand. *New Zealand Population Review, 30*(1&2), 23–42.

Hugo, G. (2006). An Australian diaspora? *International Migration, 44*(1), 105–133.

Ip, M. (2000). Beyond the 'settler' and 'astronaut' paradigms: A new approach to the study of new Chinese immigrants to New Zealand. In M. Ip, K. M. Kang, & S. Page (Eds.), *Migration and Travel Between Asia and New Zealand, Aotearoa/New Zealand Migration Research Network Research Paper* (pp. 3–17). Palmerston North: Department of Sociology, Massey University.

Ip, M. (2003a). Chinese Immigrants and Transnationals in New Zealand: A Fortress Opened. In J. C. Ma & C. Cartier (Eds.), *The Chinese Diaspora: Space, Place, Mobility and Identity* (pp. 339–358). Lanham: Rowman & Littlefield Publishers, Inc.

Ip, M. (2003b). Seeking the last Utopia: The Taiwanese in New Zealand. In M. Ip (Ed.), *Unfolding History, Evolving Identity: The Chinese in New Zealand* (pp. 185–210). Auckland: Auckland University Press.

Ip, M. (2006). Returnees and transnationals: Evolving identities of Chinese (PRC) immigrants in New Zealand. *Journal of Population Studies, 33*, 61–102.

Ip, M., & Friesen, W. (2001). The new Chinese community in New Zealand: Local outcomes of transnationalism. *Asian and Pacific Migration Journal, 10*(2), 213–240.

Ley, D., & Kobayashi, A. (2005). Back to Hong Kong: Return migration or transnational sojourn? *Global Networks, 5*(2), 111–127.

Li, W. W. (2011). Filial piety, parental piety and community piety: Changing cultural practices of elder support among Chinese migrant families in New Zealand. *The Journal of Multicultural Society, 2*(1), 1–30.

Liu, L. (2016). Intergenerational dimensions of transnational Chinese migrant families in New Zealand. *Journal of Chinese Overseas, 12*(2), 216–250.

Nonini, D. M., & Ong, A. (1997). Introduction: Chinese transnationalism as an alternative modernity. In A. Ong & D. M. Noni (Eds.), *Ungrounded Empires: The Cultural Politics of Modern Chinese Transnationalism* (pp. 3–33). New York: Routledge.

Ong, A. (1999). *Flexible Citizenship: The Cultural Logics of Transnationality.* Durham, NC: Duke University Press.

Pe-Pua, R., Mitchell, C., Iredale, R., & Castles, S. (1996). *Astronaut Families and Parachute Children: The Cycle of Migration Between Hong Kong and Australia.* Wollongong, Australia: Centre for Multicultural Studies, University of Wollongong.

Portes, A. (1999). Conclusion: Towards a new world – the origins and effects of transnational activities. *Ethnic and Racial Studies, 22*, 463–476.

Portes, A. (2001). Introduction: The debates and significance of immigrant transnationalism. *Global Networks, 1*(3), 181–194.

Rapson, V. (1998). New Zealand's migration policy: A revolving door? *People and Place, 6*(4), 52–62.

Salaff, J. W. (2008, 24–26 October). *Return Migration: The Role of Social Networks and Family Relations.* Symposium Conducted at the Meeting of the Conference on Globalisation and Chinese Culture: History and Challenges, Nanjing University, Nanjing, China.

Skeldon, R. (1994). Reluctant exiles or bold pioneers: An introduction to migration from Hong Kong. In R. Skeldon (Ed.), *Reluctant Exile? Migration From Hong Kong and the New Overseas Chinese* (pp. 3–18). Hong Kong: Hong Kong University Press.

Skeldon, R. (2006). The case of Hong Kong. In L. Pan (Ed.), *The Encyclopedia of the Chinese Overseas* (pp. 67–70). Singapore: The Chinese Heritage Centre.

Spoonley, P., Bedford, R., & Macpherson, C. (2003). Divided loyalties and fractured sovereignty: Transnationalism and the nation-state in Aotearoa/New Zealand. *Journal of Ethnic and Migration Studies, 29*(1), 27–46.

Waters, J. (2002). Flexible families? 'Astronaut' households and the experience of lone mothers in Vancouver, British Columbia. *Social and Cultural Geography, 3*(2), 117–134.

Whyte, M. K., & Ikels, C. (2004). Filial obligations in Chinese families: Paradoxes of modernization. In C. Ikels (Ed.), *Filial Piety: Practice and Discourse in Contemporary East Asia* (pp. 106–127). Stanford: Stanford University Press.

Yeoh, B. S. A., Huang, S., & Lam, T. (2005). Transnationalizing the 'Asian' family: Imaginaries, intimacies and strategic intents. *Global Networks, 5*(4), 307–315.

5 Conceptualisation of "home", identity, sense of belonging, and citizenship

Along with examining the physical transnational trajectories of highly mobile Chinese migrants, this chapter aims to explore their emotional dimension of transnational migration; namely, their emotions and feelings when they move between places (Baldassar, 2008; Mar, 2005; Ryan, 2008; Wolf, 2002). The notion of "emotional transnationalism" or "symbolic transnationalism" that addresses life experiences and feelings of migrants when they are on the move has become an important subject recently to understand human movement (Datta, 2008, 2011; Espiritu, 2003; Mitchell, 1997; Viruell-Fuentes, 2006; Wolf, 1997, 2002). The notion of "home" is at the centre of explorations of transnational migrants' identity and sense of belonging, and how they experience their migratory journey and conceive of their possible future movement (Ahmed, 1999; Basu, 2004; Haller & Landolt, 2005; Pratt, 2004; Skrbis, 2008; Wise, 2011). Citizenship on the other may add on another layer to the complicated issues surrounding migrants' mobility, home making, identity, and sense of belonging (Faist, 2000; Ip, Inglis, & Wu, 1997; Ong, 1993, 1999). In the context of transnational migration, migrants' construction of these notions may all becomes multi-dimensional and indicate migrants' lives and experience during their transnational movements.

In research practice, apart from asking the interviewees about their physical and geographical transnational movements, the Interview Questions (see Appendix 4) consists of one distinct set of questions. This set of questions explores the interviewees' sense of home, belonging, identity, and perceptions of citizenship and are used as the primary data source to construct this chapter. Two subsections are included into this chapter. The first focuses on a more rational issue – that is citizenship – and the second turns to the emotional construction of transnational migration, such as "home", identity, and sense of belonging.

Mismatch between citizenship and identity

The interviews conducted in Australia and in China revealed that different decisions on citizenship between "returnees" and "trans-Tasmam" interviewees were associated with their transnational mobility patterns. Compared to the "returnees", half of who intend to keep their Chinese citizenship to facilitate their travel to and within China, most of the "trans-Tasman" interviewees have given up their Chinese citizenship and obtained citizenship in their settlement countries of New Zealand and/or Australia. Of the ten "trans-Tasman" interviewees, all had obtained New Zealand citizenship. Five who moved to Australia before 2001 had already obtained Australian passports. The other five were recent arrivals and were either in the process of applying for Australian citizenship or waiting through the two-year-residence requirement to meet their eligibility to apply for citizenship. The reason for this decision on citizenship is institutional as well as pragmatic. In China, dual citizenship is not allowed, therefore for many "returnees", applying for a foreign passport means relinquishing their Chinese citizenship and compromising their convenient, visa-free travel between New Zealand and China. Pragmatically, many "returnees" do have an interest in re-entering New Zealand for future retirement or their children's education, and New Zealand permanent residence will enable them to do so while still keeping their ability to travel freely between New Zealand and China. With legal status as both Chinese citizens and New Zealand permanent residents, they can also be entitled to social welfare in both countries.

As many "returnees" mentioned, if their transnational activities took place primarily between China and New Zealand, there is little need for them to replace their Chinese citizenship with New Zealand citizenship, because with a New Zealand permanent Returning Resident's Visa, they can enter New Zealand as a resident at any time; and with a Chinese passport, they can avoid the hassle of applying for a visa to enter China. More importantly, to keep their Chinese citizenship means they can still enjoy many state welfare, privileged policies regarding buying houses, and their child(ren) can also enjoy state-funded compulsory education. Furthermore, it is almost impossible for one to re-apply for Chinese citizenship, if one regrets forfeiting his/her Chinese passport to become a citizen of another country. For those "returnees" who have obtained New Zealand citizenship, their willingness to seek a New Zealand passport is mainly driven by the need for convenient visa-waiver international travel. This reason echoes the finding from the research by Ip et al. (1997) on the concept of citizenship among recent Asian immigrants in Australia. It was found that a considerable number of new Asian immigrants take an instrumental or practical approach toward acquiring Australia citizenship, namely, for convenient visa-waiver international travel, for accessing social welfare, for political protection, or for educational benefits (Ip et al., 1997).

Similarly, the decision of "trans-Tasman" interviewees who took New Zealand and Australian passports was also largely an instrumental one. Since New Zealand and Australian citizens have free entry into either country and can visit, reside, work, and live in either place for an indefinite period, "trans-Tasman" interviewees' eligibility to enter Australia from New Zealand was conditioned on whether they had New Zealand citizenship. As Peter revealed,

> We arrived in Australia in a hurry. I remember that Australia's new policy came into effect in March 2001,[1] and we arrived at Australia in January. We had to apply for New Zealand citizenship before departure because it is

a necessary landing condition to reside in Australia. Otherwise, I wouldn't give up my Chinese passport.

When the interviewees were asked what an Australian/New Zealand passport meant to them, almost everyone emphasised that the passport meant "convenience for international visa-waiver travel". Other general interests that associated with citizenship, such as voting and legal rights, were rarely mentioned. This conceptualisation of citizenship has little correlation with the perception of their identity and sense of belonging or with the concept of "home". For many, their newly acquired legal status as citizens of New Zealand or Australia did not lead to a sense of full commitment and incorporation into either host society; neither do these individuals identify themselves as "New Zealanders" or "Australians". In fact, a sense of being Chinese and emotionally belonging to the Chinese homeland appears dominant among these interviewees.

First, "being Chinese" is a strong self-identification. Such identification is partly rooted in an acknowledgement of the deep and wide effects of Chinese culture and tradition in one's lives that formulated his/her values and shaped his/her aspirations. For example, Lawrence had no doubt that he saw himself as Chinese:

> I may say I am a New Zealander only because I hold the New Zealand passport. If you ask me what I feel who I am, there is no doubt that I am Chinese – definitely not New Zealander. I am Chinese because of my life experience of the previous 26 years and background of growing up in China. I know that I am quite different from the Kiwis in terms of my personal networks and lifestyle. My interactions with Kiwi or European people are only because of the need to do business and work, but it does not mean that I integrate into the mainstream well. Actually, it is hard to integrate, and also there is no need to fully integrate.

Lawrence's conscious and firm identification of himself as Chinese and his comment that "there is no need to fully integrate" provide clear evidence that contemporary transnationalism provides an alternative strategy for migrants who want to adapt and survive in a new environment (Faist, 2000; Portes, 1999, 2001, 2003; Portes, Guarnizo, & Landolt, 1999). While the traditional assimilation narrative of immigration that advocates full assimilation into a host society is the orthodox way for immigrants to survive, transnationalism provides no real need for migrants to fully integrate into their mainstream societies.

Second, regardless of whether they hold a Chinese passport or not, whether they live in China or not, the claim of "being Chinese" among the interviewees was pervasive. As first-generation migrants, to identify themselves as Chinese is one of the most natural things. Quite often, when I asked my interviewees "if you see yourself as Chinese, why do you say so and what does Chineseness mean to you", my interviewees' facial expression and body language showed that this should not be a question to ask. For example, Frank, a returnee, replied, "It is not worth to ask this question. I am Chinese is the way I was, I am, I should be and will be". Some tried very hard to explain this identity by reflecting this to some material culture, for example, Mia, a "trans-Tasman" interviewee, said, "I say I am Chinese because I eat Chinese food every day, my colleagues always commented that I am dressed like a standard Chinese, the majority of my good friends are Chinese too". One possible interpretation is that "being Chinese" is a pre-determined aspect of how PRC Chinese migrants identify themselves.

Other factors, such as the way migrants interact with the host society, China's rising international status as an emerging economic power, and the resurgence of overseas Chinese nationalism and patriotism in recent years (Liu, 2007; Yin, 2013), intensified the sense of being Chinese. For example, in Kerry's, another returnee, statement about his strong identification as being a Chinese, one can find a strong pro-China stance: "I am a Chinese, and am very proud of being a Chinese. China still has many things that are not very good, but I love her as I love my mother. Now China is rising, I am really proud of it, and I hope that it will become stronger and stronger".

In addition, the strong identification with being Chinese among the interviewees was also a self-conscious identification with others or sense of being different from others. As Jeff, another "trans-Tasman" migrant, noted,

> Other people always see me as Chinese. This is the fact that cannot be changed. For example, if I go to Hong Kong, the locals see me as Chinese. When I am in Australia, others see me as Chinese as well. If I go back to China and tell people there that 'I am an Australian', people will think that I am out of my mind.

In such a case, "being Chinese" is a perpetual status as how other people see him, which consequently reinforces his own sense of Chineseness.

As can be seen, the popular identification with being Chinese is a way of self-conscious identification as being different from others and also a way of interacting with significant others. It may be the close connection with the homeland, or it may be come from a sense of exclusion from the host society that drives this identification, or it may be a combination of both. In general, the findings here show that a large number of interviewees identified themselves strongly as "Chinese" even though a small number picked up a hybrid identity. The citizenship they hold, either New Zealand or Australia, has nothing to do with their strong identification as Chinese. As Sandy said, "If one day I obtain New Zealand citizenship, it does not mean that I will betray China". Meanwhile, their strong identification as Chinese and their legal status as New Zealand or Australia citizens are not conflicting. As Mary states, "My identification as Chinese does not mean that I lack loyalty toward the immigration host country. As a New Zealand citizen, I will never say something negative about New Zealand". The strong identification as Chinese among those PRC migrants is not political; rather, it is only evidence of the deep emotional attachment of first-generation migrants to their country of birth and their strong ties to their homeland.

Negotiation of "home", identity, and belonging in a transnational social space

Research on transnational emotions places particular emphasis on the notion of "home" to migrants because of its centrality in identity construction and formulation of the sense of belonging. The interviews therefore charts out how the concept of home, sense of identity, and social spaces are shaped during increased mobility and transnationalism among highly mobile PRC Chinese migrants.

"Home" as a spontaneous construction

Many interviewees spontaneously expressed their conceptualisation of "home" when talking about their transnational migration processes and movement plans for the future. Even though there were several questions that related to the concept of "home" in the interview process, most interviewees spontaneously raised the discussion of "home" when they explained their transnational trajectories. In the case of "returnees" for example, going back to China is primarily justified in terms of return to their home country. For them, the notion of home is heavily embedded into their explanation of their return journeys. Such homeward journeys are perceived by many first-generation migrants as being natural and logical. For example, Jane, another returnee, revealed that China is her home to which she can and should return: "My real home is China although I own a house in New Zealand. My root is here [China]. When I was in New Zealand, I dreamed a lot about returning to my home, China. Now my dream became true". Such construction of home reflects a nostalgia that often relates to a longing to be back in the place that accords with one's national identity.

As mentioned in Chapter 3, there is an inter-relationship between migrants' identity and their sense of belonging and their sense of "home". This point can be also confirmed in the interviews. Some interviewees brought out the issue "home" automatically when they were articulating the ways they identified themselves and their sense of belonging. When Sophia, a very recent "returnee", gave her reasons for quitting her job as a programme manager at a New Zealand university and returning to China to work as a trade development executive in Shanghai, she placed particular emphasis on her emotional links with China in her spontaneous narrative about "home": "I am a Chinese, and China is my country. My home is here. Returning to China means for me returning to my own home. Here [China] is a place where I feel belong. In New Zealand, even though they offered me citizenship, I could not find the feeling of being home".

"Home" as a flexible and ambiguous construction

Compared with a strong sense of identity as Chinese, the sense of "home" among the interviewees was more flexible and also more ambiguous, as "home" was conceptualised by these PRC migrants in a variety of ways. As illustrated in Chapter 1, in Chinese terms, the character home (*jia* 家) can be used in combination with other characters in different ways and as phrases that connote different meanings. This reality complicates the ways in which Chinese migrants actually conceptualise their notion of "home". Some interviewees referred to their idea of "home" as the immigration destination country, some referred to their idea of "home" as their national home (家国) – China, and some preferred to conceptualise their "home" as a single geographic locality in their places of birth and origin (家乡) – a specific locality in China where their deep emotional attachments lay. For example, Anni, another returnee, revealed firmly that "my home is Shanghai, China. I was born there and I feel my roots are there". Some referred to their "home" as a dual choice of two geographic localities, their immigration destination of New Zealand/Australia and their place of origin, China:

> It's hard to answer this question. On the one hand, China is definitely my home because I grew up here and I am deeply influenced by the Chinese culture, especially now that I am here and my whole family is here. On the other hand, I also feel that New Zealand is my home too. I got married there, had my daughter there, and established my own family there. The time I spent in New Zealand means so much to me. It was a process for me to become a woman from a young girl, to become married from a single woman, to become a mother from a daughter, to become a New Zealand permanent resident from a visitor. It is a process involving the changing of many roles I played in my life course. I believe that the most wonderful things happened to me in my life during the years I stayed in New Zealand. Based on this point, New Zealand is my home too, for sure.

While many interviewees had very firm conceptualisations of "home", some interviewees expressed confusion over the issue. Rose, who is working for a French cosmetics retail company, expressed her puzzled feelings about "home":

> When I left China for New Zealand, I left my home. Now my only emotional link with China is my parents. However, I don't feel that the 3-bedroom apartment owned by my parents in China is my home, even though they always tell me that that is. In Shanghai, I don't feel that I am at home either. Shanghai is a place for work. I don't really have a home to go back to there.

In this case, the sense of no "home" presents an emotional insecurity, but also facilitates free movement in Rose's future. Indeed, since many Chinese migrants still keep close ties with their homeland, they never quite "arrive" at their destinations because they never quite "left" the homeland. Some interviewees constructed their idea of "home" by comparing and differentiating the concepts of "home", "hometown", and workplace and still used the geographic localities to define these terms. For example, Paul conceived his "home" to be in New Zealand, where he will definitely go back to enjoy his life after retirement: "New Zealand is my home and I will finally return there and die there. Beijing is not my home; it is my workplace, and Haerbin [a provincial capital city in the far north of China] is the place where I was born. It is my hometown".

One common theme that can be drawn from the interviews is that when the interviewees conceptualise their ideas of home emotionally and flexibly, their home was finally grounded in material/physical terms. This is to say that physical/material dimensions of conceptualisation of home are significant, given the fact that most interviewees could not detach the notion of home from the reality of a particular geographic place. This way to construct home also strongly reflects the idea that home is a multi-scalar concept. It can be felt at the scale of the town, city, region, or home country, which draws attention to the layered arenas of everyday life. For migrants, home can be stretched into transnational belonging to a physical locality (Blunt, 2005; Blunt & Dowling, 2006; Blunt & Varley, 2004).

"Home" as an immaterial construction of the sense of belonging

Most studies have found that migrants employ the word "home" to refer to their immigration destination or to their place of birth or origin. Although the physical place dimension to migrants' identification with home is important (Christou & King, 2006; Lewin, 2001; Muggeridge & Dona, 2006; Wiles, 2008), it should be noted that "home" is more than just a geographic location. It can refer to the immaterial – the feeling or sense of home that may have no spatial correlation and simply "connotes an emotional place, somewhere you truly belong" (Pollock & Reken, 1999, p. 124). Richard, a "trans-Tasman" interviewee declared, "Where I'll go depends on where my home is. Home for me is not a geographic or physical concept, but where my family is and where my heart belongs". He was not the only one to convey that definition of home as a place of safety, love, familiarity, belonging, and where certain dear people are located. Mike referred to his "home" as "a place I feel really comfortable and relaxed, and a place I can turn to. 'Home', in my concept, is not a house in a certain place; it is more about people who are around me and about family".

"Home" is hard to define or redefine in the term of migration, because migration essentially means a disruption of the physical "home", given the fact that migrants do leave their old "home" and build a new "home" in the destination country. In transnational migration, however, "home" is even more problematic because transnational migration simply denotes deterritorialisation, which overrides the basis of the physical "home". However, as these interviews show, if "home" is conceptualised in an immaterial way, it can be an important indicator of what the transnational migration experience is and means. "Home" can be a place where certain cultural assumptions and expectations are met as well as a place where there are emotional links and attachments. These emotional links could have to do with where the person originally comes from and the feelings as that individual moves between places. In this sense, immigrants' sense of "home" may change, and the individuals may attach new feelings of "home" to different places as they move. Doing so involves a strong sense of self-discovery and reflection during each of the transnational movements that happen.

Home, identity, and sense of belonging: an interplay

LINDA: I am a Chinese for sure, and will be a Chinese always. No matter how long I have been overseas, I am a Chinese is a fact that cannot be changed. I eat Chinese food every day and I live in a Chinese way. But if you ask me where my home is, I would say that my home is in Australia because my family is here, and more importantly, my son is here.

JAMES: If you ask me where my home is, the first interpretation of this question that emerges in my mind is that you ask me where my root is. My answer would be "my home is in Tianjin, China". For people of my age, our links with China are so strong, and many contacts and networks are mostly in China. I am a Chinese, and I feel that I belong to China, my home country. If you ask me whether Melbourne, Australia is my home, my interpretation of this question is that you actually ask me where my family is. In this sense, home for me can be Melbourne. But really, it means more about family rather than home. Home means more for me as an emotional attachment that a person identifies with a particular place.

The quotations above illustrate an interesting interplay between the concept of "home" and interviewees' sense of identity and belonging. James, a "trans-Tasman" migrant who re-migrated to Australia with his family ten years ago, identified himself as Chinese and considered that his real home was in China despite the fact that he actually lived in Australia. Linda, who moved to Australia five years ago, also identified herself as Chinese, but did not see her home as being in China. Rather, Australia, the country she was currently residing in and where her family was, was perceived as her home. The quotations also reveal a clear trend in the sense that although there was a strong sense amongst the interviewees of "being Chinese", this identity however was not linked to their conceptualised "home". Very often, the interviewees felt strongly Chinese, but they did not necessarily see their "home" as being in China. Instead, many often referred to their "home" as the place where they currently reside. For example, the "returnees" often saw their "home" as in China, while the "trans-Tasman" interviewees often saw their "home" as in Australia.

When they de-linked their sense of identity and "home", more links between the sense of "home" and the sense of belonging were revealed. When I asked where they felt they belonged, the voices were polarised, depending on the way each interviewee treated the term "belong". Some treated the term "belong" in a cultural sense, so their answers linked to their sense of identity as Chinese. For example, Neil said, "I belong to China because I am a Chinese". Some treated the term "belong" from a geographic sense, so their answers were connected to where they currently resided. Like Joe said, "I belong to Australia. My family and my life are here, and I am working here as well". In such cases, belonging to the host countries refers to migrants' physical presence and daily engagement in the country they reside in. These respondents felt that they belonged to where their physical homes were or where their families' residential bases were. The place of residence was often referred to as home.

This interplay between PRC interviewees' conceptualisation of home, identity and senses of belonging, confirms the importance of both the physical and the emotional/cultural dimensions of home when investigating transnational migrants' identity and belonging. For first-generation migrants in a Western country, who are very aware of the distinctive differences between the Occidental and Oriental cultures, being Chinese is a perpetual part of their identity. Transnationality *per se* seems to have little effect on their strong identification as being Chinese, but it does influence and complicate the ways PRC migrants interact with others in their different social and spatial settings and articulate their sense of belonging and identification with home.

Summary

This chapter highlights the dynamic emotional journeys of the PRC Chinese migrants with transnational mobility. Such transnational manoeuverings challenge issues related to citizenship, identity formation, and the conceptualisation of "home". The dominant conceptualisation of citizenship in political theory as an institutionalised form of solidarity and in cultural studies as membership in a country that usually requires moral commitment (Faist, 2000) appears insufficient to explain the multiple attachments of PRC transnational migrants. Given the exclusionary and political feature of citizenship, a request for immigrants' full commitment and total loyalty to the immigration destiny country is problematic. As shown in these interviews, being a New Zealand or Australian citizen does not result in full incorporation with or a sense of belonging to the host society for many PRC migrants, nor does it deter the pervasive identification of being "Chinese" or the conceptualisation of "home" as an emotional longing for the place of origin.

This chapter also revealed that the highly mobile PRC transnational migrants are constantly re-negotiating their conceptions of home, and issues of identity and sense of belonging. Their conceptions of home, whether material or immaterial, are increasingly fluid and ambivalent. Home is often hard to define or re-define, and migrants continue to load new meanings onto it centered on family, social relations, and emotional attachment and investment. The interviews show that both physical/material and emotional/immaterial aspects of home are equally important when many PRC migrants constructed their ideas of home. While they inscribed their home with so many social and symbolic meanings, the physical dimension of home clearly matters too. Very often, the physical, social, symbolic, and emotional aspects of home are mutually interdependent.

There is also a critical relation between PRC migrants' identity, their sense of belonging, and their conceptualisation of home. Among the interviewees, their negotiation of home is intimately connected to the ways they construct their identity and sense of belonging. An important aspect of such a relationship is the ways in which they construct their notion of home and the associated sense of identity and belonging that are actually shaped into something tangible which is also negotiable. Sometimes, these issues converge but for most times they diverge. Both convergence and divergence reflect the complex realities of the everyday lives of these migrants in "home here" and "home there". PRC migrants share a very strong identification as being Chinese that is either self-perpetuated or externally imposed. The tensions between "here" and "there", "us" and "them" are likely to amplify the complicated reality of the migrants' simultaneous existence across two or more societies. Such migrants have to continually adopt flexible strategies to keep the ties that bind them to, and the lines that distance them from, two or more countries.

The ways in which "home" and "away", "here" and "there" are defined in the narratives are likely indications of the dilemma of choosing to stay or to return, or perhaps move elsewhere. The transnational movements described not only involve a long-range geographic move and costly air journeys across the oceans; they are also emotionally costly and involve critical, sometimes extremely difficult decision-making. It is always hard for a person to uproot themselves again to re-enter the homeland or travel to a third destination, and face inevitable re-adjustment and re-integration issues. Often, the scholarship on transnational migration discusses highly mobile migrants with a positive, even celebratory tone. Transnational migrants are usually presented as if they pass smoothly from place to place without emotional difficulty. However, this research reveals that such assumptions are inaccurate, and there is in fact a great deal of "emotional labour" involved (Skrbis, 2008, p. 237). On the one hand, transnational migration is a rational decision for Chinese migrants hoping to maximize the economic opportunities while balancing family members' different needs. On the other hand, transnational migration is an emotionally challenging task. It costs migrants deeply to constantly negotiate their relationship with different places, especially their intimate relationship with the homeland, important family members, and familiar social networks left behind.

Note

1 Before 26 February 2001, most New Zealanders were automatically granted a Special Category Visa (SCV), which allowed the holders to be eligible for Australian citizenship, access certain social welfare, or sponsor their family members for permanent residence. However, after the policy change in 2001, if a New Zealander wants to have the status of permanent residents in Australia, he/she must apply for it under the same terms as other immigrants who are not New Zealand citizens.

References

Ahmed, S. (1999). Home and away: Narratives of migration and estrangement. *International Journal of Cultural Studies*, 2(3), 329–347.

Baldassar, L. (2008). Missing kin and longing to be together: Emotions and the construction of co-presence in transnational relationships. *Journal of Intercultural Studies*, 29(3), 247–266.

Basu, P. (2004). My own island home: The Orkney coming. *Journal of Material Culture*, 9(1), 27–42.

Blunt, A. (2005). *Domicile and Diaspora: Anglo-Indian Women and the Spatial Politics of Home*. Oxford: Blackwell Publishing.

Blunt, A., & Dowling, R. (2006). *Home*. London: Routledge.

Blunt, A., & Varley, A. (2004). Introduction: Geographies of 'home'. *Cultural Geographies, 11*, 3–6.

Christou, A., & King, R. (2006). Migrants encounter migrants in the city: The changing context of "home" for second-generation Geek-American return migrants. *International Journal of Urban and Regional Research, 30*, 816–835.

Datta, A. (2008). Building differences: Material geographies of home(s) among polish builders in London. *Transactions of the Institute of British Geographers, 33*, 518–531.

Datta, A. (2011). Translocal geographies of London: Belonging and 'otherness' among polish migrants after 2004. In K. Brickell & A. Datta (Eds.), *Translocal Geographies: Spaces, Places, Connections* (pp. 73–90). Burlington, VT: Ashgate.

Espiritu, Y. L. (2003). *Home Bound: Filipino Across Cultures, Communities, and Countries*. Berkeley: University of California Press.

Faist, T. (2000). Transnationalization in international migration: Implications for the study of citizenship and culture. *Ethnic and Racial Studies, 23*(2), 189–222.

Haller, W., & Landolt, P. (2005). The transnational dimensions of identity formation: Adult children of immigrants in Miami. *Ethnic and Racial Studies, 28*(6), 1182–1214.

Ip, D., Inglis, C., & Wu, C. T. (1997). Concepts of citizenship and identity among recent Asian immigrants in Australia. *Asian and Pacific Migration Journal, 6*(3–4), 363–384.

Lewin, F. A. (2001). The meaning of home among elderly immigrants: Directions for future research and theoretical development. *Housing Studies, 16*(3), 353–370.

Liu, H. (2007). New migrants and the revival of overseas Chinese nationalism. *Journal of Contemporary China, 14*(43), 291–316.

Mar, P. (2005). Unsettling potentialities: Topographies of hope in transnational migration. *Journal of Intercultural Studies, 26*(4), 361–378.

Mitchell, K. (1997). Transnational discourse: Bringing geography back in. *Antipode, 29*(2), 101–114.

Muggeridge, H., & Dona, G. (2006). Back home? Refugees/experiences of their first visit back to their country of origin. *Journal of Refugee Studies, 19*(4), 415–432.

Ong, A. (1993). On the edge of empires: Flexible citizenship among Chinese in diaspora. *Positions, 1*(3), 745–778.

Ong, A. (1999). *Flexible Citizenship: The Cultural Logics of Transnationality*. Durham, NC: Duke University Press.

Pollock, D. C., & Reken, E. V. (1999). *The Third Culture Kid Experience: Growing Up Among Worlds*. London: Interculture Press.

Portes, A. (1999). Conclusion: Towards a new world – the origins and effects of transnational activities. *Ethnic and Racial Studies, 22*(2), 463–476.

Portes, A. (2001). Introduction: The debates and significance of immigrant transnationalism. *Global Networks, 1*(3), 181–194.

Portes, A. (2003). Conclusion: Theoretical convergences and empirical evidence in the study of immigrant transnationalism. *International Migration Review, 37*(3), 874–892.

Portes, A., Guarnizo, L. E., & Landolt, P. (1999). The study of transnationalism: Pitfalls and promise of an emergent research field. *Ethnic and Racial Studies, 22*(2), 217–237.

Pratt, G. (2004). *Working Feminism*. Philadelphia: Temple University Press.

Ryan, L. (2008). Navigating the emotional terrain of families 'here' and 'there': Women, migration and the management of emotions. *Journal of Intercultural Studies, 29*(3), 299–313.

Skrbis, Z. (2008). Transnational families: Theorising migration, emotions and belonging. *Journal of Intercultural Studies, 29*(3), 231–246.

Viruell-Fuentes, E. A. (2006). 'My heart is always there': The transnational practices of first-generation Mexican immigrant and second-generation Mexican American women. *Identities: Global Studies in Culture and Power, 13*(3), 335–362.

Wiles, J. (2008). Sense of home in a transnational social space: New Zealanders in London. *Global Networks, 8*(1), 116–137.

Wise, A. (2011). 'You wouldn't know what's in there would you?' Homeliness and 'foreign' signs in Ashfield, Sydney. In K. Brickell & A. Datta (Eds.), *Translocal Geographies: Spaces, Places Connections* (pp. 93–108). Burlington, VT: Ashgate.

Wolf, D. (1997). Family secrets: Transnational struggles among children of Filipino immigrants. *Sociological Perspectives, 40*(3), 457–483.

Wolf, D. (2002). There is no place like 'home': Emotional transnationalism and the struggles of second-generation Filipinos. In P. Levitt & M. C. Waters (Eds.), *The Changing Face of Home: The Transnational Lives of the Second Generation* (pp. 255–294). New York Russell Sage Foundation.

Yin, H. (2013). *Chinese-Language Cyberspace: Overseas Chinese Cyber Nationalism and Migrant Identity.* (PhD), University of Auckland. Retrieved from https://researchspace.auckland.ac.nz/handle/2292/21638.

6 Does the economic factor still matter? – trans-Tasman migration of new PRC migrants

"Back-door" migration is a negative comment often used in Australia referring to the sharp increase of New Zealand citizens, especially those who had been born in Asia re-immigrated to Australia after gaining New Zealand passports (Bedford, Ho, & Hugo, 2003). In February 2001, the Australian government introduced stricter controls over access to welfare provisions to New Zealand citizens who arrived in Australia, but not under Australia's immigration programme. This policy change explicitly aimed at New Zealand citizens, including those born in countries of Asia and made many of them ineligible for social security support for a period of time after arriving in Australia and tried effectively to reduce the "back-door" migration (Bedford, Ho, & Lidgard, 2005). Previous studies indicate that the largest percentage increases of New Zealand citizens who were born overseas and engaged into the trans-Tasman migration between 2002 and 2009 were amongst those born in countries in Africa, the Middle East, and Asia. New Zealand citizens born in China was the main group of overseas-born New Zealand citizens from Asia. The other two main groups were from South Africa and India (Bedford, Callister, & Didham, 2010a). Based on a detailed analysis on the Permanent and Long-term (PLT) arrival and departure data from INZ and information from an online survey conducted by the author, this chapter examines the trans-Tasman migration of new PRC Chinese migrants. It focuses on the volume and intentions of PRC migrants' trans-Tasman migration flow.

This chapter starts from an overview of the issue of trans-Tasman migration, which aims to provide a backdrop to the following examination of the PRC migrants' trans-Tasman migration flow. It draws the results from quantitative analysis on the New Zealand PLT arrival and departure data from previous studies to show the trend of trans-Tasman migration of New Zealand citizens to Australia. This overview is followed by a brief introduction of the research approach and methodology. The following two sections are based on the author's original research. The first part is based on a detailed analysis on the PLT arrival and departure data of New Zealand citizens who were born in the PRC and entered into Australia as against to New Zealand local-born citizens and other overseas-born citizens who were significant contributors in trans-Tasman migration to Australia. The second part is based on an online survey conducted among New Zealand's PRC migrants. These two sections can provide factual evidences to show the precise reality of the PRC migrants' trans-Tasman migration and intention.

Trans-Tasman migration to Australia: an overview

The issue of trans-Tasman migration is nothing new. Based on the Trans-Tasman Travel Arrangement, New Zealand and Australia had pursued less restrictive immigration controls between each other, and migration flows between the two countries had been less regulated for a long time before the 2001 policy change in Australia (Bedford, Ho, & Lidgard, 2000). Even though this movement is essentially international, "in many respects it is more similar to internal migration within Australia', at least from an Australian perspective" (Hugo, 2004, p. 35). By the late 1990s, citizens of either country were free to work and settle in the other without any requirements for a visa, and were entitled almost all the educational and welfare benefits available to permanent residents of both countries (Birrell & Rapson, 2001).

However, situation changed in the late 1990s when there was an immigrant influx from Asian countries to New Zealand. This immigrant influx to New Zealand was coincided with a sharp increase in the share of trans-Tasman migrants to Australia in 1999 and 2000 (Bedford et al., 2003). This sharp increase of trans-Tasman migration to Australia stimulated the issue of trans-Tasman migration had been the subject of considerable debate. The long-standing migratory connection between these two countries was heavily criticised within Australia during the late 1990s due to this so-called "back-door" migration, referring to the trans-Tasman migration from New Zealand to Australia of New Zealand citizens who were born outside of New Zealand and entered into Australia without having to meet the standards set by the official migration programme (Birrell & Rapson, 2001; Rapson, 1998). In New Zealand, this movement has been criticised as disloyal and a problem of the loss of talents (Spoonley, Bedford, & Macpherson, 2003). This phenomenon also attracted a great deal of media hype, such as that New Zealand citizens who were born outside of New Zealand used this country as a "revolving door" to step into Australia (Rapson, 1998, p. 56).

In February 2001, the Australian government introduced stricter controls over access to welfare provisions to New Zealand citizens who arrived in Australia, but not under Australia's immigration programme. In a wider context of trans-Tasman relations as Birrell and Rapson (2001) pointed out, this policy change "heralds a new era in the relationship between these two countries" (p. 2). More specifically related to migration, Bedford et al. (2003) suggest that this change signals a significant contraction of the privileged migratory relationships that citizens of both countries had when resident in the other that the previous Trans-Tasman Travel Arrangement reinforced. Australian government's concern was not so much with the volume of immigration of New Zealand citizens *per se*; rather, "it was with the mix of people who were entering as New Zealand citizens . . . especially Pacific Islanders, people from countries in Asia, and refugees accepted by New Zealand from Africa and the Middle East" (Birrell & Rapson, 2001, p. 53), and the related cost on Australian government of the social security benefits that citizens of New Zealand entitled when they reside in Australia.

INZ data shows that between April 1997 and March 2001, the number of New Zealand citizens crossing the Tasman, with the intention of staying away for 12 months or more, was high over 120,000 (see Appendix 5). Bedford et al. (2003) pointed out that in 2000 just before the 2001 policy change, the number of New Zealanders who entered Australia was particularly high. This influx of New Zealanders into Australia was associated with the advanced warning of the 2001 policy change in Australia. Before the enforcement of the new policy in Australia, there was a rush to enter this preferable immigration destination. Otherwise, latter acquisition of Australian permanent residence or citizenship would become a much longer and more complex application process. This policy change in Australia made many New Zealanders who chose to reside in Australia were not eligible for many Australia's social security benefits; thus, efficiently reduced the volume of out-migration to Australia within the following immediate years. Between April 2001 and March 2005, the number of the PLT departures of New Zealand citizens dropped by just under 24,000 (19.5 per cent). The number of overseas-born New Zealand citizens leaving for Australia in particularly fell sharply after June 2001 and, by the year ended June 2003, totally only 3,968 by comparison with 11,427 in the period between October 2000 and June 2001 (Bedford et al., 2010a). The biggest reduction in overseas-born New Zealanders moving to Australia after the policy change was among those born in countries in Asia. Between October 2000 and June 2001, 4,524 Asia-born New Zealand citizens moved to Australia for 12 months or more. This was 3.5 times more than the 1,282 who moved over the following 12 months to June 2002. In the year ending June 2003 there had been a further fall to 802 (Bedford et al., 2003).

The 2001 policy change in Australia did discourage trans-Tasman migration of New Zealand citizens to Australia in the immediate following years; however, Bedford et al. (2003) argued,

> It is highly unlikely that the policy changes *per se* will have much impact on the long-established movements to Australia of New Zealanders. Australia remains the favoured destination for New Zealanders moving overseas for period of 12 months or more, and trans-Tasman migration will continue to contribute more people to Australia than New Zealand in the foreseeable future.
>
> (p. 61)

The fact shows that such estimation is correct. In the four-year period between April 2005 and March 2009, the numbers of New Zealand citizens leaving for Australia increased markedly – from 96,745 (2000–2005) to 142,786 (2006–2009). Among the trans-Tasman New Zealanders, overseas-born comprises a large number. A recent work done shows an overall picture of the trans-Tasman migration of New Zealand citizens born locally compared with New Zealand citizens born in overseas (Bedford, Callister, & Didham, 2010b). During the eight years between April 2002 and March 2009, the overall PLT net loss of 171,156 New Zealand citizens to Australia included 34,382 people who had been born in other countries. This work also examines the net losses to Australia of New Zealand citizens born overseas by broad region of birth, the largest increases from 2002 to 2009 were among those born in countries in Africa and the Middle East (85.4 per cent) and in Asia (55.3 per cent, including South Asia) (Bedford et al., 2010a) (also see Appendix 6).

Recent studies by Sanderson (2009) furthered the research on trans-Tasman migration patterns by using the dataset from the Australian Department of Immigration, Multicultural and Indigenous Affairs (DIMIA) to not only look at the PLT arrivals of New Zealand citizens, but also examine the short-term movement patterns of New Zealanders, especially those who stated intentions to remain in Australia for at least 12 months in the passenger card (Sanderson, 2009). The results show that the pattern of trans-Tasman migration is much more complicated than the classic perception of "back-door" migration. Based on the statistical analysis, the author suggests that migration from New Zealand to Australia is strong, but not a one-way movement, evidenced by the repeat and return migration and migration to a third destination. Other research provides similar views. Using a longitudinal dataset on New Zealand citizens arriving for a stay of 12 months or longer between 1 August 1999 and 31 July 2002, Poot and Sanderson (2007) tracked all subsequent moves of these migrants out of and back into Australia, up to July 2005. The most significant result is that the 2001 policy change in Australia not only reduced the inflow of New Zealanders to Australia, but increased the probability of remigration from Australia to other destinations among those who had intended to settle down permanently (Poot, 2010; Poot & Sanderson, 2007).

Methodological notes

This chapter aims to examine the trans-Tasman migration of New Zealand's PRC migrants through two ways. First, a detailed analysis of the PLT data from INZ will show the trend of the trans-Tasman migration to Australia that New Zealand's China-born citizens engaged in from 2002 onwards. Second, based on the information from an online survey the author conducted, this chapter will show the PRC migrants' intention to move to Australia.

Since October 2000 there has been birthplace question on New Zealand's customs arrival and departure cards,[1] New Zealand citizens who moving to and from Australia can be identified and monitored by country of birth. Therefore, the examination of the trans-Tasman migration trend of the PRC migrants is feasible. To do so, the author used the PLT arrival and departure data to take account of both arrival and departure numbers to establish the net loss of New Zealand's PRC-born citizens to Australia from 2001 onwards. In order to capture the full picture of the trans-Tasman migration of the PRC-born migrants, this trans-Tasman migration flow is placed in a comparative context with the trans-Tasman migration flow of New Zealand local-born citizens and other overseas-born citizens who were also significant contributors in trans-Tasman migration to Australia, such as citizens who were born in Pacific Island countries (including Fiji, Samoa, and Tonga), UK, India, and South Africa.

The online questionnaire survey provides quantitatively indicative data of the trans-Tasman intention among the PRC migrants and also the factors that determine their trans-Tasman movements. In general, this survey targeted all PRC migrants with New Zealand permanent residency or citizenship no matter where they resided at the time of survey.[2] The survey was administered using the "Survey Monkey" (www.surveymonkey.com) online service. It was officially launched on 1 December 2008, and closed on 15 July 2009. Several Chinese community networks, Chinese-language newspapers, and Internet websites in New Zealand and Australia,[3] Auckland University Alumni, and the author's personal network were used to recruit respondents. In general, this survey targeted all PRC migrants with New Zealand permanent residence or citizenship no matter whether they were in New Zealand or not. In total, 477 respondents completed the survey. Due to the different locations of the potential respondents, the targeted respondents were carefully framed as four groups: "returnees", "settlers", "transnationals", and "commuters".[4] The online survey questionnaire was written in both English and Chinese, and respondents could choose to use either language to complete the survey. Most of the questions were close-ended with provided answer selections (see Appendix 7). The first half of the survey asked questions about a respondent's basic demographic information, such as gender, age, place of birth, marital status, highest education level, where that highest education level obtained, residence/citizenship status, type of visa on first arrival in New Zealand, and immigration category. The second half of the survey asked different respondent groups' employment and income status, main reasons for choosing different movement trajectories, and their future movement and settlement intentions. The last part addresses respondents' economic connection between country of origin and the immigration destination.

As for the data analysis of the online survey, this chapter provides some important between-group comparisons. Through these between-group comparisons, the different dimensions of each surveyed group's decision-making of taking different transnational movements and future plans of further movement intentions can be revealed; thus, some important dimension of choosing to leave New Zealand to move to Australia can emerge. Comparisons were also made among the "transnational" group to compare the employment and income status before and after they moved Australia. It also needs to be pointed out that the small sample size of this survey, especially the groups of "returnees" (26), "transnationals" (45), and "commuters" (13) prevented this survey from providing statistical data that represented the overall PRC migrant population. Also, the "settler" respondents were age-biased and mainly young adults. Therefore, the survey only aims to provide indicative and illustrative data and analysis, and enhance the overall interpretation of the trans-Tasman migration of the PRC migrants.

What does the PLT arrival and departure data tell us?

Table 6.1 shows the net loss of New Zealand citizens to Australia divided by birth places. The immediately following two years after the 2001 policy change in Australia (2002–3 and 2003–4), the volume of trans-Tasman migration across all groups apparently declined. The net loss of local-born New Zealanders dropped sharply from 12,297 between the year of 2001 and 2002 to 9981 between the year of 2002 and 2003. In the same period of time, the net loss of the PRC-born New Zealand citizens to Australia also dropped dramatically from 429 to only 86. As for other important migrant groups who contribute greatly in New Zealand's immigration intake and who were born outside of New Zealand, such as those who were born in Pacific countries, and born in UK, India, and South Africa, the net loss of them to Australia also decreased but not as dramatic as those PRC-born New Zealand citizens.

However, one can also find that the influence of the 2001 policy change in Australia was short-lived rather than long-term. After April 2004, the size of trans-Tasman migration of both local-born and overseas-born New Zealand citizens recovered and increased. The size of the trans-Tasman migration of some groups, such as the local-born, Pacific-born, and South Africa-born, were even over the pre-2002 numbers. The net loss of those local-born New Zealanders to Australia reached a new peak, at 32,057 between April 2011 and April 2012. During the same period of time, the number of the PRC-born New Zealanders who moved to Australia increased slowly but has never reached the same level of the period between 2001 and 2002 (see Table 6.1).

Figure 6.1 shows the changing trans-Tasman migration flow to Australia of some groups of overseas-born New Zealand citizens between 2001/2002 and

Table 6.1 Net loss of New Zealand citizen to Australia divided by birthplaces

Birth place	New Zealand	Pacific island countries	UK	PRC	India	South Africa
April 2001–2002	12297	657	664	429	384	380
April 2002–2003	9981	507	545	86	160	320
April 2003–2004	10353	619	482	134	187	293
April 2004–2005	15400	776	523	116	203	448
April 2005–2006	17809	790	604	204	272	506
April 2006–2007	18967	622	713	226	568	690
April 2007–2008	24357	813	749	269	708	887
April 2008–2009	27635	1076	783	276	667	665
April 2009–2010	12538	724	408	198	374	368
April 2010–2011	21262	965	628	208	624	540
April 2011–2012	32057	1488	946	310	797	804
April 2012–2013	29006	2116	790	239	733	823
Total 2001–2013	**231662**	**11153** (4.8%)*	**7835** (3.4%)	**2695** (1.2%)	**5677** (2.5%)	**6724** (2.9%)

(Note *: Compared with New Zealand born cohort, expressed as percentage in the brackets.)

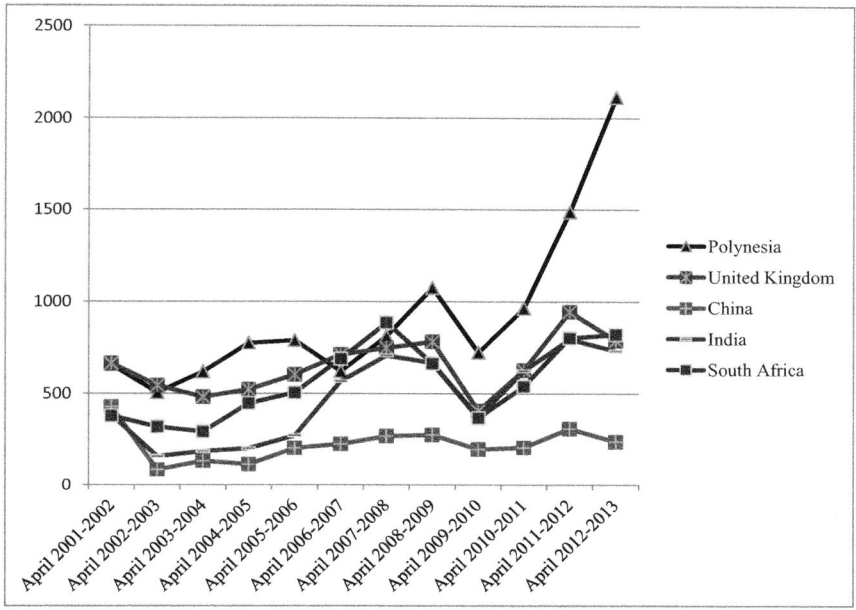

Figure 6.1 Changing situation of the trans-Tasman migration of New Zealand's
overseas-born citizens by birth places between 2001/2002 and 2012/2013
(Source: Immigration New Zealand)

2012/2013. While the net loss of New Zealand citizens who were born in UK, China, India and South Africa remained relatively steady with some fluctuations, the volume of trans-Tasman migration of those who were born in Pacific countries increased dramatically since 2009. This may be closely related to the quick development of the mining industry in Australia, which requires a large number of mining and labour workers. However, the true reason of such sharp increase warrants further in-depth investigation.

The author believes that this significant increase of the trans-Tasman migration of the Pacific migrants may be related to the distinctive demographic profile of this group of migrants. Compared with the PRC new migrants, or migrants from UK, India, and South Africa who usually come to New Zealand under the skilled or business categories with high-education and better finance, a large number of the Pacific migrants came to New Zealand via special categories, such as the Samoa Quota or the Pacific Access Category (Bedford et al., 2010a; Bedford et al., 2005). The overall economic and educational profile of this group of migrants is lower compared with those skilled and business migrants. They are more likely to work in the low-skilled labour market rather than working as professionals or entrepreneurs. When seeing the fast growth labour market of Australia's mining industry, many of them moved to Australia for job opportunities.

In summary, the number of the PRC-born New Zealand citizen does not feature prominently in the trans-Tasman migration flow. However, the perception that Australia is a better place to work and live of the general New Zealand population may influence PRC-born New Zealanders' perception. Many of them may consider moving to Australia for better career development and income when opportunities arise. Overall, Australian's policy change in 2001 did not reduce the trans-Tasman number of New Zealand citizen, including those overseas-born ones. Australia seems to remain a desired destination for many New Zealand citizens.

What have been found from the online survey?

Respondents' profile

Among those 477 online survey respondents, most were below the age of 50; only 2.3 per cent of respondents age 50 or over (see Table 6.2). This age bias was likely caused by three factors, 1) Chinese immigrants to New Zealand are mainly young adults; 2) young people were more likely to use a computer and access the online survey; and 3) young people are more interested in browsing Internet communities, forums, and bulletin board systems (BBS), and therefore, more likely to encounter the survey advertisement placed in those systems. It also should be noted that the biggest group among the respondents is the age group between 25 and 29 (51.1 per cent), followed by the groups between 20 and 24 (14.2 per cent) and between 30 and 34 (14.2 per cent).

In terms of the place of birth, most of the respondents were born in urban cities in China. In Table 6.3, it can be seen that half of the respondents were married (48 per cent married + 2 per cent civil union), and another half (50 per cent) were single.

In terms of highest education, 75 per cent of the respondents had bachelor or higher degrees compared with the national average of 14.2 per cent of New Zealand population having bachelor degrees or higher. Moreover, almost 30 per cent of the respondents had postgraduate or higher degrees (see Table 6.4). This finding is in line with the 2006 Census which shows that ethnic Chinese born in China are one of the best-educated groups in New Zealand (Liu, 2011).

In terms of where respondents obtained their highest degree, about 76 per cent obtained their highest degrees in New Zealand (see Table 6.5). This finding indicates the fact that many Chinese intend to spend a period of time to pursue

Table 6.2 Age distribution of the online survey respondents

Age	20–24	25–29	30–34	35–39	40–44	45–49	50–54	55–59	60 and over
Respondents (%)	14.2%	51.1%	14.2%	7.4%	5.9%	4.8%	1.5%	0.3%	0.5%

Table 6.3 Marital status of online survey respondents

Marital Status	Single	Married	Separated	Divorced	Widow or Widower	Civil Union
Respondents (%)	48.3%	44.8%	2.0%	2.8%	0.3%	1.8%

Table 6.4 Highest education level of online survey respondents

Highest Degree Obtained	Lower than Bachelor Degree or New Zealand Level 7	Bachelor Degree or New Zealand Level 7	Post-graduate/ Honours Degree	Master's Degree	PhD or equivalent or higher
Respondents (%)	25.7%	47.1%	9.2%	15.0%	3.1%

Table 6.5 Location where online survey respondents gained their highest degree

Places Highest Degree Obtained	Respondents (%)
China	22.4%
New Zealand	75.6%
Other Locations	2.0%

a New Zealand education after they immigrate to New Zealand. Obtaining a higher degree in a Western country like New Zealand is a way for many Chinese migrants to accumulate personal human capital and improve their performance in the job market or facilitate future movements.

As for the residential status, about 74 per cent of the online survey respondents were New Zealand permanent residents and 26 per cent of them were New Zealand citizens. For those holding permanent residency, two-thirds (67 per cent) wanted to apply for a New Zealand passport in the future. Upon arriving first time in New Zealand, 68.1 per cent of respondents were holding Student Visas, 21 per cent of them were on Permanent Residence Visas, 5.5 per cent of them were on Visitor Visas, 2.3 per cent of them used Work Visas, and 1.9 per cent of them used the Family Reunion Visa (see Table 6.6). The survey found that there was a high percentage of Student Visa entry which confirms what has been suggested in previous research findings, namely, that PRC migrants intend to apply for permanent residency on-shore rather than off-shore (Ip, 2006). This finding also reflects that the current main route of immigration for PRC migrants moves from study to getting a degree, finding work, and gaining residency. Especially after 2003, the new selection system was introduced, under which one criteria requires a definite job offer, which seems to be the most difficult obstacle for

Table 6.6 Visa type on first arrival in New Zealand

Visa Type	Respondents (%)
Student Visa	68.1%
Permanent Residence Visa	21.0%
Visitor Visa	5.5%
Work Visa	2.3%
Family Reunion Visa	1.9%
Other (i.e. refugee etc)	0.8%

PRC applicants. Therefore, being on-shore gives those applicants more time, space, and opportunity to obtain a job offer. In addition, a large number of Chinese international students obtained Job Search Visas after finishing their studies in New Zealand and were subsequently approved for residence (Ho, 2005). This group also contributed to the large number of the respondents whose first arrival in New Zealand with Student Visas.

In terms of the time of first arrival of the respondents in New Zealand, that timeframe varied from 1981 to 2009; however, the majority of them landed in New Zealand after 1997. The average time of residence in New Zealand following first landing was 8.5 years for all respondents. As for the immigration categories, most respondents obtained permanent residency under the Skilled Migrant Category (SMC) (77 per cent, see Table 6.7). That category was followed by the Family Category (spouse, parents, or children, 14 per cent). Work to Residence category totalled 4.8 per cent, and Business/Investment Category totalled 3.1 per cent, statistics consistent with the discussions in other literature, indicating that most PRC migrants come to New Zealand under the SMC (Ho, 2003). Of the respondents, 76 per cent were the principal applicants when they applied for residency, while the remaining respondents were mainly co-applicants and family members.

Of the 477 respondents who completed the survey, 393 (82 per cent) were living in New Zealand ("settlers"); 45 (9.4 per cent) were living in a third country ("transnationals"); 26 (5.5 per cent) were living in China ("returnees"); and 13 (2.7 per cent) were commuting between China and New Zealand ("commuters"). For those living in a third country, the majority were now in Australia (82 per cent, 37), and the remaining group were located in the US (8.9 per cent, 4), Canada (4.4 per cent, 2), and Taiwan (4.4 per cent, 2).

In general, this profile of the respondents reflects a group of new migrants who possess rich human capital, as evidenced by their very young age and high education qualifications. Most of them were able to meet the entry criteria as skilled immigrants. Such positive human capital is necessary for them to become desirable workforce globally. It should be acknowledge that one major bias in the sample is the age bias that respondents who aged between 20 and 29 comprised 65.3 per cent of the total number of respondents.

Table 6.7 Immigration category for online respondents immigrating to New Zealand

Immigration Category	Overall Response (%)
Skilled	76.9%
Work to Residence	4.8%
Investment/Business	3.1%
Family: Parents/Children	4.6%
Family: Spouse	9.4%
Other (i.e. refugee etc)	1.0%

Survey findings

New Zealand's attractions

To investigate why the respondents immigrated to and stayed in New Zealand are necessary questions in this survey, because it would be meaningless to try to chart migrants' trans-Tasman and/or further movement intentions without understanding how and why the initial immigration took place. Therefore, the survey asked for reasons from those 393 "settler" respondents who chose to immigrate to and to stay in New Zealand. Answers for such question can be used as an indicative comparative parameter against why some respondents who chose to re-migrate to a third destination and who chose to return to the homeland – China. The two major reasons for those 393 "settler" respondents to immigrate to New Zealand and stay were: 1) "I feel more comfortable in NZ" (57 per cent), and/or 2) "I like NZ's social and natural environment" (58 per cent) (Figure 6.2). While the economic factor ("I can earn more in NZ") was ranked third at 21 per cent, of the 70 people who chose "other" and gave specific reasons, 21 of the answers, including "lifestyle", "children's education", "safer", "give parents a good living environment", and "NZ is beautiful", can be categorised and placed within reasons 1) or 2) above (see Figure 6.2).

Other major reasons given by those 70 people who chose "other" included "waiting for permanent Returning Resident's visa", "waiting for passport to go to Australia or other places", "further education", "gain experience to facilitate future movement", and "scared of returning to China where competition is fierce". These answers show a strong tendency of leaving New Zealand to move to other places, including moving to Australia. They show that transnational movement was executed at a specific time to suit either personal and/or the family's needs. Some reasons for "settler" respondents to choose to stay in New Zealand indeed illustrate this point. The specific time for some "settler" respondents to leave New Zealand was probably after they accumulated necessary social and human capitals, such as educational qualifications, work experience, and New Zealand residence or citizenship status. These social and human capitals potentially allowed them to forge a transnational migratory life. Many PRC migrants clocked their time to start transnational movements after obtaining New Zealand

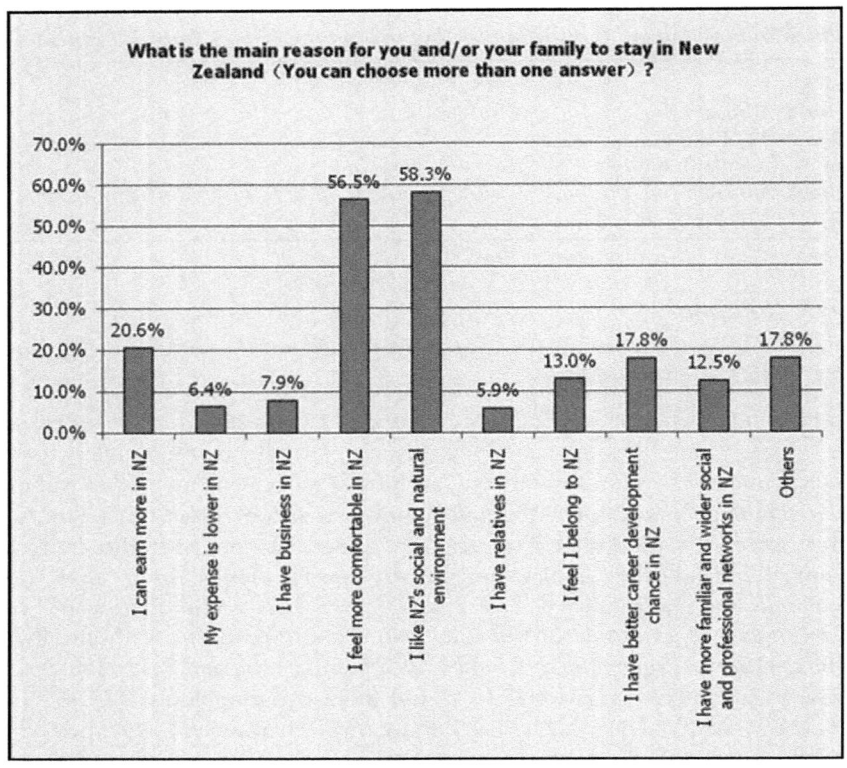

Figure 6.2 Main reasons to immigrate to and stay in New Zealand

permanent residence or citizenship or after obtaining a higher education degree and some New Zealand work experience. These answers indicate that strategic onward movements that many PRC migrants engaged in were often based on a rational assessment of whether their personal and family situation allowed them to proceed. More specifically, the kind of residential and citizenship status they held did determine the scope of their mobility in terms of cross-border travel. New Zealand citizenship allows them to go to many third countries without visa issue. New Zealand permanent residency ensure those who left New Zealand to go back to the homeland can travel freely between China and New Zealand at any time they want without visa issue. New Zealand qualifications and work experience are valuable credentials for those who are ambitious to compete in the international job market.

These answers also suggest that respondents' current stay in New Zealand is largely utilitarian and temporary. Once they reach these utilitarian goals, they might leave New Zealand. Apparently, such reasons as "waiting for passport to go

Australia", "further education", and "gain experience to facilitate future move-ment" indicate that staying in New Zealand may only be a transitional stage to be well prepared to leave and re-locate somewhere else. These utilitarian reasons suggest a time-consuming process of capital accumulation, which is necessary and prepares the PRC migrants to pursue further movement. Therefore, for some respondents, settling down in New Zealand for a while is their strategy. Once they have obtained enough human capital, they will be on the move. This finding confirms certain points suggested by other scholars that New Zealand is more likely a destination for short-term or mid-term immigration settlement than it is for long-term settlement (Bedford et al., 2000).

More strikingly, these results show that economic consideration is not the most important reason for PRC migrants to stay in New Zealand. They place lifestyle choice high but economic and career development factors are still important con-siderations. Interestingly, almost 13 per cent of the respondents picked "I have more familiar and wider social and professional networks in NZ". This result may be because quite a large proportion of respondents came to New Zealand as students when they were young and then developed their social and professional networks in New Zealand. This focus is obviously different than that of those older and mature migrants who came to New Zealand in their late twenties, whose main social and professional networks remained still in China. This find-ing may also explain why some of the respondents indicated they were "scared of returning to China where competition is fierce" and "I have no idea what I can do back in China", because they have very limited network of their own in China. Owning a business and/or having family/relatives in New Zealand were also reasons for some respondents to stay in New Zealand, but that reason was only important to a small proportion (about 8 per cent and 6 per cent, respectively, see Figure 6.2).

The pull factor from a third destination

When examining the trans-Tasman migration, one should understand that mov-ing to Australia after immigrating to New Zealand is one of many choices that the PRC migrants have to step into a third immigration destination. Therefore, the PRC migrants' trans-Tasman migration should be viewed within the wider context of the transnational migratory mobility. Out of the 477 respondents, there are 45 "transnational" respondents who left New Zealand to move to a third country, and the majority of them were now in Australia (82 per cent, 37), and the remaining group were located in the USA (8.9 per cent, 4), Canada (4.4 per cent, 2), and Taiwan (4.4 per cent, 2). The highest rated reason for them to leave New Zealand to a third destination was "there are more and better oppor-tunities for my career development there" (69 per cent, Figure 6.3). Another major reason with a 38 per cent selection rate was "I can earn more here than in New Zealand". The third major reason was "I could not find a satisfactory job in New Zealand" (27 per cent). Other reasons were relatively minor, all having less than 20 per cent selection. Also, six respondents gave different reasons, such as

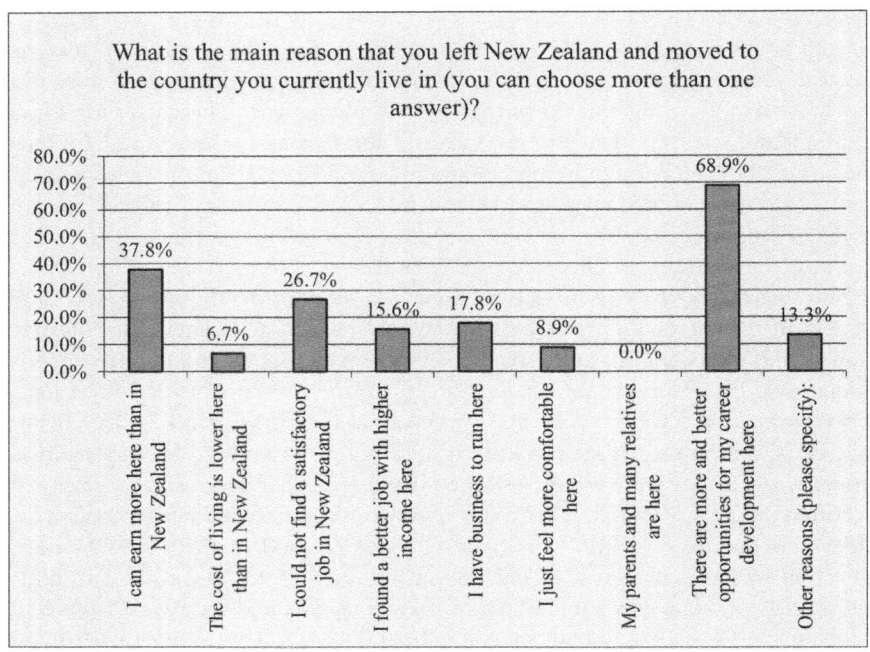

Figure 6.3 Main reasons to leave New Zealand and step into a third destination

"close to USA", "for study", "better weather here than in New Zealand", "for children's education", "reunion with family", and "self- expatriation because of separation (broken marriage)".

It is interesting to compare the respondents who stepped into a third destination with those who returned to China after several-year staying in New Zealand. The comparison shows that the percentage of respondents who indicated that the reason for them to leave New Zealand to enter another country is for "more and better opportunities for my career development" was almost identical to those who returned to China who chose the same reason (see Figure 6.4). For the majority of both "returnee" and "transnational" groups, the reason for them to leave New Zealand is exactly the same, namely to advance career development where their human and financial capitals can be maximised. The difference however, is the choice of a place to relocate. One group choose the homeland as their place of relocation, and another group choose a third country to move to. These results from the "returnee" group and the group who re-migrated to a third country firmly point to the reason for many PRC migrants to leave New Zealand being largely economically related.

Results from further survey questions about these respondents' employ status and income confirm that the employment situation and income profile for

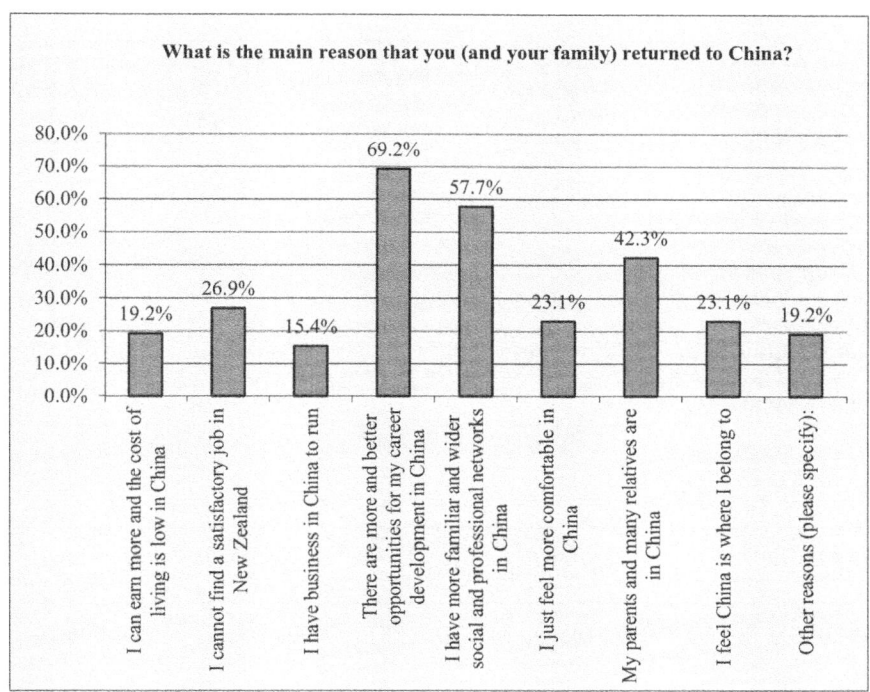

Figure 6.4 Main reasons to leave New Zealand and return to China

"transnational" respondents improved greatly after they moved away from New Zealand. Taking a close look at the unemployment rates before and after leaving New Zealand, the different is apparent. The unemployment rate for this group of respondents before leaving New Zealand was 15.6 per cent, but after moving to a third country the unemployment rate was 0 (see Table 6.8).

As for the income profile of the "transnational" respondents, the percentage of them earning more than NZ$70,000 per year significantly increased from 8.8 per cent to 37.7 per cent after they left New Zealand for a third destination while the percentage of them earning between NZ$10,001–25,000 per year decreased dramatically from 28.8 per cent to 8.8 per cent (see Table 6.9). As living costs in Australia, the US, and Canada are not very different from New Zealand, such increased net-earnings may have been a reason for those "transnationals" to move to the current country to work and live. All these factors correlate well with the argument made before that economical consideration is an important factor to contribute to the decision to move to another country.

Further question which asked about when those "transnational" respondents made the plan to leave New Zealand and to move to Australia or other countries, 62 per cent of them indicated that further movement they took or planned

Table 6.8 Employment status of the "transnational" respondents at different times and locations

Employment Status	"Trans-nationals" in NZ before moving away (n = 45)	"Trans-nationals" in third country after moving (n = 45)
Employee	57.8%	60.0%
Employer	11.1%	24.4%
Self-employed without employees	4.4%	6.7%
Unpaid family worker	0.0%	0.0%
Un-employed	**15.6%**	0.0%
In school	6.7%	0.0%
Not in labour force (housewife or retired person etc)	4.4%	8.9%

Table 6.9 Annual income profile for "transnational" respondents

Annual Income	Below NZ$10,000	NZ$10,001–25,000	NZ$$25,001–70,000	Over NZ$70,000
"Transnationals" in NZ before moving away (*n* = 45)	8.9%	28.8%	53.3%	8.8%
"Transnationals" in the third country (*n* = 45)	2.2%	8.8%	51.1%	**37.7%**

was not deliberately made before they immigrated to New Zealand; rather, such plan of further movements was made after they arrived and live in New Zealand for a while. These statistics contrast to the prevalent assumption of "back-door" migration that many Asian migrants made the deliberate plan to use New Zealand as a "revolving door" or a "stepping stone" to Australia (Rapson, 1998, p. 56) ahead of their migration to New Zealand.

The trans-Tasman intentions

The survey shows that the trans-Tasman intention is great among the PRC migrants. This is particularly evidenced when one takes a close look at the "settler" respondent group. The questionnaire asked about their short-term further movement plan. The actual question is "Do you plan to go to another country to live or work"? The "settler" respondents showed a great immediate further movement (going to a third country) intention. Of the 393 "settler" respondents, more than half of the respondents had plans to go to another country to live and work (see Table 6.10). Among those respondents who had plans to go

Table 6.10 Short-term future movement intention of the "settler" respondents (*Question: Do you plan to go to another country to live or work?*)

Short-term Further/Future Movement Intention	Response
Respondents who do **not** have plans to go to another country to live and work.	48.6%
Respondents who **do** have plans to go to another country to live and work.	51.4%
Top destinations for those who plan to go to a third country (country with highest picks is first)	Australia, China, USA

Table 6.11 Short-term future movement intention of all groups of respondents (*Question: Do you plan to go to another country to live or work?*)

Further/Future Movement Intention	"Settlers" (n=393)	"Returnees" (n=26) ()	"Transnationals" (n=45)	"Commuters" (n=13)
Respondents who do **not** have plans to go to another country to live and work.	48.6%	73.1%	68.9%	61.5%
Respondents who **do** have plans to go to another country to live and work.	51.4%	26.9%*	31.1%**	38.5%
Top destinations for those who plan to go to a third country (country with highest picks is first)	Australia, USA, China	Australia, USA, Canada/ UK	USA, China	Australia, China, UK/USA

another country (202 out of 393 respondents), 48 per cent (97 respondents) indicated that they wanted to move to Australia, 26 per cent (53 respondents) would like to go back to China, and 19 per cent (38 respondents) wanted to go to US. Apparently, Australia is the most favourable destination for those PRC migrants, same as for those local born New Zealanders (Bedford et al., 2003).

A comparison between different surveyed groups showed some interesting patterns of further movement intentions. It can be found that the "settler" group had greater further movement (going to a third country) intention than that of the "returnee", "transnational", and "commuter" groups (see Table 6.11). However, the lower percentage of "returnees", "transnationals", and "commuters" who have no plans to move to another country in the immediate future should not be read in the way that these three respondent groups are less mobile than the "settlers"; rather, these three groups are already on track for transnational movement.

Back to New Zealand: a high possibility?

While there is an obvious intention of trans-Tasman migration among New Zealand's PRC migrants, the survey also found that the pulling effect of New Zealand's natural and social environment and lifestyle for those who moved to a third destination country or returned to the homeland is strong. About 22 per cent respondents who moved to Australia and nearly half of respondents who returned to China intended to go back to New Zealand to settle down in the future. More than 35 per cent of "settlers" indicated they would stay in New Zealand without any movement, while 38.5 per cent "commuters" wanted to settle down in New Zealand, either after a few years or after their retirement (see Table 6.12). Even though Australia, the US, and Canada have generally been considered by many PRC migrants as preferred immigration destination countries, the large number of respondents across all the respondent groups who indicated they would like to settle in New Zealand in the future is a clear evidence that New Zealand's environment and lifestyle is a significant attraction and draws many PRC migrants to settle in this country permanently. Especially for the "returnee" and "transnational" respondents, even though they did leave New Zealand to relocate to the homeland, Australia or another third country, a significant proportion still intended to return to New Zealand and settle down. This view may be due to the fact that they can compare countries in terms of living experiences. That

Table 6.12 The intended place and time-frame for respondent long-term settlement in the future (*Question: Where and when will you settle down permanently eventually?*)

Final Destination and Time-frame	"Settlers" (n=393)	"Returnee" (n=26)	"Transnational" (n=45)	"Commuters" (n=13)
I'll always stay in New Zealand	28.2%	N/A*	N/A	N/A
I'll always stay in China	N/A*	7.7%	N/A	N/A
I'll settle down here (the third country)	N/A	N/A	28.9%	N/A
China, after a few years	12.2%	N/A	6.7%	23.1%
I'll stay in China for a few years, but will return to New Zealand to live then	N/A	23.1%	N/A	N/A
New Zealand, after a few years	N/A	N/A	4.4%	15.4%
China, after my retirement	2.5%	0.0%	6.7%	0.0%
New Zealand, after my retirement	6.9%	23.1%	17.8%	23.1%
Don't know	37.7%	30.8%	28.9%	30.8%
Other plan (please specify):	12.5%	15.3%	6.7%	7.7%

(Note *: N/A or not applicable, which means the choice was not available for the group surveyed.)

opportunity may strengthen the attractiveness of New Zealand's natural living environment in their minds.

It also should be noted that the percentage of "unknown" selection was high (38 per cent). These relatively high percentages of respondents who were uncertain about their future movement reflected the existence of a strong transnational dimension among the respondents. It reveals the variety of transnational options that they have and that their transnational movements are not highly planned ahead of time but highly contingent on their changing situation.

A concluding comment

There are four important findings from the statistical analysis and questionnaire survey. First, compared with the volume of New Zealand local-born citizens, the trans-Tasman migration of China-born New Zealand citizens is not large in number. The number of Chinese trans-Tasman migrants is even lower than migrants born in Indian and South African, despite that Chinese migrant population is higher than Indian and South African (Statistics New Zealand, 2014). Therefore, it is fair to say that the stereotyping of Asian "back door" migration creates a false impression in the public media in the early 2000s.

Second, it can be found that Australia's change in policy of controlling the access of social security benefits for New Zealand citizens did have an immediate impact on the trans-Tasman migration to Australia. Chinese migrants from the PRC were inevitably influenced by this policy change. Clear evidence can be found from the detailed analysis of the PLT arrival and departure data on the PRC population. However, the influence was short-lived. Given the long-term existence of the trans-Tasman connection, one can conclude that Australia still remains to be a favoured destination for New Zealanders moving overseas.

Third, the online survey reveals that economic consideration was not the primary reason for the PRC migrants to choose to immigrate to and stay in New Zealand. Instead, some non-economic reasons, especially New Zealand's good social and natural environment, appeared to be the dominant reasons for their decisions to choose to move to and reside in New Zealand. However, economic-related reasons contributed significantly for those respondents who made the decision or plan to move to Australia or another third country, or return to China. The author argues that these economic and non-economic considerations in immigration and remigration are not contradictory. First, although the PRC migrants' motives for immigrating to New Zealand were primarily not economic, to secure employment with reasonable income in the new land was their preferred goal. Therefore, when they could not meet their basic economic needs, they would choose to leave and head to where the employment and business opportunities were more abundant. Trans-Tasman migration to Australia is just one of many PRC migrants' choices to re-locate to a preferable place to explore job/business opportunities or secure employment. Indeed, the onward movements of many PRC migrants do take place worldwide, depending on where opportunities are and how social networks are stretched. Moreover, those non-economic considerations in immigrating to New Zealand just reflect the fact that immigrating to New Zealand is a transitional stage for many PRC migrants. For many of them, immigrating to New Zealand and the later acquisition of New Zealand passport means that they can enjoy many benefits as New Zealand citizens, such as more free and convenient international travel to other countries without visa issue. They also can obtain New Zealand qualifications and work experience. All of these non-economic considerations are actually a good preparation for them to accumulate enough human capital towards the goal of moving to a more economically viable destination for career development, better income, or an overall well-being for their families. Although as the survey shows that leaving New Zealand for another country was rarely pre-meditated before actual immigration to New Zealand for most respondent, that movement was executed at a specific time to suit either personal and/or the family's needs.

Lastly and most importantly, this part of research reveals a circulatory feature of the PRC migrants' trans-Tasman migratory movements, as evidenced by the fact that a significant number of the "transnational" respondents indicated that they would come back to New Zealand in future. Bedford et al. (2003) pointed out that the long-term future of population flows between the two countries should not ever be read as a one-way movement. Migration back to New Zealand has always been an important part of the trans-Tasman migration system. The findings strongly confirm this point. Often, residing in New Zealand for a specific length of time is a capital accumulation process for many PRC migrants who do desire to pursue their further economic well-being. Once they have completed their human capital accumulation, they leave New Zealand to move to a third country with a larger economy that then enables them to make full use of their human capital and secure life savings quickly. In this sense, moving to Australia or another third country may not be the end point of these migrants' movement trajectories. In terms of seeking a desirable place for retirement or enjoyment of lifestyle, New Zealand is an ideal destination for many migrants. Therefore, after the life savings are secured, these migrants may move back to New Zealand for final settlement.

In addition, Australia and New Zealand have been two important competitors in the market for skilled migrants. The Integration of Immigrants Programme 2007–2012 conducted through collaboration of three New Zealand universities proposed the idea of "lifestyle migrants" and indicated that the most positive aspects of immigrating to New Zealand is lifestyle, climate, environment, education for children, and personal safety. However, one negative aspect is a clearly perceived lack of opportunity for career development (Spoonley, Meares, Ho, & Bedford, 2009). Comparatively, Australia remains a favourable destination in terms of advancing a career for many New Zealanders. For those who are struggling to find employment at home, the Australian labour market is an alternative well worth exploring. Hugo proposed the possibility that New Zealand and Australia might draw each country's advantages to establish joint activities to attract skilled migrants, and especially in harmonisation of regulations and processes relating to this movement. Remembering that 20 per cent of New Zealand's four million residents is living overseas, with more than 10 per cent (around 460,000 New Zealand citizens) living in Australia while Australia has a similar sized diasporic population, both of these two countries face similar situation in which they are experiencing a substantial emigration of the brightest and the best among their young people. However, these two countries have many shared values and interests in international migration, especially the integrated labour market of both countries might be an advantage for both countries to work together with respect to meeting shortages of skills. International migration, permanent or temporary, may be one of the strategies to meet these shortages would be part of this collaboration both in terms of encouraging trans-Tasman exchanges but also in recruitment of skilled migrants from elsewhere (Hugo, 2004).

Notes

1 On New Zealand's customs arrival and departure cards, there had been a birthplace question until 1987 when a very short-sighted and ill-advised decision was taken to remove this question. In 2000, the birthplace question was restored on the arrival and departure cards.
2 The criteria for being a respondent were: 1) one must be ethnic Chinese originally from the PRC; 2) one must be an adult over 20 years old; 3) one must have either New Zealand permanent residence or New Zealand citizenship.
3 With some funding support, survey advertisements and a website link were put on those newspapers and Internet websites. Two Chinese-language newspapers used to advertise the survey were The New Zealand Chinese Herald (先驅報) and Australian Chinese Daily (澳洲新報). One New Zealand-based Chinese-language website (www.skykiwi.com), two Australia-based websites (www.snowpear.com and www.ozchinese.com), and one North American-based website (www.6park.com) were all used to advertise. The choice of these websites was due to their popularity among the overseas Chinese community, especially new Chinese migrants who have Chinese language skills. With all these efforts, of the 1,575 responses, 477 were found to be complete and valid.
4 "Returnees" in this study refer to those Chinese who returned to China from New Zealand and now have had a long-term stay in China. "Settlers" refers to those Chinese who have had a prolonged stay in New Zealand without any significant absence. "Transnationals" refers to those Chinese with New Zealand permanent residence or citizenship who moved to a third destination, i.e. Australia, Canada, the US, etc. "Commuters" means those Chinese who travel between New Zealand and China frequently (at least twice a year).

References

Bedford, R., Callister, P., & Didham, R. (2010a). Arrivals, departures and net migration, 2001/02–2008/09. *New Zealand and International Migration, 22,* 50.
Bedford, R., Callister, P., & Didham, R. (2010b). Arrivals, departures and net migration, 2001/02–2008/09. In A. Trlin, P. Spoonley, & R. Bedford (Eds.), *New Zealand and International Migration: A Digest and Bibliography, Number 5* (pp. 50–103).
Bedford, R., Ho, E., & Hugo, G. (2003). Trans-Tasman migration in context: Recent flows of new New Zealanders revisited. *People and Place, 11*(4), 53–62.

Bedford, R., Ho, E., & Lidgard, J. (2000). *International Migration in New Zealand: Context, Components and Policy Issues* (Discussion Papers No. 37). Hamilton, New Zealand: Population Studies Centre, University of Waikato.

Bedford, R., Ho, E., & Lidgard, J. (2005). From Targets to outcomes: Immigration policy in New Zealand, 1996–2003. In A. Trlin, P. Spoonley, & N. Watts (Eds.), *New Zealand and International Migration: A Digest and Bibliography, Number 4* (Vol. 4, pp. 1–43). Palmerston North: Department of Sociology, Massey University.

Birrell, B., & Rapson, V. (2001). New Zealanders in Australia: The end of an era? *People and Place, 9*(1), 2–15.

Ho, E. (2003). Reluctant exiles or roaming transnationals? The Hong Kong Chinese in New Zealand. In M. Ip (Ed.), *Unfolding History, Evolving Identity: The Chinese in New Zealand* (pp. 165–184). Auckland: Auckland University Press.

Ho, E. (2005, Tuesday, October 18). *From Students to Residents: Policy Initiatives, Data Issues and Research Findings in New Zealand.* Symposium Conducted at the Meeting of the The 10th International Metropolis Conference's Workshop on International Students as Immigrants, Metropolitan Toronto Convention Centre, Toronto, Canada.

Hugo, G. (2004). Future immigration policy development in Australia and New Zealand. *New Zealand Population Review, 30*(1&2), 23–42.

Ip, M. (2006). Returnees and transnationals: Evolving identities of Chinese (PRC) immigrants in New Zealand. *Journal of Population Studies, 33,* 61–102.

Liu, L. (2011). New Zealand case sstudy of PRC transnational migration: Returnees and trans-Tasman migrants. In M. Ip (Ed.), *Transmigration and the New Chinese: Theories and Practices From the New Zealand Experience* (pp. 57–101). Hong Kong: The Centre of Asian Studies of the University of Hong Kong.

Poot, J. (2010). Trans-Tasman migration, transnationalism and economic development in Australasia. *Asian and Pacific Migration Journal, 19*(3), 319–342.

Poot, J., & Sanderson, L. (2007). Return and onward migration, attachment and travel of New Zealand migrants to Australia. *Journal Ekonomi Malaysia, 41,* 61–90.

Rapson, V. (1998). New Zealand's migration policy: A revolving door? *People and Place, 6*(4), 52–62.

Sanderson, L. (2009). International mobility of new migrants to Australia. *International Migration Review, 43*(2), 292–331.

Spoonley, P., Bedford, R., & Macpherson, C. (2003). Divided loyalties and fractured sovereignty: Transnationalism and the nation-state in Aotearoa/New Zealand. *Journal of Ethnic and Migration Studies, 29*(1), 27–46.

Spoonley, P., Meares, C., Ho, E., & Bedford, R. (2009). *Attracting, Supporting and Retaining Skilled Migrants: Experiences of Recently Arrived British and South African Migrants.* Symposium Conducted at the Meeting of the Rising Dragons, Soaring Bananas International Conference, University of Auckland, Auckland.

Statistics New Zealand. (2014). *2013 Census QuickStats About Culture and Identity – Birthplace and People Born Overseas.* Retrieved March 21, 2017 from www.stats.govt.nz/Census/2013-census/profile-and-summary-reports/quickstats-culture-identity/birthplace.aspx

7 Point of return – a quantitative data analysis from a comparative perspective

"Return migration" is an important manifestation of PRC migrants' transnational mobility (Liu, 2009, 2011). To convey the picture of return migration of the PRC migrants in New Zealand, this chapter takes an unconventional approach – that is through a quantitative comparison. The first section of this chapter is based on an analysis of New Zealand's Permanent and Long-term Travel (PLT) data. This section aims to compare the volume, pattern, and timing of returning to China and their associated reasons and social implications with return migration of New Zealand's other four major immigrant groups from the Asia-Pacific region (i.e. South Korea, Taiwan, India, and Pacific Island region including Fiji, Samoa, and Tonga). Through comparison, the distinct feature of return migration patterns of the PRC migrants can be revealed.

This part of research contributes to recent calls in return migration studies for more macro-level analysis and an integrated approach that can connect several related themes together to produce a broader picture of return migration (Oxfeld & Long, 2004). This approach to return migration has potential to illuminate the changing power relations between migrant-sending and receiving countries in the economic realm and associated positioning in the world migration system. These power relations and different positioning in the world migration system implicate various aspects of migration, return migration, re-migration, and circulatory migration. The most important point is that return migration contributes to emerging themes, such as how issues resulting from competing policies and the competition for skills in the global migration system play out at both the level of the migrant and of the state.

The second section of this chapter is based on the same online survey discussed in Chapter 6, to reveal some tangible economic linkages, including remittance, and financial and real-estate investment of the "returnee" respondents compared with that of the "settler", "transnational", and "commuter" respondents. These economic linkages are an important manifestation of their transnationalism.

Methodological notes

Methods used for the PLT data analysis

The PLT migration data, by age, sex, citizenship, country of birth, and destination, for the period April 2001 to April 2015, were obtained from Statistics New

Zealand (www.immigration.govt.nz/about-us/research-and-statistics/statistics). From the data the gross and net flows of people and direction of travel direction were derived for the targeted migrant groups. The final analysis results are listed in Table 7.1 and Table 7.2. The formation of Table 7.1 is based on Tables 1, 2, 3, 4, and 5 in Appendix 8, and Table 7.2 is based on Tables 6, 7, 8, 9, and 10 in Appendix 8. In both Table 7.1 and Table 7.2, each net gain/loss was derived from total number of people for a chosen country who arrived in New Zealand from their original country compared with the total number of people who left New Zealand to return to the same original country.

Apart from investigating the PRC returnee group, four other migrant groups, with or without New Zealand citizenship, were chosen for the purpose of comparison, including South Korean, Taiwanese, Indian, and Pacific Islanders (from Fiji/Tonga/Samoa). South Korea, India, and the three Pacific countries (Fiji, Tonga, and Samoa) are among the eight major source countries for New Zealand's immigrant intake (Bedford & Liu, 2013) and are in the same Asia-Pacific region as China and with which New Zealand has close ties (Brady, 2008). In addition, migrants from these countries include members of visible ethnic minority groups in New Zealand (in terms of both number and percentage in the total population). Therefore, these three immigrant groups form a perfect benchmark for comparison with the PRC Chinese migrants. Taiwan is also involved into this comparison. Although it is not among the eight major source countries, it is another major source of New Zealand's Chinese migrant intake, especially during the 1990s and early twenty-first century. It is also ranked as the 6th on the absentee list (see Appendix 1). Since Hong Kong is included in the PRC migrant population in the data of INZ, Taiwan offers a useful comparator to examine the uniqueness of the return migration pattern of New Zealand PRC Chinese migrants. Through this kind of comparison, similarities and/or distinctions of return migration patterns across major five immigrant groups can be shown.

In the following section, the analysis of the PLT data is considered from two perspectives: 1) comparison of the return migration patterns of the five chosen groups of migrants who have obtained New Zealand citizenship; and 2) comparison of the return migration patterns of the five chosen groups of migrants who have not obtained New Zealand citizenship but are holders of New Zealand permanent residence or other types of long-term or mid-term residence status, such as holders of Student Visa, Work Permit, Work to Residence Visa, Job Search Visa, and Working Holiday Visa. Although the traditional migrants in migration studies do not usually refer to people who have no permanent residence or citizenship of the immigrant-receiving country, the working term, "migrants", in this chapter include people who stay in New Zealand without permanent residence but with the long-term or mid-term temporary residence status. In the New Zealand Residence Programme (NZRP), there are two streams: 1) the Residence Streams and 2) the Temporary Streams. The Residence Streams refer to all immigration categories leading to permanent residence, including three sub-streams: 1) Skilled/Business Stream (including Skilled Category and Business Category); 2) Family Sponsorship Stream (including Dependent Children

Category, Spouse/Partner Category, Parent Category, Adult Child(ren) Category, and Sibling Category); and 3) International/Humanitarian Stream. The Temporary Streams, especially Student, Skilled Work, Work to Residence, Job Search, and Working Holiday schemes, provide people long-term and mid-term residence status. People with such temporary residence status are not considered as permanent residents in New Zealand for migration purposes, but are included as "usual residents in New Zealand"[1] if their stay is intended to be for 12 months or more when counted by the New Zealand Census.

The reason for including the long-term and mid-term temporary residence status into this quantitative data analysis is because in recent years, the revised Temporary Streams provides a platform for many usual residents who have an intention of permanent immigration to make their immigration applications on shore and to transit their temporary residence status to the status as permanent immigrants in New Zealand (Bedford, Ho, & Bedford, 2010). Since the human mobility patterns are undergoing tremendous change as part of increasing globalisation, along with the traditional routes that channel immigrants through permanent-based immigration categories, many states have started to explore other alternative and flexible pathways for potential immigrants. The traditional route intends to enforce a one-way selection of qualified immigrants; namely, a state government enforces selection criteria as to who can immigrate and who cannot. The flexible and innovative immigration legislation on the other hand provides a framework of diversifying the immigration routes and liberating a two-way choice for immigration. Potential immigrants arrive in a country with a temporary status first to live, travel or work, which gives them a chance to understand the local society and to make a rational choice as to whether they want to seek a more permanent-based residence status. This kind of innovation in immigration legislation also aims to remedy a country's short-term labour shortage in some specific industries or to obtain economic benefits from the tourism industry (Bedford et al., 2010).

In the case of New Zealand, the enforcement of the new Temporary Stream in 2009 is a part of the New Zealand government's plan of having an innovative immigration programme to deliver a comprehensive service to meet market needs and provide chances to further this country's economic development through promoting human mobility beyond the traditional routes. Apart from usual and direct routes to obtain permanent residence through the Residence Streams (such as applying for permanent residence under the Business or Skilled Categories), some non-conventional, transitional routes for permanent immigration emerge. Transitions from temporary permits to permanent residence have become increasingly popular routes to permanent residence (Bedford et al., 2010). The 2000s has been a decade when a range of pathways to residence in New Zealand was introduced, extended and became better known and understood within and outside the country. New Zealand official data shows that during the period 2003 to 2008, 69 per cent of the applicants approved for residence in all of the streams had held a temporary work permit during the year, 22 per cent a visitor's permit, and 9 per cent a student permit (Bedford et al., 2010).

In migration studies, people on these transitional pathways are increasingly form a component in an expanded conceptualisation of traditional "migrants", which traditionally only referred to people with the legal status as permanent residents along with people born in a different country who had been granted citizenship. During the last two decades, migration researchers and policy makers recognised that links between temporary movements and permanent immigration were very strong and that increasing numbers of migrants were moving from one type of permit to another when they reside in an immigrant-receiving country (Bedford et al., 2010). A better understanding of their experiences and behaviour necessitated a more integrated approach of the analysis on population movement which incorporated the growing importance of transitions to residence from temporary work, study, temporary family categories, or visits.

Methods of the online questionnaire survey

Since the Chapter 6 has already provided a general discussion of the online questionnaire survey, it is not necessary to repeat it again. However, some questions of this survey are designed to explore patterns of respondents' money transactions between country of origin and immigration destinations and places of their financial and real-estate investment (see Appendix 7).

Return migration for those with New Zealand citizenship

In this section I compare the returning migration pattern of the Chinese migrants with New Zealand citizenship with four other chosen groups of migrants who were born overseas, have migrated to New Zealand, and have lived there long enough to have been granted New Zealand citizenship during the period of April 2001 to April 2015. The final analysis results are listed in Table 7.1. The gain of 1,660 Chinese from China to New Zealand and loss of 612 Chinese who left New Zealand to return to China (predominantly in age groups 20–24 and 25–29) resulted in a net gain of 1,048 Chinese who had New Zealand citizenship but were born in China, from China to New Zealand (see Table 1 in Appendix 8).

The explanation for this phenomenon lies in the common trend that has been identified in transnational migration studies. People with greater economic resources and human capital are more likely to forge transnational linkages (Portes, 1999, 2001). Human capital includes the relatively young ages of people who have high levels of transnational mobility. Ip's (2000) study of Chinese transnational migrants in New Zealand also argues that the very qualities many Chinese migrants possess not only make them desirable migrants to New Zealand as "young, high-educated, highly trained professionals, technocrats and business entrepreneurs" (p. 8) but also make them desirable to other countries of further immigration, including the countries from which they emigrated. People aged between 20 and 29 are also a well-educated group who have finished their tertiary education, possess university qualifications and relevant working. Most importantly, people in this age combine an adventuring spirit and an ambition for

Table 7.1 Long term and permanent arrival and departure of New Zealand citizens who were born overseas, by age and place of origin, in the period from April 2001 to April 2015

Age	Net gain from China* to NZ	Net gain from Taiwan to NZ	Net gain from South Korea to NZ	Net gain from India to NZ	Net gain from Pacific Islands* to NZ
Under 5 years	303	87	53	47	145
5–9 Years	131	5	14	–25	208
10–14 Years	125	69	4	2	391
15–19 Years	100	47	–35	16	430
20–24 Years	–417	–302	–185	–34	156
25–29 Years	–194	–125	–51	–29	115
30–34 Years	138	65	10	–105	114
35–39 Years	192	40	13	–91	63
40–44 Years	240	23	4	–14	75
45–49 Years	183	21	–18	–17	63
50–54 Years	91	42	–12	–6	54
55–59 Years	57	85	–12	–7	78
60–64 Years	57	125	5	9	100
65–69 Years	10	33	4	8	–16
70–74 Years	18	15	–2	–10	36
75–79 Years	9	10	4	5	24
80–84 Years	6	7	0	4	16
85–89 Years	–1	–1	0	–2	–1
90–94 Years	0	0	0	0	3
95 Years and Over	0	0	0	0	–1
Total	1,048	246	–204	–249	2,053

(Note *: China = included the Mainland and Hong Kong, Pacific Islands = Fiji/Tonga/Samoa)

career advancement. Going overseas is a popular option to accelerate their career development and to accumulate professional credentials and economic capital for financial security. Overseas work experience is a bonus. In addition, this group of people have fewer family obligations tying them to one locality; allowing this group of migrants greater mobility. Their decision to return to China is also driven by the strong pull-factor of "China rising" (Li, Sleigh, & Nunes, 2008) and its associated huge demand for skilled professionals.

Four other migrant groups from the Asia-Pacific region with similar or different homeland conditions were also analysed. It can be observed that Taiwan has a similar pattern to China with a net gain of 246 people, the largest net loss of migrants from New Zealand to Taiwan is in the 20–29 age group (427), but a 674 gain of migrants in other age groups (except group of 85–89). The similarity of the age structure here with that seen in the China flows is related to the similar economic drivers for young Taiwanese migrants returning to their homeland. From the 1990s to the early twenty-first century, Taiwan was viewed as a member of the group of "Four Asian Dragons" (also known as the "Four Asian Tigers" comprising of Taiwan, Korea, Singapore, and Hong Kong) – the four developed economies in Asia with an exceptionally high growth rates and rapid industrialization. While the economy of Taiwan slowed down because of the 1997 financial crisis in Asia and 2008 global financial crisis, the legacy of being a member of the "Four Asian Dragons" remains. This plus Taiwan's recent re-engagement with China in the economic sector drives Taiwan's recovery from that financial crisis and continuous economic prosperity (The Economist, 2015). For many young migrants from Taiwan, returning to their homeland is about riding the wave of the stunning economic growth of the "Greater China" region offering a more vibrant labour market for better employment and business opportunities.

South Korea is another significant migrant source country for New Zealand from the East Asian region. The 2013 Census counted 30,171 people of Korean ethnicity usually resident in New Zealand, of who 26,171 were migrants born in Republic of Korea (Statistics New Zealand, 2014). Compared with the overall net gain of Taiwanese and PRC migrants, Table 7.1 shows that New Zealand does not have a net gain of Korean migrants with New Zealand citizenship. However, Korean migration flows are a more recent feature of New Zealand population dynamics than PRC migration, and it takes time to grow a New Zealand-citizen migrant population. During this period, New Zealand lost 204 New Zealand-citizen Korean migrants than it gained. The age profile of return migration among the Koreans is very different from that of China and Taiwan. Unlike Taiwan and China where the net loss of migrants from New Zealand only occurs in two age groups (20–24 and 25–29), the net loss of Korean migrants occurs across many age groups, including younger groups such as groups aged 15–19, 20–24, and 25–29, and older groups such as groups aged 45–49, 50–54, 55–59 and 70–74. The 20–24 age group had the biggest volume of returning migration with a 185 net loss to Korea, followed by the 25–29 age group with 51 net loss and the 15–19 age group with 35 net loss.

India is the source of another sizeable Asian migrant group in New Zealand (Statistics New Zealand, 2014), however the Indian migrants' return migration patterns are very different from their PRC and Taiwanese counterparts, but share many similarities with the Koreans. First, rather than having a net gain of migrants, New Zealand has the net loss of migrants to both South Korea (204) and India (249). Second, the age profile of return migration among Indian migrants is similar to that of Korean migrants, but different from the Taiwanese and the PRC migrant groups. Return migration rate is high among only two age groups (groups aged 20–24 and 25–29) for the PRC and Taiwanese migrant groups. However, the net loss of the Indian migrants to India and the net loss of the Korean migrants to Korea are seen across many age groups, with losses for all age groups 5–9, 15–59, and 70–89. Indian migrants aged between 30–39 forms the biggest contributor to the return migration volume (196 net outflow to India for the group aged 30–39) (see Table 7.1). The age profile of return migration is slightly older than that of the PRC and Taiwanese migrants, but part of the underlying reason is economically driven. Comparable with China and Taiwan's economic boom, India is another rapidly growing economy in the

Asian region (Zhao, 2013). India's economic performance, especially in the tele-communication industry (Xiang, 2004, 2006), creates numerous opportunities for more experienced and skilled Indians for high- and senior-level employment or personal advancement, and draws them back to their home country. As these senior and skilful Indian returnees are more experienced through years of work-ing, they are therefore naturally older.

One of the key factors in this difference is the relative sizes of the receiving and sending pools of potential migrants: there are relatively more New Zealand citizens born in India living in New Zealand than there are living in India. This is a factor that needs to be considered with all the flows discussed here, especially with respect to the Pacific countries. Apart from the return migration patterns, one can find that there is a large contrast between the overall number of the return movement of the New Zealand-citizen India-born migrants (1,052) com-pared with that of the New Zealand-citizen PRC-born migrants (3,084) (see Table 1 and Table 4 in Appendix 8). Considering that the overseas-born Indian population (67,171) is the second largest Asian migrant group in New Zealand, which closely follows the PRC-born Chinese population (89,121) (Statistics New Zealand, 2014), this is a large disparity.

The Pacific islands, represented here by Fiji, Tonga, and Samoa, have very dif-ferent histories, population resources, and socio-economic potential. Almost all age groups show a net gain to New Zealand of New Zealand-citizen island-born migrants, with relatively small gross flows to their birth countries, even in the age group of 20–39 who might be assumed to exhibit greater transnational mobil-ity (see Table 7.1). This one-way migratory traffic is closely associated with the economic status of these South Pacific island nations and the cost of travel. These countries have relatively undeveloped economies and smaller markets compared with New Zealand. They are also typical "remittance societies" (Barber, 2000) which heavily depend on overseas remittances generated by its diaspora in much more developed economies to support the backbone of the national economy and transformation of the local development (Vertovec, 2004). The migrant's families living in their homelands also depend on the remittances to improve their living standard (Brown, 1994, 1995). Migrants from these remittance societies have to work mainly in richer migrant-receiving countries to make their living and have less inclination and ability to return for extended periods to their home-lands, which offer very limited opportunity for personal economic advancement.

Return migration of those without New Zealand citizenship

In this section I compare the New Zealand-citizen flows with those who have not been granted New Zealand citizenship during the period of April 2001 to April 2015. The final analysis results are listed in Table 7.2. For those PRC Chi-nese without New Zealand citizenship, the return movement pattern is different from those with New Zealand citizenship (see Table 7.2 and Table 7.1). In the following, these PRC Chinese without New Zealand citizenship are referred to

Table 7.2 Long term and permanent arrival and departure of migrants who were born overseas and without New Zealand citizenship, by age and place of origin, from April 2001 to April 2015

Age	Net gain from China* to NZ	Net gain from Taiwan to NZ	Net gain from South Korea to NZ	Net gain from India to NZ	Net gain from Pacific Islands* to NZ
Under 5 years	1668	75	348	2908	3934
5–9 Years	1974	147	422	2314	3818
10–14 Years	3563	471	–279	1927	3910
15–19 Years	27532	653	44	10488	6153
20–24 Years	16761	462	1966	24106	4268
25–29 Years	2233	1556	904	12947	4274
30–34 Years	4976	353	203	6053	3293
35–39 Years	4717	171	51	3284	2573
40–44 Years	3328	311	92	1960	2229
45–49 Years	1755	246	–18	1254	1122
50–54 Years	1379	193	–27	897	54
55–59 Years	2573	118	106	868	659
60–64 Years	2573	96	91	922	634
65–69 Years	1565	40	87	625	383
70–74 Years	903	20	64	357	207
75–79 Years	325	18	22	201	37
80–84 Years	72	12	–8	54	3
85–89 Years	7	1	–4	11	–13
90–94 Years	5	1	–1	3	–11
95 Years and Over	1	0	1	0	3
Total	77910	4944	4064	71179	37476

(Note *: China = included the Mainland and Hong Kong, Pacific Islands = Fiji/Tonga/Samoa)

as "PRC residents" of New Zealand. The flow direction is mainly from China to New Zealand. New Zealand has the 77,910 net gain of this group of migrants during the indicated period, and there is no net loss of the PRC migrants to China across all age groups, even in the age group of 20–39 who in theory should have high return or transnational movement mobility. This trend is actually not surprising given the fact that New Zealand is taking in both a large number of Chinese international students[2] (New Zealand Herald, 2015) and of skilled and business migrants as permanent residents. Moreover, the recent innovations of the range of transitional pathways to permanent residence that have been discussed in the "Methodological notes" also drive this one-way inflow.

Migrants from Taiwan without New Zealand citizenship, unlike those New Zealand citizens born in Taiwan and China, show no strong return migration trend (see Table 7.2 and Table 7.1). In all age groups, the flow is from Taiwan to New Zealand, which means New Zealand has a net gain of people with Taiwan citizenship in all age groups. One possible driver for males to migrate at a young age and to remain overseas may be related to the desire to avoid compulsory military service in Taiwan. Taiwan allows for dual citizenship, and Taiwanese aged between 18 and 22 with both Taiwan and foreign passports are required to be enlisted for one-year military services (Chiang, 2011).

As with migration flows of New Zealand citizens born in Fiji/Tonga/Samoa, the non-New Zealand-citizen permanent, long-term, and mid-term residents from these three Pacific Island countries predominantly form one-way traffic – that is from those Pacific islands towards New Zealand. Return migration rate is minimal (9,974) compared with the significant immigration inflow to New Zealand across all age groups (47,450; see Table 8 in Appendix 8), which results in a net gain of 37,474 to New Zealand over the period of this study (see Table 7.2). Again, this reflects the economic status of these Pacific countries as "remittance societies" (Barber, 2000; Brown, 1994, 1995).

Flows of permanent, long-term, and mid-term residents without New Zealand citizenship from India, also tend to be dominated by flows from India to New Zealand across all age groups, with a net gain of this group of Indian residents to New Zealand across all age groups (see Table 7.2). This migration flow is in line with the Pacific Islanders included in this study, but different from Indian migrants with New Zealand citizenship whose number of PLT departing New Zealand (1,052) is much larger than the number of PLT arriving in New Zealand (803) (see Table 4 in Appendix 8). And as in the case of the New Zealand citizen flows, the relative sizes of the sending and receiving country pools of potential migrants in this category has a bearing on the net flows.

There is a similar pattern with the South Korean migrants. Unlike the South Koreans with New Zealand citizenship whose number of PLT departures (866) is greater than arrivals (662) (see Table 3 in Appendix 8), the general flow of the South Korean residents in New Zealand without New Zealand citizenship is from South Korea to New Zealand, resulting in an overall net gain of South Korean migrants to New Zealand (4,064, the result of 25,446 arrivals and 21,382 departures) (see Table 7.2 and Table 10 in Appendix 8). Although there is a net immigration gain from South Korea for New Zealand, loss of South Korean migrants from New Zealand to South Korea is observed in the groups of 10–14, 45–49, 50–54, 80–84, 85–89, and 90–94. Nevertheless, even for these groups, while the number of PLT departing New Zealand does exceed those leaving for these age groups, the net represents the difference between large flows and are predominantly in the secondary school ages and the age groups where one would expect to find their care-giver parents and grand-parents. Among these groups, the aged-patterned return migration is different from that of the South Korean migrants with New Zealand citizenship. For the South Korean return migrants with New Zealand citizenship, the top three age groups were 20–24 (with 267 departures to Korea), 25–29 (with 205 departures), and 45–49 (with 64 departures). The ranking of the age groups of 20–24 and 25–29 as the top two groups with large returning migration volume compares with the age pattern of the return migration among the PRC, Taiwan and Indian migrants with New Zealand citizenship. This is to say that people in their twenties and thirties are the most sought after group in their homeland labour market, which offers great work and business opportunities for returnees.

Military service requirements, commented on with regard to Taiwanese citizens, may also play some part in the migration pattern of Koreans, at least for males. In the case of Koreans, the acquisition of New Zealand citizenship does make a difference to military service obligations. This may affect the return migration pattern of Koreans with New Zealand citizenship compared with Koreans without New Zealand citizenship. Korea does not generally allow dual citizenship, and compulsory military service applies to the male Korean citizens aged between 18 and 35. This is to say that Korean migrants with New Zealand citizenship who are in this age range are not subject to the military services. This institutional regulation provides those Korean migrants with New Zealand citizenship confidence to return to the homeland without worrying about the obligation of military services. This fact may explain the weak return migration trend among Koreans without New Zealand passport in the 20–39 age group, which is subject to military service, when we would expect the economic and social drivers to generate much higher return migration. In other age groups which are not subject to the military services there is high return migration, suggesting that the state's institutional regulation is affecting return migration.

The significant volume of return migration in the age group of 10–14 is particularly interesting but hard to interpret. One reason is perhaps educationally related. South Korean parents might choose to send their children back to South Korea to study in a Korean language environment, especially if they have been in the New Zealand school system and have acquired a high level of skill in English. This age group equates to the early secondary school years. The net loss of Koreans in the age groups of 45–49 and 50–54 are likely to, as noted above, to include the care-givers of these children, but will also include those moving to new careers or preparing for retirement in familiar surroundings after a period of time of staying in New Zealand. For people in these two age groups, the process of returning to South Korea would be easier since their children, if returning with them, are likely to be approaching adulthood and increasingly independent. There is a small net loss of Korean migrants who are aged 80 years and over. As with return migration to other countries, ageing among migrant populations is complicated, especially for transnationals (Heikkinen & Lumme-Sandt, 2013), and may involve return home. For South Koreans, this is often related to the strong cultural tradition of returning to one's cultural roots before death, a factor that also influences return migration for people born in the Pacific who become terminally ill (Blakely, Richardson, Young, Callister, & Didham, 2009)

Cross-border investment and financial transactions in comparison

The location of respondents' choice of placing their finance and property investments is an important parameter that can reflect their transnational linkage with different places. Table 7.3 offers such information. As shown in the table, the

Table 7.3 Financial and real estate investment of respondents in different countries

Investment types and in different locations	"Settlers" (n=393)	"Returnees" (n=26)	"Transnationals" (n=45)	"Commuters" (n=13)
Real estate property in NZ (% and average value)	43% $512,000	23% $306,000	22% $687,000	46% $725,000
Real estate property in China (% and average value)	46% $582,000	69% $1,795,000	36% $501,000	77% $300,000
Real estate property in a 3rd country (% and average value)	N/A	N/A	47% $669,000	N/A
Other forms of financial investment in NZ (% and average value)	15% $348,000	19% $600,000	11% $288,000	15% $500,000
Other forms of financial investment in China (% and average value)	24% $66,000	65% $494,000	31% $274,00	46% $467,000
Other forms of financial investment in a 3rd country (% and average value)	N/A	N/A	20% $518,000	N/A

percentage of "returnees" (23 per cent) and "transnationals" (22 per cent) who own property in New Zealand was significantly lower than for the "settlers" (43 per cent), which correlates with their current residence locations. However, since "returnees" and "transnationals" were not living in New Zealand, the rates of these two groups (23 per cent for "returnees" and 22 per cent for "transnationals") who owned properties in New Zealand is quite substantial. Strikingly for "returnees", "transnationals", and "commuters", the percentage who owned real estate properties in China was higher than the percentage having property in New Zealand. Overall, the percentage of respondents having properties in China was higher than for those in New Zealand, irrespective of their current locations.

As for other forms of investment, such as stocks and bonds, the percentage of respondents in all groups with investment in China was higher than in New Zealand, indicating a stronger financial interest in and connection with China than with New Zealand (see Table 7.3).

"Transnationals" are a unique group. Since they are in a third country, their transnational linkages spread across three countries: China, the homeland; New Zealand, the first immigration country; and the third country where they currently reside. The percentage of involvement in real estate investment for this group occurred in the order of: the country of current residence > China > New Zealand. For other forms of financial investment, however, the order becomes

Table 7.4 Money flow between countries

Money flow	"Settlers" (%) (n=393)	"Returnees" (%) (n=26)	"Transnationals" (%) (n=45)	"Commuters" (%) (n=13)
No money flow between countries	50.9%	65.4%	71.1%	30.8%
Mainly from China (or a third country) to New Zealand	41.0%	30.8%	8.9%	69.2%
Mainly from New Zealand to China (or a third country)	8.1%	3.8%	4.4%	0.0%
Other	0.0%	0.0%	15.6%	0.0%

China > the country of current residence > New Zealand (see Table 7.3). Obviously, financial involvement with New Zealand is the lowest among these three countries, and the financial linkage with China and current country of residence are stronger.

As for the money transaction between places, Table 7.4 shows that over 50 per cent of "returnee" respondents did not have money transactions between New Zealand and China. This is consistent with the "settler" and "transnational" respondents. For those respondents with money transactions between China and New Zealand, the money flow runs mainly from China to New Zealand. The percentage of people who have a money flow from China to New Zealand was greater than those with money flow from New Zealand to China across all four groups. "Settler" and "commuter" groups had particularly higher percentages (41 per cent and 69 per cent, respectively) of people who send money from China to New Zealand.

Detailed analysis shows that for all respondents with money transactions between China and New Zealand, most have occasional transactions, and very few have regular transactions. The reasons for these transactions are mainly family related, and business reasons are rare. For the "commuters", the high percentage who sends money from China to New Zealand is closely related to the "commuting" transnational strategy in which they engaged, which is one family member works in China to provide financial support to other family member(s) to live in New Zealand.

Detailed analysis also shows that for those respondents who transfer money from New Zealand or a third country to China, all of them are in the age band of 40–49. This small group of respondents represents a group of overseas PRC Chinese who left China in early 1990s. They are different from the most recent Chinese migrants who immigrated to Western countries after 2000 mainly for seeking a desirable place for retirement or enjoyment of lifestyle rather than economic prospects (Ip, 2006b). They are among a group of Chinese migrants who immigrated to overseas immediately after China's relaxation of its restrictive control over international migration in the early 1990s. Most of this group of migrants immigrated to overseas mainly for pursuing better income, receiving Western tertiary education, and job perspective in Western countries; and many of them went to the US and Japan, and a small proportion went to Australia and New Zealand (Xiang, 2003). They were also highly unlikely to be able to bring their parents to New Zealand because all of them were born before the enforcement of China's "one-child" policy and majority have siblings; therefore they were not qualified to be as the sponsors to bring their parents to New Zealand under the Family (Parents) category. Their money transactions from New Zealand or a third country to China are occasional, and the reason of such transactions is personal, mainly to show their financial support and filial piety to their parents during the time of their absence.

From this information, it is clear that the PRC migrants are bringing money and investment into New Zealand. The majority transacts money from China to New Zealand instead of remitting money back to the homeland. This trend of the money flow contrasts with that to immigrants of other developing countries. For example, Philippines and Caribbean nations are regarded as classic examples of a "remittance society" (Barber, 2000). Mexican migrants in the US sending regular remittances back to their villages is a well-known practice (Durand, Kandel, Parrado, & Massey, 1996). Closer to the New Zealand context is the example of the remittance flow of Pacific Islanders – another major transnational population in New Zealand. Their remittance flow pattern is similar to that of migrant groups from the Philippines and Latin American countries. The remittance flow is usually from the migrant receiving countries to their homelands where the economies are less developed. Relatives in their homelands depend on the remittances to improve their living standard (Brown, 1995). However, the new PRC migrants show a difference pattern to this more conventional trend.

This scenario also confirms to the middle-class status of many new PRC migrants and their families. Instead of remitting money back to China, the contemporary situation shows a reverse remittance transaction channel, from China to New Zealand to support migrant family members settling down in New Zealand. Such reverse remittance from China to New Zealand also testifies to the economic take-off of China in the last decade. Overseas remittances supported the backbone of the economy of many coastal home villages in China in the early twentieth century (Ip, 2006a), but that is no longer the case in contemporary PRC Chinese migration in the twenty-first century.

This survey took place just before the global financial crisis. The indication here is that New Zealand drew substantial capital from new PRC immigrants which might drive its economic growth. This may be one of the reasons (along with the increasing business development between New Zealand and China during the past decade) why New Zealand was less destructed by the global economic crisis compared with many other developed countries (Murphy, 2011).

This also reflects the fact that, as an immigrant-receiving country, New Zealand's economy may be influenced by migrants' overseas connections.

Comparison between different respondent groups shows that many PRC migrants are still keeping a relatively strong financial interest in China, in the form of real estate properties or financial investment, such as the China's stock market. This strong economic tie to China has the potential to draw more immigrants back to China to pursue their own economic welfare, whether long-term or short-term. The assets they keep in China also may make their homewards movement much easier as well. After all, this strong financial tie to the homeland is an important orientation in directing their decision-making regarding any future movement. On the other hand, the investment in China also has implication to New Zealand. Should those migrants decide to retire in New Zealand after earning sufficient money, those investments will become capitals or funds in New Zealand eventually, whose economy will benefit from that.

Discussion

In summary, there are four important findings that can be drawn from above analysis. The first and foremost is that a strong return migration trend for the PRC migrants with New Zealand citizenship. However, this strong return migration trend only affects a relative small percentage of all migrants, and mainly observed among those young people aged between 20 and 29. Return migration, even for this age group, does not dominant the migrant flow as a whole, with strong positive flows from China to New Zealand. While immigration to New Zealand as permanent residents contributes to the size of the migrant inflow, other Temporary Streams (such as Student Visa, Work Permit, Work to Residence Visa, Job Search Visa, and Working Holiday Visa) also contribute significantly to New Zealand's migrant inflows. Many PRC people arrive in New Zealand without permanent resident status, but later apply for permanent residence on shore. It seems that the new immigration legislation in 2009 works particularly well in terms of providing diversified routes to channel in potential migrants. Immigration resulting from this new legislation provides alternatives to return migration among the PRC Chinese. The same applies to Taiwanese, Indian, and Korean migrants without New Zealand citizenship. Two competing strategies in the global need to attract and retain skills can be seen. On the one hand, some traditional migrant-sending countries take advantage of their growing economic status to develop policies and incentives to attract their diasporic population back to the homelands. On the other hand, traditional immigrant-receiving countries, usually with developed economies, simultaneously develop innovative polices to retain their migrant population and proactively recruit potential new migrants.

Second, age structure of return migration (which is highest in the 20–29 year age group) among the PRC migrants is also observed in the three other major migrant source countries/regions from East and South Asia. Taiwanese migrants with New Zealand citizenship share exactly the same pattern as PRC migrants; Indian and Korean migrants with New Zealand citizenship also have a similar pattern in that young people are more likely to return to their home countries for extended periods or permanently. However, there are also some differences. For both Korean and Indian migrants, strong return migration trend appears not only among younger people in their twenties or thirties, but there is also a net loss to New Zealand across many other age groups. For Indian migrants with New Zealand citizenship, the biggest volume of return migration was found in the slightly older age groups (in the 30–39 age group rather than 20–29).

These differences are a significant reflection of relative success of different diasporic strategies in the context of the national economic scenarios in different migrant-sending countries. The distribution of return migration across various age groups among South Korean migrants may be linked with Korea's diaspora policy which provides a comprehensive package and generous allowance to facilitate successful re-settlement into Korean society (Lee, Friesen, & Kearns, 2015). In China, the development of a diaspora policy and strategy started to develop only in 1990s, which is rather late compared with Korea and even Taiwan. The famous "Hundred Talent Scheme" and "Thousand Talent Scheme" funded by the Chinese central government only started in 1994 and 2008 respectively, and these schemes only concentrate on attracting top-class scientists and engineers back to China. These policies tend to target older experienced people with established expertise. Strategies to attract younger returnee entrepreneurs and high-level professionals in private sector, especially those in high-tech and financial industries, only took place after 2000, and most of the high-tech industrial parks that especially target returnee entrepreneurs are initiated at the local government level (Zhu, 2013; Zweig, 2006).

Such recent returnee schemes only target a small number of relatively young returnees with world-class skills. This is perhaps one factor contributing to the large number of the PRC returnees among young age group of 20–29. Arguably, returnees in this age group are the most highly sought after candidates for work with foreign companies in China, with Chinese firms going global, and with private companies in innovative industries in the high-tech sector. The contemporary diasporic policies of China can be seen as an extended exertion of this country's modernity, rising international status, remarkable economic achievement, and ambition in foreign diplomacy. Along with China's changing labour market demands, in which the private sector, foreign investments, and joint ventures occupy a significant space, the young returnees with overseas qualifications and experience win themselves high status and are an important force in China's professional labour market and are in huge demand.

Third, among migrants from three Pacific Island countries, a strong return migration trend is not seen. This is so for both those with New Zealand citizenship and those without it. This is in stark contrast to migrants from the large growing economies, such as China, Taiwan, Korea, and India, where the homeland offers "an alternative adaptation path" (Portes, Guarnizo, & Landolt, 1999, p. 228) or the so-called "non-conventional pathway" (Portes et al., 1999) to economic survival and success. The conventional path largely relies on the degree and speed of migrant acculturation and integration into the mainstream society of the migrant-receiving country; however, the non-conventional path is cultivating strong social and economic networks across national borders to create a transnational social field in which economy security can be achieved, followed by a gradual lift in social status in the host society (Portes, 1999). The majority of the migrants from these three Pacific nations immigrated to New Zealand via special bilateral arrangements such as the Samoan Quota and the Pacific Access Category.[3] These special immigration categories provide much more relaxed and privileged assessment criteria for people from selected Pacific countries. These migrants are a part of migrants under the International/Humanitarian immigration scheme, which is designed to provide access for people from relatively disadvantaged economic backgrounds who would not be eligible under other categories, and include neither skilled nor business migrants. These migrants are also likely to lack the financial resources for continued mobility. Geo-politically, the economic conditions in their home countries do not offer an alternative adaptation path for immigrant survival and success, which consequently results in little incentive to move back to their homelands.

Last, the online survey found that transnational connections that respondents built up with their homeland – China – remained extremely strong. This is manifested when looking at respondents' cross-border financial activities, such as their cross-border financial transaction patterns and financial and property investment. Such strong economic ties with the homeland may mean on-going strong personal, social, and cultural connections with China. These strong connections with the homeland commonly existed among first-generation migrants and may be significant when orientating their personal future movement intention. The reverse direction of remittance transactions from China to New Zealand that many PRC migrants engaged is evidence that New Zealand can enjoy the strong economy of China via the PRC migrants who bring money from China into New Zealand's economy. These migrants can bring with them a substantial flow of capital and funds that sometimes can influence a country's economic prospect, especially smaller countries like New Zealand.

For example, many countries' housing price suffered significant decrease during the global economic downturn; however, the housing price in New Zealand was stable and even increased in the Auckland region. This is largely related to immigration because a large number of newly arrived wealthy immigrants increased the demand of housing, which drives the price of real estate (Murphy, 2011). In many countries, including New Zealand, immigration policy mainly focuses on economic benefits from migrants (Bedford, 2003). Given the fast growing economy of China, it is highly likely that people from the PRC will continuously and significantly contribute to the migration flow to New Zealand as skilled or business migrants, and these migrants and their families have so much to offer to New Zealand. Apart from the booming real estate industry, this survey found that remittances from New Zealand to China are not a usual practice among recent PRC migrants; rather, remittance flows are from immigration-sending country (i.e. China) to immigration-receiving country (i.e. New Zealand). This is another way that the PRC migrants can channel financial funds from China to New Zealand.

Notes

1 Everyone residing, or intending to reside, in New Zealand for 12 months or more is defined as "usual residents" by New Zealand Census. The census data records country of birth and ethnicities, but does not contain information on a person's citizenship(s).
2 International students are defined as "usual residents" in New Zealand because most of them intend to study in New Zealand for at least 12 months.
3 The Pacific Access Category allows up to 650 citizens from Fiji, Tuvalu, Kiribati, and Tonga to come to New Zealand as permanent residents each year, while the Samoa Quota offers 1,100 Samoan citizens permanent residence each year. The Pacific Access Category and Samoa Quota are run by ballot (www.immigration. govt.nz/employers/employ/lowerperm/pacific/). Once resident, these people can apply to bring other family members to New Zealand under the Family Sponsored and partnership streams.

References

Barber, P. G. (2000). Agency in Philippine women's labour migration and provisional diaspora. *Women's Studies International Forum, 23*(4), 399–411.
Bedford, R. (2003). *New Zealand: The Politicization of Immigration.* Retrieved December 9, 2012 from Migration policy Institute www.migrationinformation. org/profiles/display.cfm?ID=86
Bedford, R., Ho, E., & Bedford, C. E. (2010). Pathways to residence in New Zealand, 2003–2009. In A. Trlin, P. Spoonely., & R. Bedford (Eds.), *New Zealand International Migration. A Digest and Bibliography, Number 5* (pp. 1–49). Palmerston North, New Zealand: Massey University Printery.
Bedford, R., & Liu, L. (2013). Parents in New Zealand's family sponsorship policy: A preliminary assessment of the impact of the 2012 policy changes. *New Zealand Population Review, 39,* 25–49.
Blakely, T., Richardson, K., Young, J., Callister, P., & Didham, R. (2009). Does Mortality Vary Between Pacific Groups in New Zealand? Estimating Samoan, Cook Island Maori, Tongan, and Niuean Mortality Rates Using Hierarchical Bayesian Modelling. *The New Zealand Medical Journal,* ISSN 1175–8716. Retrieved from www.otago.ac.nz/wellington/otago024010.pdf
Brady, A. (2008). New Zealand-China relations: Common points and differences. *New Zealand Journal of Asian Studies, 10*(2), 1–20.
Brown, R. (1994). Migrants' remittances, savings and investment in the South Pacific. *International Labour Review, 133*(3), 347–367.
Brown, R. (1995). Hidden foreign exchange flows: Estimating unofficial remittances to Tonga and Western Samoa. *Asian and Pacific Migration Journal, 4*(1), 35–54.
Chiang, L. H. N. (2011). Return migration: The case of the 1.5 generation of Taiwanese in Canada and New Zealand. *China Review, 11*(2), 91–124.
Durand, J., Kandel, W., Parrado, E. A., & Massey, D. S. (1996). International migration and development in Mexican communities. *Demography, 33,* 249–264.
The Economist. (2015). *Taiwan's Economy: Straitened Circumstances.* Retrieved November 15, 2015 from www.economist.com/news/finance-and-economics/ 21678276-weaker-growth-exposes-downside-ties-china-straitened-circumstances
Heikkinen, S. J., & Lumme-Sandt, K. (2013). Transnational connections of later-life migrants. *Journal of Aging Studies, 27*(2), 198–206.

Ip, M. (2000). Beyond the 'settler' and 'astronaut' paradigms: A new approach to the study of new Chinese immigrants to New Zealand. In M. Ip, K. M. Kang, & S. Page (Eds.), *Migration and Travel Between Asia and New Zealand, Aotearoa/New Zealand Migration Research Network Research Paper* (pp. 3–17). Palmerston North: Department of Sociology, Massey University.

Ip, M. (2006a). New Zealand. In L. Pan (Ed.), *Encyclopedia of Chinese Overseas* (pp. 286–291). Singapore: Curzon.

Ip, M. (2006b). Returnees and transnationals: Evolving identities of Chinese (PRC) immigrants in New Zealand. *Journal of Population Studies, 33,* 61–102.

Lee, J. Y., Friesen, W., & Kearns, R. A. (2015). Return migration of 1.5 generation Korean New Zealanders: Short-term and long-term motives. *New Zealand Geographer, 71*(1), 34–44.

Li, G., Sleigh, A., & Nunes, F. (2008). China rising. *Outlook: The Journal of High-Performance Business.* Retrieved May 11, 2017 from www.criticaleye.com/insights-servfile.cfm?id=395

Liu, L. (2009). Home is calling? Or home is on the move? Return Chinese immigrants of New Zealand as transnationals. *New Zealand Journal of Asian Studies, 11*(2), 164–171.

Liu, L. (2011). New Zealand case study of PRC transnational migration: Returnees and trans-Tasman migrants. In M. Ip (Ed.), *Transmigration and the New Chinese: Theories and Practices From the New Zealand Experience* (pp. 57–101). Hong Kong: The Centre of Asian Studies of the University of Hong Kong.

Murphy, L. (2011). The global financial crisis and the Australian and New Zealand housing market. *Journal of Housing and the Built Environment, 26*(3), 335–351.

New Zealand Herald. (2015). *NZ Reputation at Risk From Indian Student Exploitation.* Retrieved November 21, 2015 from New Zealand Herald www.nzherald.co.nz/business/news/article.cfm?c_id=3&objectid=11548482

Oxfeld, E., & Long, L. D. (2004). Introduction: An ethnography of return. In L. D. Long & E. Oxfeld (Eds.), *Coming Home? Refugees, Migrants, and Those Who Stayed Behind* (pp. 1–15). Philadelphia: University of Pennsylvania Press.

Portes, A. (1999). Conclusion: Towards a new world – the origins and effects of transnational activities. *Ethnic and Racial Studies, 22*(2), 463–476.

Portes, A. (2001). Introduction: The debates and significance of immigrant transnationalism. *Global Networks, 1*(3), 181–194.

Portes, A., Guarnizo, L. E., & Landolt, P. (1999). The study of transnationalism: Pitfalls and promise of an emergent research field. *Ethnic and Racial Studies, 22*(2), 217–237.

Statistics New Zealand. (2014). *Census QuickStats About Culture and Identity – Asian Ethnic Group.* Retrieved December 1, 2016 from www.stats.govt.nz/Census/2013-census/profile-and-summary-reports/quickstats-culture-identity/asian.aspx

Vertovec, S. (2004). Migrant transnationalism and modes of transformation. *International Migration Review, 38*(3), 970–1001.

Xiang, B. (2003). Emigration from China: A sending country perspective. *International Migration, 41*(3), 21–48.

Xiang, B. (2004). Indian information technology professionals' world system: The nation and the transnation in individuals' migration strategies. In B. S. A. Yeoh & K. Willis (Eds.), *State/National/Transnation: Perspectives on Transnationalism in the Asia-Pacific* (pp. 161–178). London: Routledge.

Xiang, B. (2006). *'Body Shopping': An Indian International Labour System in the Information Technology Industry*. Princeton: Princeton University Press.

Zhao, H. (2013). China and India: The world is big enough for both. In G. Wang & Y. Zheng (Eds.), *China: Development and Governance* (pp. 415–422). Singapore: World Scientific Publishing.

Zhu, J. (2013). China attracting global top talent: Central and local government initiatives. In G. Wang & Y. Zheng (Eds.), *China: Development and Governance* (pp. 361–368). Singapore: World Scientific Publishing.

Zweig, D. (2006). Competing for talent: China's strategies to reverse the brain drain. *International Labour Review, 145,* 65–89.

8 "Local" or "Global"? – situating Chinese transnational migration in the world migration system and global modernity

In this final chapter, I first pull the qualitative and quantitative research together to draw major research findings. Based on the most significant findings of the research, this chapter offers summarising remarks about the recent trends of Chinese international migration and transnational migration, and a reflection of these new trends to the vastly changing global situation, and rethinks about notions like Chinese modernity, transnationalism, and globalisation. To summarise the major findings of this research, I offer five themes that have emerged within and across the different chapters from the compilation of the research effort: 1) the reasons and driving forces for PRC migrants to engage in transnational movements and cross-border migratory activities; 2) further movement intentions and plans for final settlement; 3) family influence/considerations in migration and re-migration; 4) transnational linkages and connections that PRC migrants build with China, New Zealand, and/or other countries to which they move; and 5) the interplay for how PRC migrants self- identify and conceptualise of the full notion of "home" and citizenship, and a sense of belonging.

Summary of major research findings: comparing the qualitative and quantitative research

Why "transnationals"? situating PRC transnational migration in the world migration system

This research shows that the transnational movements that many PRC migrants engage in are the result of a combination of personal/family-related reasons and macro-level economic-political driving forces. Both the qualitative interviews and the quantitative online survey reveal that even though many PRC migrants originally immigrated to New Zealand for non-economic considerations, economic-related reasons contributed significantly to the decision to engage in later cross-border movements. The patterns of PRC migrant transnational movements are varied and diverse, but the primary reason for such transnational movement is essentially economic. For example, "returnees" and "transnationals" both left New Zealand because of more and better career and business development opportunities in the homeland or a third country where the market was bigger, and the economy thriving. "Commuters" chose to work in China, but still made periodic visits to New Zealand where their families remained to enjoy New Zealand's lifestyle or advanced educational system and thus not compromising the family's overall economic well-being.

Behind these personal economic-related motivations were the dynamic geo-economic conditions of globalisation, which now places China and New Zealand in different quite positions in the world migration system. Beginning in the 1970s, the PRC government made a strategic decision to send Chinese scholars overseas for academic and scientific training with the expectation they would eventually return to China and make positive contributions to the homeland. This was also the period when the PRC started to loosen its restrictive border control over its nationals. Attracted by Western freedom, better work conditions and higher income, the liberation of the PRC's policy on travel overseas led to a massive increase in the number of people going overseas, and indeed many did return to China after their foreign training.

By the early 1990s, the PRC was an immigrant sending country in the world migration system, characterised by large emigration flows of students or young professionals to the developed West (Skeldon, 1996, 2004; Zweig, 1997). This large outflow of Chinese nationals to the developed West was often described as "brain drain" (Zweig, 1997) that let the developed countries rob valuable human talent and the best and brightest people from China. This large flow of Chinese to the West engendered both a counter flow of return migration to China and a large settlement of permanent residents in Western countries. The military assault in Tiananmen Square on 4 June 1989, increased the desire of overseas Chinese to stay in the West. However, from the mid- to late-1990s, the number of returnees started to increase; and since 2000, that rate of increase has risen sharply (Zweig, 1997, 2006). The recent fast-growing economy in China re-defines the country's position in the world migration system as a desired return destination for Chinese expatriates (Iredale, Guo, & Rozario, 2002; Luo, Guo, & Huang, 2003). The PLT data analysis presented in Chapter 7 has shown that there is a strong return migration trend among PRC migrants in New Zealand. This trend toward return migration flow has recently reversed the "brain drain" to a "brain gain" or even a "reverse brain drain" (Zweig, 1997, 2006).

The defining factor behind this position of the PRC in the world immigration system is mainly economic, but it is also political. Adding to a booming economic pull factor is the PRC central government's pro-active policies toward returning expatriates. Following the successful paths of the Republic of Korea and Taiwan where both thriving economies and liberalised polices turned "brain drains" into "brain gains", the Chinese government recognised that overseas PRC migrants did have the potential to contribute to their domestic economy, and introduced a series of policies and programmes to attract skilful Chinese expatriates and persuade them to return to the homeland (Zweig, 1997, 2006). In the context of PRC migrants to New Zealand, leaving New Zealand after several years of residence to return to China simply was a case of immigrants choosing to ride the tide of China's growing home economy.

As for New Zealand, an immigrant receiving country, the factors that attract immigrants are often not economic, but rather environmental, educational, and social. Especially for skilled migrants with economic ambitions, New Zealand might not be an immigration destination to pursue economic and career advancement. However, in terms of seeking a desirable place for retirement or enjoyment of lifestyle, New Zealand is the ideal destination for many migrants. The idea of "lifestyle migrants" (Spoonley, Meares, Ho, & Bedford, 2009) mentioned in Chapter 6 supports the argument made above for New Zealand's unique positioning in the world migration system.

The different positions of China and New Zealand in the world migration system then indicate that the residence of many PRC migrants in both countries is not permanent. Both the interviews and the survey results show that immigrating to New Zealand is a transitional stage for many PRC migrants in order to improve their social and economic situation and then move to a more preferable destination. Often, residing in New Zealand for a specific length of time to study or work is also a capital accumulation process for many PRC migrants who do desire to pursue their further economic well-being. Once they have completed their human capital accumulation, they leave New Zealand to return to China or move to a third country with a larger economy that then enables them to make full use of their human capital and secure life savings quickly. In this sense, returning to China may not be a permanent settling back to the homeland, and moving to a third country may not be the end point either for those PRC migrants to New Zealand. For many of them, after their life savings are secured, they may move back to New Zealand for retirement or final settlement. This part of finding coincides with the argument that recent Chinese "emigration is in fact a form of class-based consumption, a strategy for class reproduction, and a way to convert economic resources into social status and prestige" (Liu-Farrer, 2016, p. 499).

Apart from the economic factors that are motivating PRC migrants to engage in transnational movements, non-economic factors, such as family considerations, patriotic pride, cultural alienation from the host society, and emotional linkages to China, are also important motivating factors for returning or onward migration to another country. Both the interviews and the online survey conducted within the "returnee" group showed that family factors, especially the location of parents, do play a significant role in many PRC migrants' decision to return to China. This finding will be further elaborated on in the next section.

Mobility potential, further movements, and settlement intention

Another finding of this research is that PRC migrants possess great transnational mobility potential. Apart from an examination of PRC transnational migrant motivations behind the existing mobility patterns, this research particularly focused on investigating the long-term transnational intentions of PRC migrants. Both the qualitative interviews and the quantitative survey found strong evidence to indicate further movement for many PRC migrants are contingent on various factors. For example, a large number of "settlers" intend to leave New Zealand

and return to China or go to a third destination. For "returnees" or people who have moved to a third destination, return migration and step-migration does not mean permanent re-location in the homeland or even in a third country. Rather, many migrants continue to show their intention to undertake further movement.

Examining this general trend of on-going movement, this research found that the transnational mobility of PRC migrants is actually nuanced and often characterised by different patterns of movement, such as frequent commuting between the homeland and host countries, returning to the homeland, and relocating to a third country. The strong intention to return to New Zealand among "returnees" was seen in both the interviews and the online survey, and the so-called "double return" (Ley & Kobayashi, 2005) was particularly referred to and discussed in Chapter 4, revealing a circular migratory movement across the ocean, first from New Zealand to China for economic advancement, and then back to New Zealand for children's education or retirement. In the case of the "trans-Tasman" interviewees, although many of them regard the country in which they currently reside (i.e. Australia) as their residential "home" base, their intentions for either temporary and short-term re-location to China or another destination are also strong. Similar to the "returnees", some even plan to return to New Zealand in later years for retirement as shown in the online survey.

Family influence/considerations in migration and re-migration

This research also found that family factors play a significant role in motivating PRC migrant transnational movements. The online survey revealed a significant trend, namely, that a large number of respondents intend to engage in cross-border movements with their immediate family members. The qualitative interviews particularly demonstrated that, when necessary, many PRC migrant families are willing to take on family separation and multi-locational residences to satisfy and meet each family member's different needs as well as the general economic well-being of the entire family. A strong sense of family unity during these transnational movements, as engendered from the online survey responses and the courage and/or willingness to take on strategic family dispersal revealed in the in-depth interviews, are not mutually exclusive for understanding PRC migrant transnational movements within the family context. Both trends did show that family consideration is often the number one priority by PRC migrants in the decision-making process regarding transnational moves. The qualitative interviews in particular showed that their mobility patterns and transnational intentions for further movement are significantly affected by individual's family circumstances as well as specific socio-economic forces affecting the place of residence at any given time.

Different family structures and dynamics and individual family members' different needs at different life stages indeed do determine the particular strategic transnational arrangement of many migrant families. Consideration of certain family members, especially older parents and school-age children holds the key to such decision-making. Incorporated into an overall consideration of each family's collective well-being, family members will pursue divergent trajectories and locate in different countries as a "home" base to best suit personal circumstances. Decisions on re-location are often based on consideration of career development, maintenance of a family's financial well-being, children's educational needs, childcare support, and provision for aging parents. Therefore, strategic family separation, multi-locational residences and onward movement can take place. In any negotiation of family transnational plans, a balanced decision is made based on individual family members' personal needs and the family's overall well-being.

Such strategic plans for onward movement or multi-locational residence can also be seen from the survey results. There were two different trends regarding PRC migrants' timing of re-location. The first follows obtaining New Zealand qualifications or professional work experience, and the second follows securing a New Zealand permanent Returning Resident's Visa or citizenship. Both findings do indicate that strategic onward movement that many PRC migrants engage in is often taken based on a rational assessment of whether their own human and social capital is sufficient and will facilitate that smooth relocation.

Since every individual family's circumstance and structure does change constantly, the transnational migratory strategies that many PRC migrants have adopted also change based on circumstances. This finding means that what PRC transnational families seem to constantly undergo is an incessant cycle of family dispersal, translocality, and reunion. This cycle results in a constant change of "home" base for many PRC migrants. Sometimes the "home" base is the homeland, China, and sometimes the "home" base is in New Zealand or a third country. As argued before, since PRC migrants may have different "home" bases, "home" for them may be an emotional sense of longing for "home" or a sense of family unity that these migrants just carry with them when they move between their many different "home" bases.

Transnational linkages across borders

Both the interviews and the survey found that if the transnational connections of PRC migrants are based on just the physical linkages that migrants build up across borders, such as family networks, cross-border physical travel, or economic linkage, the transnational connection that PRC migrants establish with their homeland – China – is extremely strong. However, their connection with New Zealand appears to be relatively weak compared with their connection to China. For example, the interviews showed that less "trans-Tasman" interviewees intended to re-locate to New Zealand for short-term purposes, while more of the group did intend to make a temporary re-location to China. Such an intention of re-locating to China is clear evidence of their strong interest in building a close connection with the homeland, particularly a common phenomenon that exists pervasively in first-generation migrants. This strong connection to China is also evidenced by the substantial business connections that "returnees", "commuters", and some "trans-Tasman" interviewees established with China and their strong attachment to China as an emotional "home".

The online survey provides further evidence of the strong connection that many PRC migrants have with their country of origin. The online survey showed that all migrant groups have greater financial interest and/or stake in China than in New Zealand or a third country, in the form of property or other financial investments.

As discussed in Chapter 3, many kinds of transnational social connections that migrants established, such as emotional connections to certain places through memory, nostalgia, or imagination, may possibly exist without geographic movements and physical engagement (Levitt & Glick-Schiller, 2004). This research found that the scenario of transnational connections of PRC migrants with New Zealand becomes stronger if the above is taken into consideration. As I have pointed out in the last section, a large number of respondents across all four groups plan to return to New Zealand for retirement or final settlement. This intention of returning to New Zealand indirectly suggests that while PRC migrants keep a strong tie with China, their connections with New Zealand cannot be under-estimated. Interview findings particularly show that consideration of children's education and lifestyle are important driving forces for many PRC migrants to plan to come back to New Zealand. Based on such considerations, it can be said that many PRC migrants would like to or need to keep connections with New Zealand in order to secure a life-style option for the future.

Identity, sense of belonging, "home", and citizenship

In general, there is a strong sense of "being Chinese" among PRC transnational migrants. Regardless of whether they hold a New Zealand passport or not, the qualitative interviewees reveal that the claim of "being Chinese" is prevalent. Such strong identification derives from the strength of Chinese cultural influences, since most first-generation PRC adult migrants have grown up in China and been educated under the Chinese system. Other factors, such as the way migrants interact with the host society, China's rising international status and its growing profile as an emergent economic power, and the resurgence of overseas Chinese nationalism in recent years intensifies the sense of being Chinese.

There is an intriguing dynamic about the ways different respondent groups identify themselves. First, the strong identification as being Chinese among different respondent groups varies. Fewer "returnees" and "commuters" identify themselves as being Chinese compared with "settlers" in New Zealand and "transnationals" in a third immigration country. As well, more "returnees" and "commuters" claimed a hybrid identity (being both Chinese and New Zealander) compared with "settlers" and "transnationals". This interesting pattern suggests that external social factors, especially the way in which people envisage their social status in different social settings, play a decisive role in the self-identification as Chinese. The strong identification as being Chinese among "settler" and "transnational" groups correlates to their awareness of being ethnic immigrant minorities in a Western country. As this has been referred to in the interviews, the way that many mainstream New Zealanders perceived migrants as "different others" has significant impact on how Chinese migrants identify themselves. For "returnees" and "commuters", a hybrid identity involving being a New Zealander may provide social privileges in Chinese society; therefore, most of them intend to identify themselves as both Chinese and New Zealanders.

One salient part of this research also found that the strong identification as being Chinese among PRC migrants does not mean that they would strongly identify themselves as belonging to China. In many cases, research participants see themselves as Chinese, but perceive that they belong to their host countries, or to both the host countries and China. In many such cases, belonging to the host countries refers to migrants' physical presence and daily engagement in the country they reside in, while belonging to China refers more to their emotional belonging to their country of origin. In the interviews, this clear separation from interviewees' sense of identity and sense of belonging has been reflected by the way the interviewees conceptualised the notion of "home". Very often, interviewees could feel strongly Chinese but not necessarily see their "homes" as being in China. However, the interviews show that how PRC migrants perceive their sense of belonging to some extent is in line with the ways that they conceptualise the notion of "home" or the immediate communities around "home". Although many interviewees conceptualised their "home" as an emotional terrain, irrespective of where they physically live, some of them strongly felt that they belong to where their physical "homes" are or where their families' residential bases are. In many such cases, the family residential base was often referred to as their "home".

Another notable finding is that the citizenship that PRC migrants hold has no direct effect on how they identify themselves or their sense of belonging. For many of their newly acquired legal status as citizens of New Zealand or a third country is a means to use to engage in convenient, visa-free international travel and simply is social capital to help them reach a higher living standard or greater social status. This finding seriously challenges the dominant expectations of the immigrant-receiving country toward offering citizenship to immigrants. From the point of view of the government of an immigrant-receiving country, immigrants are expected to make a full commitment to the immigrant- receiving country. What this research shows, however, is that there can be a sense of belonging to New Zealand among many PRC migrants, but that sense of belonging does not originate from the legal status they gain from being New Zealand citizens or permanent residents; instead this sense of belonging to New Zealand relates more to social factors, such as how long they have settled in New Zealand, whether their immigration experience in New Zealand has been positive or negative, and even more importantly, how the New Zealand mainstream population/society perceives and interacts with them.

The implications: Chinese modernity, globalisation, transnationalism, and the world migration system

The mobility of the new PRC Chinese migrants reveals the economic, social, and political transformations that have occurred in both New Zealand and China.

On the one hand, the strength of the economic and political development in "Greater China" seems to place powerful strings on these migrants, pulling them back to Asia (Studwell, 2003; Wang, Wong, & Sun, 2006; Zeng & Williamson, 2003). This characteristic is not only witnessed in New Zealand, but also in other countries of immigration such as Canada, Australia, and the US (Hugo, 2005). On the other hand, New Zealand's economy "has turned about from a highly protected economy toward one of the most open market economies" (Lidgard, Bedford, & Ho, 1995, p. 16). It is characterised by extensive overseas linkages in addition to high export dependency, which has significantly impacted patterns of international migration, including Chinese migration. Moreover, the increasing competition for skilled migrants, often from much larger economies, will ensure that New Zealand remains relatively low on the list of priorities for potentially long-term high-skilled settlers. Short to medium-term residents will increasingly dominate its skilled immigrant flow (Bedford, Ho, & Lidgard, 2000).

The implications drawn by this study in the New Zealand context can be extended beyond New Zealand. The subject of this research – transnational PRC Chinese migrants from New Zealand – is an important component of "global citizens" in the modern world, and it is a great force that is actively participating in the transnational circulation (Liu, 2014, 2015). With their transnational habitats, they have developed strong connections with their homeland, while they might also have multiple citizenships and permanent residences in various countries. The scenarios of return migration among this migrant group in particular pose intriguing questions in Chinese migration studies. It is possible that other traditional Chinese immigrant-receiving "White Settler" societies share similar positioning as New Zealand in the world migration system. These Chinese immigrant-receiving countries (i.e., Australia, Canada, and US) face challenges to develop effective policy in accommodating and retaining their Chinese immigrants. At the same time, China, the homeland, actively engages with its diasporic population, because this population plays a vital role in connecting China with the international community. The policy of China with respect to its diaspora reflects a multilayered and complicated relationship between this re-emerging world power and the global North, a term referencing developed economies. What also can be seen from the case study of transnational PRC Chinese migrants in Oceania is that "China rising" has resulted in a significant shift and change in the world migration system.

The centre-periphery model of immigration implies an enduring trajectory of immigration from South to North, as the flows from developing countries to the economically well-developed countries has been dubbed (Massey et al., 1997; Massey et al., 1993; Massey, Goldring, & Durand, 1994). This model is insufficient to explain the recent return migration process from the economically well-developed countries to the developing or newly developed countries, such as China and India (Xiang, 2006; Zweig, 2006). This is to say that both the traditional immigrant-receiving and sending countries are undergoing a change in their position in the world migration system.

Many traditional migrant-sending countries with a relatively more advanced economy invest significant resources to engage with their diasporic population, at the same time immigrant-receiving countries work hard to develop flexible and innovative immigration programme to compete for human resources. These immigrant-receiving countries face double challenges in competition for skilled migrants to remedy domestic skilled labour shortages and to enhance human and cultural capital for economic development. First, these countries have to continuously compete with each other for skilled migrants (Bedford, Lidgard, & Ho, 2003; Luo et al., 2003); and second, competition also come from their migrant-sending countries which are very keen to exert their rising economic powers and implement efficient policies to attract their diasporic population back. The competing strategies in immigrant sending and receiving countries within a globalised transnational context is perhaps a new dimension in the world migration system, responding to a renewed global competition for human capital identified as a crucial underpinning factor for continuing national economic and social development. This reconfigures concepts, such as nation states and population boundaries, to incorporate emerging senses of place, space, and belonging.

The last implication from this research is more practical. On the policy level, this research has produced a knowledge base about contemporary Chinese migration to New Zealand, which may over time facilitate more positive policy adjustment. Despite decades of Chinese immigration to New Zealand, this country's awareness of Chinese immigration remains inadequate. Like other immigrant-receiving countries where much policy making is formed based on the philosophy of promoting permanent settlement of migrants and by the model of calculative rationality, which simply weighs up various factors and chooses the best and most efficient means to attain a present policy goal (van Dalen & Henkens, 2005), New Zealand's post-1987 immigration policy has not yet adequately accommodated the ongoing migration needs of many migrants including Chinese migrants. First, there is an incomplete understanding among policy-makers to issues associated with migrants' potential to engage in transnational movements. It is not well appreciated that under the skilled and business immigration categories, the targeted immigrants with professional skills, high educational levels, and considerable investment capital are naturally the most mobile immigrant group whose very financial and human capital can make their settlement both fluid and dynamic. Second, the precise position of New Zealand in the world migration system as an immigration destination for short- or medium-term residence rather than long-term residence (Bedford et al., 2000, p. 29) is yet to be fully addressed by the immigration policy.

Recently, there has been a progressive shift in immigration policy to accommodate temporary migration of skilled migrants (Bedford, Ho, & Bedford, 2010). Furthermore, considerable attention on the subsequent mobility of immigrants has been reflected by some reports produced by the Department of Labour (Merwood, 2008; Shorland, 2006). This present research can hopefully further facilitate a fuller understanding of the transnational dimension of immigration by highlighting the data derived from this country's second largest immigrant group. Based on a comprehensive understanding, this research further suggests a need for policy makers to incorporate the transnational aspect of immigration in future policy development, and then to ensure future policy can reflect the transnational realities of immigration.

More importantly, when formulating policies, the New Zealand government and its policymakers must shift their thinking away from focussing only on the permanent migration settlement. Only when the view towards this widely-accepted but increasingly problematic traditional model is widened and updated, the country's immigration policy can become beneficial for all parties. What should be kept in mind is that migration is ultimately a flow of people who carry with them to a location all their aspirations for life and family. Migrants should not be treated as economic chips in any government's policy agenda. Before making such policies, full understanding of migration and empathy toward migrants should be cultivated and used as an ethics and moral compass. It should be remembered as well that migrants are far easier to be legislated out of the country than legislated in. In this free-choice age in which we live, immigration policy should focus on considerations of how best to accommodate migrants during their period of residence in New Zealand and seek better ways to maximise and utilise the resources of migrants, so they do make positive contributions to this country.

References

Bedford, R., Ho, E., & Bedford, C. E. (2010). Pathways to residence in New Zealand, 2003–2009. In A. Trlin, P. Spoonely, & R. Bedford (Eds.), *New Zealand International Migration. A Digest and Bibliography, Number 5* (pp. 1–49). Palmerston North, New Zealand: Massey University Printery.

Bedford, R., Ho, E., & Lidgard, J. (2000). *International Migration in New Zealand: Context, Components and Policy Issues* (Discussion Papers No. 37). Hamilton, New Zealand: Population Studies Centre, University of Waikato.

Bedford, R., Lidgard, J., & Ho, E. (2003). International migration during election years: The evidence for 1996, 1999 and 2002. *New Zealand Journal of Geography*, *115*, 26–43.

Hugo, G. (2005). The new international migration in Asia. *Asian Population Studies*, *1*(1), 93–120.

Iredale, R., Guo, F., & Rozario, S. (2002). Introduction. In R. Iredale, F. Guo, & S. Rozario (Eds.), *Return Skilled and Business Migration and Social Transformation* (pp. 1–19). Wollongong, Australia: Centre for Asia Pacific Social Transformation Studies, University of Wollongong.

Levitt, P., & Glick-Schiller, N. (2004). Conceptualizing simultaneity: A transnational social field perspective on society. *International Migration Review*, *38*(3), 1002–1039.

Ley, D., & Kobayashi, A. (2005). Back to Hong Kong: Return migration or transnational sojourn? *Global Networks*, *5*(2), 111–127.

Lidgard, J., Bedford, R., & Ho, E. (1995). Situating international migration within world-system analysis: Relevance for Aotearoa/New Zealand. In R. Bedford, E. Ho, J. Lidgard, S. N. Kim, & J. Young (Eds.), *International Migration in New Zealand: Perspectives on Theory and Process*. Discussion Papers No. 7 (pp. 11–17). Hamilton, New Zealand: Population Studies Centre, University of Waikato.

Liu, L. (2014). PRC Chinese transnational migration in the case of New Zealand: Returnees and trans-Tasman migrants. *The International Journal of Diasporic Chinese Studies, 6*(1), 41–71.

Liu, L. (2015). Examining trans-Tasman migration of New Zealand's new immigrants from the People's republic of China: A quantitative survey. *Asia Pacific Viewpoint, 56*(2), 297–314.

Liu-Farrer, G. (2016). Migration as class-based consumption: The emigration of the rich in contemporary China. *The China Quarterly, 226,* 499–518.

Luo, K., Guo, F., & Huang, P. (2003). China: Government policies and emerging trends of reversal of the brain drain. In R. Iredale, F. Guo, & S. Rozario (Eds.), *Return Migration in the Asia Pacific* (pp. 88–111). Cheltenham, UK: Edward Elgar Publishing Limited.

Massey, D. S., Arango, J., Hugo, G., Kouaouci, A., Pellegrino, A., & Taylor, J. E. (1997). Migration theory, ethnic mobilization and globalization. In M. Guibernau & J. Rex (Eds.), *The Ethnicity Reader: Nationalism, Multiculturalism and Migration* (pp. 257–269). London: Policy Press.

Massey, D. S., Arango, J., Hugo, G., Kouaouci, A., Taylor, J. E., & Pellegrino, A. (1993). Theories of international migration: A review and appraisal. *Population and Development Review, 19,* 431–466.

Massey, D. S., Goldring, L., & Durand, J. (1994). Continuities in transnational migration: An analysis of nineteen Mexican communities. *American Journal of Sociology, 99,* 1492–1533.

Merwood, P. (2008). *Migration Trends 2006/07.* Wellington: Department of Labour.

Shorland, P. (2006). *People on the Move: A Study of Migrant Movement Patterns to and From New Zealand.* Wellington: Department of Labour.

Skeldon, R. (1996). Migration from China. *Journal of International Affairs, 49*(2), 434–455.

Skeldon, R. (2004). *China: From Exceptional Case to Global Participants.* Retrieved August 6, 2009 from www.migrationinformation.org/Profiles/display.cfm?ID=219

Spoonley, P., Meares, C., Ho, E., & Bedford, R. (2009). Attracting, supporting and retaining skilled migrants: Experiences of recently arrived British and South African migrants. *Rising Dragons, Soaring Bananas International Conference.* Retrieved October 2, 2010 from www.waikato.ac.nz/wfass/populationstudiescentre/09-pathways/november2/Spoonely-Ho-Cooper.pdf

Studwell, J. (2003). *The China Dream: The Quest for the Last Great Untapped Market on Earth.* New York: Grove Pres.

van Dalen, H. P., & Henkens, K. (2005). The rationality behind immigration policy preferences. *De Economist, 153*(1), 67–83.

Wang, C., Wong, S. L., & Sun, W. B. (2006). Haigui: A new area in China's policy toward the Chinese diaspora? *Journal of Chinese Overseas, 2*(2), 294–309.

Xiang, B. (2006). *'Body Shopping': An Indian International Labour System in the Information Technology Industry.* Princeton: Princeton University Press.

Zeng, M., & Williamson, P. J. (2003). The hidden dragons. *Harvard Business Review, 81,* 1–10.

Zweig, D. (1997). To return or not to return? Politics vs. economics in China's brain drain. *Studies in Comparative International Development, 32*(1), 92–125.

Zweig, D. (2006). Competing for talent: China's strategies to reverse the brain drain. *International Labour Review, 145,* 65–89.

Appendixes

Appendix 1 Rates of long-term absence by source country as of 30 June 2013 for migrants approved for residence 2005/2006–2011/2012 (Adapted from *Migration Trend and Outlook 2012/13* by Ministry of Business, Innovation and Employment, 2013: 106)[*1]

Source country	Number approved for residence[*2]	Long-term absent (No.)[*3]	% long-term absent
United States	8,892	2,364	27%
Canada	3,139	809	26%
Singapore	1,460	366	25%
Taiwan	1,019	227	22%
Netherlands	2,415	522	22%
China	41,577	8,450	20%
Hong Kong	1,004	201	20%
France	1,632	320	20%
Malaysia	4,506	877	19%
Germany	4,700	898	19%

Notes

[*1] see www.mbie.govt.nz/publications-research/research/migration/MigrationTrend-and-Outlook-12-13.pdf

[*2] This number does not include those migrants who were approved for residence but never arrived in New Zealand. Only source countries with a total approval count of 1,000 or more are shown.

[*3] Long-term absence in this report in defined as: on the Department of Labour survey day, a migrant had spent a period or periods of time overseas for more than six months after his/her arrival as a resident.

Appendix 2 New Selection System – Expression of Interests (EOI) was pronounced on media in 2013

In July 2003, the Minister of Immigration, Lianne Dalziel suddenly announced that a new Skilled Migrant Category (SMC) would come into force in December 2003 to replace the General Skills Category (GSC). The Immigration Minister

Dalziel's 2003 package of press releases, as cited below, reflects the essence of the new selection system:

> Instead of lodging applications for residence, potential migrants will, in future, register an expression of interest, based on the existing pre-requisites of health, character and English language. In order to register, a minimum number of points will be required. The current points system will be expanded to include bonus points, for example, by meeting a specific skill shortage or having a skilled job offer in a region outside Auckland. . . . Those who register their interest will be pooled, and those achieving the highest level of points will be invited to apply for residence. Where no invitation to apply has been issued by the end of the registration period, the registration will lapse. This will probably occur quarterly. Once an application for residence is lodged, two streams will emerge. The first stream will consist of those who have already demonstrated that they can settle and do well here. For example, they may have successfully studied or worked in New Zealand, or they have a killed job offer, which demonstrates that a New Zealand employer has made that assessment. People in this stream will follow through to residence. The second stream will consist of those who have not yet demonstrated their ability to settle in New Zealand. . . . The majority of these will be managed through a two year work-to-residence programme, rather than gaining residence outright. This will enable them to demonstrate their ability to settle and gain relevant employment. This essentially means that they carry the risk of not achieving this outcome rather than the New Zealand welfare system that has to meet the cost of failure until now.[*]

Appendix 3 Settlement Strategies Initiated by Government before and after the 1999 National Election

1   Between 1997 and 1999, several initiatives undertaken by the NZIS's Settlement Information Programme between 1997 and 1999 included:

- The publication of a regular newsletter sent to all new immigrants (*Linkz. Making Your Way in New Zealand*, first issue, spring 1997) with a range of stories about immigrant experiences and advice about negotiating work, business, education, accommodation, and access to public services.
- In 1998, the *Settlement Kit* – a package covering issues such as finding a home, working in New Zealand, education system, government and judicial systems and laws, and the taxation system – was launched by Bradford. Special booklets providing guides for teenagers and older people were also released along with a guide to migrant services provided at the local government level.

- An ambitious longitudinal survey of immigrants, modelled on the Longitudinal Survey of Immigration in Australia (LSIA), had been scoped and approved by the National government in 1999 for piloting in 2000.*

2   In 1999, the settlement pilots developed by NZIS after the Labour Government came into power involved:

- Collaborations between communities groups delivering services to refugees and migrants, and the Government;
- A NZIS-commissioned research on migrant settlement.

3   In May 2000, Cabinet approved four pilots with varying levels of funding for asylum seekers and refugees, the families of refugees and migrants. Three pilots, each including several projects, ranging from providing emergency assistance for asylum seekers to catering for the employment needs of highly skilled migrants and the business development requirement needs of entrepreneurs, were funded during 2001.

Appendix 4 Interview Questions

Interviewee:
Code:
Interviewer:
Interview date:
Interview Place:
Remarks:

Section I: participant personal information

1   Gender _____

2   Age group: 15–19 ☐   20–24 ☐   25–29 ☐   30–34 ☐
                     35–44 ☐   45–54 ☐   55–64 65 plus ☐

3   Place of birth: Hong Kong ☐   Taiwan ☐
                        PRC ☐   Others (please specify) _____

4   Citizenship: A. Which citizenship(s) do you hold?
                         Australia ☐   New Zealand ☐   Taiwan ☐
                         Hong Kong ☐   PRC ☐
                         Others (please specify) _____

                     B If you have not taken Australia or New Zealand citizenship, do you intend to take it in the future?
                         Yes   ☐   No ☐
                     C Why?

5   **Year of first landing Australia or New Zealand as permanent resident:** _____

6   **Migration category:** Skilled
    Business   ☐
    Family spouse   ☐
    Family parent   ☐
    Others (please specify): _____

7   **Personal geographical movements prior and subsequent to landing Australia or New Zealand:**

	Duration	*Location*
Movements prior to landing Australia or New Zealand		
Movements subsequent to landing Australia or New Zealand		
When did you move to your current location?	What is your current location?	

8 A   Education Background:

Highest education qualification before arrival (including the major)	
Current education qualification (including the major)	

8 B   Detailed education history

Year	*Qualification*	*Major*	*Where did you get this qualification?*

9 A   Profession & work history (ask income level to ascertain possible economic factors)

Last occupation before arrival (income level?)	
First occupation in Australia or New Zealand (income level?)	
Current occupation (income level?)	

9 B   Detailed work history

Duration	Occupation	Employment situation	Where?

10 English proficiency (ask if participant has not mentioned it)

11 A   Family composition

	Spouse	*Children*	*Parents*	*Grandparents/ grandchildren*
Marital status: single □ married □		divorced □		widowed □
Age group				
Education				
Current occupation				
Current location				

11 B   Overview of movement pattern of family members:

Duration	*Family member*	*Location*

Section II: migration movements, decision & experiences

1   Initial immigration to Australia or New Zealand

Please elaborate on the reasons of immigrating to Australia or New Zealand

> A   Why did you choose Australia or New Zealand as your first immigration destination country?
> B   Who initiated the immigration idea?
> C   Tell us more about other family members' input in the migration decision.

2   Pattern of further movements (opportunities & challenges)

Now we are talking about the further movement that you and your family pursuit. For example, now you/your family have returned to your original place/commute between Australia/New Zealand and your original place,

A   Why did you decide to return to your original place?/ Why did you decide to move to Australia?

B   Why did you pursuit the regular commuting between Australia/ New Zealand and your original place?

C   Is the plan of further movement deliberately chosen before immigration or decided after your arrival?

D   What is the opportunity? What is the challenge?

E   How has immigration experience in Australia/New Zealand affect you so far (e.g. strength to cope with challenges, different life perspectives. . . .)

F   Your movement differs from your family, can you elaborate on the decision making processes?

Section III: home, belonging, identity & citizenship

1   **Family network (to explore pattern of interaction)**

A   How do you keep contact with your family?

B   How often do you contact with your family?

C   How often do you and your family reunite together?

D   Are you happy with this kind of contact?

E   Do you feel you need more?

F   Do you feel you are close with your family?

2   **Social network**

A   Whom do you intend to turn to when you need help or you want to share a happy moment?

B   Do you have close friends who are not where you are?

C   Are you happy with such situations?

D   Is your professional network mainly in

Australia ☐   NZ ☐   Hong Kong ☐   Taiwan ☐   PRC ☐
others (please specify)?

Elaborate if necessary. . . .

E   Who and where do you socialize after work?

3   **Economic networks**

A   You are now in location A, do you and/or your family still have economic links with location B?

B   Please specify (e.g. owning property, owning other investments etc.)

C   Do you still keep the business network back there (PRC, Taiwan, HK, NZ, Australia)?

4   **Sense of home**

    A   Where is your home? Give 3 images of the place you call 'home'.

    B   In your everyday conversation, when you say "home", which place are you referring to?

    C   If you regard your home is in AUS/NZ/HK/TW/PRC, do you feel [another place e.g. AUS/NZ/HK/TW/PRC is your home too?

    D   Is your 'home' different from that of your family's?

5   **Sense of belonging**

    A   What do you think you are? Why?

    B   Where do you feel you belong to?

    C   When you say you belong to AUS/NZ/HK/TW/PRC, do you feel you belong to [another place] AUS/NZ/HK/TW/PRC as well?

    D   When you say you are Chinese/Taiwanese/NZer/Australian. . . . , do you consider yourself as (CH, TA, NZer. . . .) as well?

    E   Do you consider yourself 'Chinese'? What does Chinese . . . mean to you?

6   **Citizenship**

What does citizenship mean to you?

Section IV: the future

1   **Your plan for the next 5 years?**

    A   Where will you and your family members be for the next 5 years?

    B   What is the ideal scenario? Why?

    C   What is the most likely scenario? Why?

    D   Do you have plans to re-enter New Zealand/AUS and settle down for the long term? Why?

2   **Your plan after 10 years?**

    A   Where will you and your family members be after 10 years?

    B   What is your ideal scenario? Why?

    C   What is the most likely scenario? Why?

    D   Do you have plan to re-enter New Zealand/AUS and settle down for long time? Why?

Appendix 5 Trans-Tasman migration by citizenship and birthplace, March Years 1998–2009 (Bedford, Callister, & Didham, 2010, p. 67)*

Citizenship and birthplace	Arrivals	PLT migration Departures	Net migration	Sex ratio Net migration
NZ citizens				
1998–2001	27,299	120,244	–92,945	1.099
2002–2005	35,016	96,745	–61,729	1.021
2006–2009	33,359	142,786	–109,427	1.070
Other citizens				
1998–2001	15,720	13,897	1,823	1.106
2002–2005	19,555	13,379	6,176	1.075
2006–2009	19,912	17,946	1,966	1.646
NZ born				
1998–2001	n.a.	n.a.	n.a.	n.a.
2001–2005	30,505	78,141	–47,636	1.028
2006–2009	28,944	117,377	–88,433	1.078
Overseas born				
1998–2001	n.a.	n.a.	n.a.	n.a.
2002–2005	23,860	30,972	–7,112	0.946
2006–2009	24,168	42,462	–18,294	0.991

Note
* See literature by Bedford, R., Callister, P., & Didham, R. (2010). Arrivals, departures and net migration, 2001/02-2008/09. In A. Trlin, P. Spoonley, & R. Bedford (Eds.), New Zealand and International Migration: A Digest and Bibliography, Number 5 (pp. 50-103).

Appendix 6 Net migration losses to Australia of overseas-born New Zealand citizens by region of birth, March Years 2002–2009 (Bedford, Callister, & Didham, 2010, p. 68)*

Birthplace	Period 2002–05	2006–09	Percentage change
Numbers			
Pacific Islands	–2,595	–3,377	30.1
UK/Ireland	–2,263	–2,887	27.6
Other Europe	–965	–1,417	46.8
Asia	–4,763	–7,398	55.3
Africa/ME	–2,368	–4,390	85.4
Americas	–390	–532	36.4

Note
* See literature by Bedford, R., Callister, P., & Didham, R. (2010). Arrivals, departures and net migration, 2001/02-2008/09. In A. Trlin, P. Spoonley, & R. Bedford (Eds.), New Zealand and International Migration: A Digest and Bibliography, Number 5 (pp. 50-103).

Appendix 7: Online Survey Questionnaire

Page 1

Language Selection （语言选择）

1 **Please select a language** （请先选择问卷语言）

☐ English （英语）
☐ Chinese （中文）

Page 2

This survey is a part of my PhD study (entitled "Homeland on the Move – New Chinese Immigrants to New Zealand as Transnationals"), which will explore your experience, feelings and opinions as a migrant to New Zealand. This research only relates to migrants who immigrated to New Zealand after 1987 from the People's Republic of China. Your contribution will help my studies greatly. Your answers will be kept strictly confidential and anonymous. It will take you about 15 minutes to complete this survey. If you have any question about this research, please contact me, the principal investigator. For any queries regarding ethical concerns you may contact the University of Auckland Human Participants Ethics Committee, the University of Auckland, Private Bag 92019, Auckland 1142.

Telephone 09 373–7599 extn. 87830.
Investigator: Ms. Liangni Liu
PhD candidate
School of Asian Studies
The University of Auckland.
Email: laingni.liu@auckland.ac.nz

Before you start the survey, please answer the following question. If your answer is "yes", the web browser will take you into the survey when you click "next". If your answer is "no" to any part of the question, please click "exit this survey" link at the top-right corner of this webpage.

1   **I am over 20 years old, I am originally from People's Republic of China, and I have either Permanent Residency or Citizenship of New Zealand. (If you are not, please click top right link of this page to exit this survey, thanks!) this survey**

*   ☐   Yes

Page 3

Now I'll start by asking you some questions about yourself. Those questions are based on Census questions. Again, your participation is anonymous and none of the information you provide here will be used to trace back to you.

1   **Please select your gender:**

    ☐ Male
    ☐ Female

2   **Please select your age range:**

    ☐ 20–24
    ☐ 25–29
    ☐ 30–34
    ☐ 35–39
    ☐ 40–44
    ☐ 45–49
    ☐ 50–54
    ☐ 55–59
    ☐ 60 and over

3   **Your place of birth?**

4   **What is your marital status?**   ☐ Single   ☐ Married/De facto

    ☐ Separated   ☐ Divorced   ☐ Widow/widower   ☐ Civil union

5   **What is the highest education level that you have completed?**

    ☐ None
    ☐ New Zealand Level 1 Certificate
    ☐ New Zealand Level 2 Certificate
    ☐ New Zealand Level 3 Certificate
    ☐ New Zealand Level 4 Certificate
    ☐ New Zealand Level 5 Diploma
    ☐ New Zealand Level 6 Diploma
    ☐ Overseas secondary school qualification
    ☐ Bachelor degree or New Zealand Level 7 qualification
    ☐ Postgraduate/Honour degree
    ☐ Masters degree
    ☐ Doctorate degree

6   **Where did you gain your highest degree/your highest education?**

    ☐ China   ☐ New Zealand   ☐ Somewhere else (please specify):

    3   **General Information (Page 1)**

Page 4

*7 **Are you a citizen or permanent resident (PR) of New Zealand?**

☐ Citizen
☐ Permanent Resident (PR)

Page 5

1   If you are not a New Zealand citizen, do you intend to apply for New Zealand passport in future?

☐ Yes
☐ No
☐ Maybe
☐ Don't know

2   What passport do you hold currently?

4   Citizenship General information continues (Page 1 continues)

Page 6

1   When did you first arrive in New Zealand (Please use the format DD/MM/YYYY, for example 21/11/2002. If you cannot remember the exact date, please give a roughly close date)?

DD MM YYYY   Date//

2   Under what type of visa did you first arrive at New Zealand?

☐ Student Visa
☐ Permanent Resident Visa
☐ Visitor
☐ Working
☐ Family Reunion
☐ Other (please specify):

3   Under which immigration category did you immigrate to New Zealand?

☐ General Skills
☐ Work to Residence
☐ Business/Investment
☐ Family (parent)
☐ Family (spouse)
☐ Other (please specify):

4   Were you the principal applicant?

☐ Yes   ☐ No

Page 7

1   What is your relationship with the principal applicant? Relation to Principal applicant (Page 2 continues)

Page 8

1   **Whose decision was it for you (and/or your family) to immigrate to New Zealand?**

☐ Mine
☐ My spouse's/partner's
☐ Both of mine and my spouse's/ partner's
☐ My parents
☐ My spouse's parents
☐ Joint family decision
☐ Someone else (please specify):

2   **Which country are you living in now?**

☐ New Zealand
☐ China
☐ Commuting between New Zealand and China
☐ A third country (please specify which country):

Page 9

1   **Which area are you living in now?**

□ Northland Region
□ Auckland Region
□ Waikato Region (Hamilton)
□ Bay of Plenty Region
□ Gisborne Region
□ Hawke's Bay Region
□ Taranaki Region
□ Manawatu-Wanganui Region
□ Wellington Region
□ West Coast Region
□ Canterbury Region (Christchurch)
□ Otago Region
□ Southland Region
□ Tasman Region
□ Nelson Region
□ Marlborough Region
□ Area outside Region (Such as Chatham Islands etc)

2   **What is your current status in labour force?**

□ Employed full time
□ Employed part time
□ Unemployed
□ Not in Labour force (e.g. retired or studying or staying at home; for example, housewife)

Page 10

1   **What is your current status in employment?**

   ☐ Paid employee
   ☐ Employer
   ☐ Self-employed without employees
   ☐ Unpaid family worker

2   **How many hours do you work per week (Please enter a number only)?**

   9   **Detailed employed status (Page 4 continues)**

Page 11

1   **What is your current study participation?0. Detailed study participation**

☐ Full time study
☐ Part-time study
☐ Not studying (e.g. retired or staying at home; for example, housewife)

Page 12

1   What is your current occupation?

2   What is your estimated personal annual income now (all ranges shown below are in NZ$)?

☐ Below NZ$5,000
☐ NZ$5,001 – NZ$10,000
☐ NZ$10,001 – NZ$15,000
☐ NZ$15,001 – NZ$20,000
☐ NZ$20,001 – NZ$25,000
☐ NZ$25,001 – NZ$30,000
☐ NZ$30,001 – NZ$35,000
☐ NZ$35,001 – NZ$40,000
☐ NZ$40, 001 – NZ$50,000
☐ NZ$50,001 – NZ$70,000
☐ NZ$70,001 – NZ$100,000
☐ NZ$100,001 – NZ$150,000
☐ Over NZ$150,000

3   Do you have a spouse/partner?

☐ Yes ☐ No

Page 13

1   What is your spouse's/partner's current status in labour force?

☐ Employed full time
☐ Employed part time
☐ Unemployed
☐ Not in Labour force (e.g. retired or studying or staying at home; for example, housewife)

Page 14

1 **What is your spouse's/partner's current status in employment?**

☐ Paid employee
☐ Employer
☐ Self-employed without employees
☐ Unpaid family worker

2 **How many hours does your spouse/partner work per week (Please enter a number only)?**

13 **Detailed employed status (Page 5 continues)**

Page 15

1   **What is your spouse's/partner's current study participation?4. Detailed study**

   ☐ Full time study
   ☐ Part-time study
   ☐ Not studying (e.g. retired or staying at home; for example, housewife)

Page 16

1   What is your spouse's/partner's current occupation?

2   What is your spouse's/partner's estimated personal annual income now (all ranges shown below are in NZ$)?

☐ Below NZ$5,000
☐ NZ$5,001 – NZ$10,000
☐ NZ$10,001 – NZ$15,000
☐ NZ$15,001 – NZ$20,000
☐ NZ$20,001 – NZ$25,000
☐ NZ$25,001 – NZ$30,000
☐ NZ$30,001 – NZ$35,000
☐ NZ$35,001 – NZ$40,000
☐ NZ$40, 001 – NZ$50,000
☐ NZ$50,001 – NZ$70,000
☐ NZ$70,001 – NZ$100,000
☐ NZ$100,001 – NZ$150,000
☐ Over NZ$150,000

3   Where is your spouse/partner now?

☐ New Zealand
☐ China
☐ Commuting between New Zealand and China
☐ A third country (please specify which country):

Page 17

1   When did your spouse/partner start to commute between New Zealand and China (Please use the format DD/MM/YY, for example, 25/10/2003, if you cannot remember the exact date, please give a roughly close date)?

DD MM YYYY   Date//

2   When was the decision made for your spouse/partner to commute between New Zealand and China while you stay in New Zealand?

☐ Before I/we/she/he applied for NZ residency
☐ After I/we/she/he arrived in NZ
☐ After I/we/she/he obtained NZ residency
☐ After I/we/she/he obtained NZ citizenship
☐ Other time (please specify):

3   How often does your spouse/partner commute between China and New Zealand?

☐ less than once a year
☐ once a year
☐ twice a year
☐ three times a year
☐ more frequently

4   Who made the commuting decision?

☐ Me
☐ My spouse/partner
☐ Both mine and my spouse's/partner's decision
☐ Joint family decision
☐ Someone else (please specify):

Page 18

1   What was your last occupation in China before you immigrated to New Zealand?

2   What was your estimated personal annual income in China before you immigrated to New Zealand (please use a rough conversion: NZ$1 = RMB 4 & all ranges shown below are in NZ$)?

☐ Below NZ$5,000
☐ NZ$5,001 – NZ$10,000
☐ NZ$10,001 – NZ$15,000
☐ NZ$15,001 – NZ$20,000
☐ NZ$20,001 – NZ$25,000
☐ NZ$25,001 – NZ$30,000
☐ NZ$30,001 – NZ$35,000
☐ NZ$35,001 – NZ$40,000
☐ NZ$40, 001 – NZ$50,000
☐ NZ$50,001 – NZ$70,000
☐ NZ$70,001 – NZ$100,000
☐ NZ$100,001 – NZ$150,000
☐ Over NZ$150,000

3   Is any of your family member(s) in New Zealand to be with you (You can choose more than one answer)?

- My spouse/partner
- My child(ren) My own parents
- My parents-in-law
- My sibling(s)
- None

4   What is the main reason that you (and your family) are now in New Zealand (You can choose more than one answer)?

- I can earn more in New Zealand
- The cost of living here is lower than in China
- I have business in New Zealand to run
- I just feel more comfortable in New Zealand
- I like the social and natural environment of New Zealand
- My parents and relatives are in New Zealand
- I feel New Zealand is where I belong to
- There are more & better opportunities for my career development in New Zealand
- I have more familiar and wider social and professional networks in New Zealand
- g Other reasons (please specify):

Page 19

5   **How often do you visit China?**

☐ Never been back to China since immigration
☐ Less than once every 3 years
☐ Once every 3 years
☐ Once every 2 years
☐ Once a year
☐ Twice a year
☐ Three times a year
☐ More frequently

6   **Have you had a student loan in New Zealand?**

☐ Yes   ☐ No

Page 20

1   **Please select the following statement about student loan which fits you:**

☐ I have repaid my loan
☐ I am in the process of repaying my loan
☐ I have not repaid my loan but I intend to do so later on
☐ I have not repaid my loan and I do not intend to repay it anyway

Page 21

1   **Do you have any plan to go to another country to work or live?**

☐ No, I plan to stay in New Zealand
☐ Yes, I have plan to go to another country (please specify which country):

2   **Where do you intend to settle down ultimately to work or live for long term in the future and when?**

☐ I'll always stay in New Zealand
☐ China, after a few years
☐ China, after my retirement
☐ New Zealand, after my retirement
☐ Somewhere else, after a few years
☐ Somewhere else, after my retirement
☐ Don't know
☐ Other plan (please specify):

Page 22

1 My/Our family money flow situation:

☐ Money remittance is mainly from China to New Zealand
☐ We/I do not have any significant money transaction between places
☐ Money remittance is mainly from New Zealand to China

Page 23

1   My/Our family money remittance situation:

☐ Money remittance is frequent
☐ Money remittance is occasional
☐ Other patterns of money remittance (please specify):

2   What are the reasons for the money transaction?

○   Regular business/investment transactions
○   Regular family/personal transactions
○   Occasional business/investment transactions
○   Occasional family/personal transactions
○   Other reasons (please specify):

Page 24

1   Do/does you/your spouse have/has property in New Zealand?

    ☐ Yes   ☐ No   ☐ I/we/she/he used to have, but sold it out later on

2   If you/your spouse have/has property in New Zealand now, what is its current value (Please provide NZ$ number only)? (optional question) NZ$

3   Do you/your spouse have/has any other investment in New Zealand (for example, investment in share market)?

    ☐ Yes   ☐ No   ☐ I/we/she/he used to have, but sold it out later on

4   If you/your spouse have/has other investment in New Zealand now, how much is it (Please provide NZ$ number only)? (Optional question) NZ$

5   Do you/your spouse have/has property in China?

    ☐ Yes   ☐ No   ☐ I/we/she/he used to have, but sold it out later on

6   If you/your spouse have/has property in China now, what is its current value (Please provide NZ$ number only)? (Optional question) NZ$

7   Do you/your spouse have/has any other investment in China (for example, investment in share market)?2. Settler's property and investment (Page 8 continues)

    ☐ Yes   ☐ No   ☐ I/we/she/he used to have, but sold it out later on

Page 25

8   If you/your spouse have/has other investment in China now, how much is it (Please provide NZ$ number only)? (Optional question)
NZ$

Page 26

1 **In general, your experience in New Zealand is:**

☐ Pleasant and valuable
☐ Unpleasant but valuable
☐ Pleasant but not valuable
☐ A waste of time

2 **Do you consider yourself as a:**

☐ Chinese   ☐ New Zealander   ☐ Both ☐ Other (please specify):

3 **Are you proud to be a Chinese?**

☐ Yes   ☐ No

4 **Are you proud to be a New Zealander?**

☐ Yes   ☐ No

5 **When China is doing well on the international stage (in economic, political, or major sporting fields), do you feel:**

☐ Proud   ☐ Jealous   ☐ Envious   ☐ Resentful   ☐ Don't care

6 **When New Zealand is doing well on the international stage (in economic, political, or major sporting fields), do you feel:**

☐ Proud   ☐ Jealous   ☐ Envious   ☐ Resentful   ☐ Don't care

7 **I feel a sense of belonging to:**

☐ New Zealand
☐ China
☐ Both New Zealand and China
☐ Not any country in particular
☐ I don't want to deal with this question
☐ Other (please specify):

Page 27

8   Do you agree with the statement, "It does not matter to me which country I am a citizen of, as long as I can maintain a high standard of living"?

☐ Strongly agree   ☐ Somewhat agree   ☐ Neutral
☐ Somewhat disagree   ☐ Strongly disagree

9   **Please rate your feeling towards the below countries:**

New Zealand: Love absolutely, Like, Neutral, Dislike, Resentful
China: Love absolutely, Like, Neutral, Dislike, Resentful

Page 28

1   When did you return to China to live or work for long-term (Please use the format DD/MM/YYYY, for example, 23/10/2003. If you can't remember the exact date, please give a roughly close date)?

DD MM YYYY   Date//

2   **When did you make the decision to return to China?**

☐ Before I/we/he/she applied for NZ residency
☐ After I/we/he/she arrived in NZ
☐ After I/we/he/she obtained NZ residency
☐ After I/we/he/she obtained NZ citizenship
☐ Other time (please specify):

3   **Who made the return decision?**

☐ Me
☐ My spouse/partner
☐ Both mine and my spouse's/partner's decision
☐ My parents
☐ My spouse's/partner/s parents
☐ Joint family decision
☐ Someone else (please specify):

4   **What was your last occupation in New Zealand before you returned to China?**

5   **What was your estimated personal annual income immediately before you returned to China (all ranges shown below are in NZ$)?**

☐ Below NZ$5,000
☐ NZ$5,001 – NZ$10,000
☐ NZ$10,001 – NZ$15,000
☐ NZ$15,001 – NZ$20,000
☐ NZ$20,001 – NZ$25,000
☐ NZ$25,001 – NZ$30,000
☐ NZ$30,001 – NZ$35,000
☐ NZ$35,001 – NZ$40,000
☐ NZ$40, 001 – NZ$50,000
☐ NZ$50,001 – NZ$70,000
☐ NZ$70,001 – NZ$100,000
☐ NZ$100,001 – NZ$150,000
☐ Over NZ$150,000

Page 29

6 **What was your status in labour force immediately before you returned to China?**

☐ Employed full time
☐ Employed part time
☐ Unemployed
☐ Not in Labour force (e.g. retired or studying or staying at home; for example, housewife)

Page 30

1   What was your status in employment immediately before you returned to China?

    ☐ Paid employee
    ☐ Employer
    ☐ Self-employed without employees
    ☐ Unpaid family worker

2   How many hours did you work per week for your last job in New Zealand (Please enter a number only)?

Page 31

1 **What was your study participation?**

☐ Full time study
☐ Part-time study
☐ Not studying (e.g. retired or staying at home; for example, housewife)

Page 32

1   Which city/area are you living in now in China?

2   What is your current occupation?

3   What is your current employment status?

    ☐ Paid employee
    ☐ Employer
    ☐ Self-employed without employees
    ☐ Unpaid family worker
    ☐ Unemployed
    ☐ Not in labour force (studying)
    ☐ Not in labour force (retired or staying in home; for example: housewife)

4   How many hours do you work per week (Please enter a number only)?

5   What is your estimated personal annual income now (please use a rough conversion: NZ$1 = RMB 4 & all ranges shown below are in NZ$)?

    ☐ Below NZ$5,000
    ☐ NZ$5,001 – NZ$10,000
    ☐ NZ$10,001 – NZ$15,000
    ☐ NZ$15,001 – NZ$20,000
    ☐ NZ$20,001 – NZ$25,000
    ☐ NZ$25,001 – NZ$30,000
    ☐ NZ$30,001 – NZ$35,000
    ☐ NZ$35,001 – NZ$40,000
    ☐ NZ$40, 001 – NZ$50,000
    ☐ NZ$50,001 – NZ$70,000
    ☐ NZ$70,001 – NZ$100,000
    ☐ NZ$100,001 – NZ$150,000
    ☐ Over NZ$150,000

6   Do you have a spouse/partner?

    ☐ Yes   ☐ No

Page 33

1   What is your spouse's/partner's current status in labour force?. Partner's

    ☐ Employed full time   ☐ Employed part time   ☐ Unemployed
    ☐ Not in Labour force (e.g. retired or studying or stay at home; for example, housewife)

Page 34

1   **What is your spouse's/partner's current status in employment?**

☐ Paid employee
☐ Employer
☐ Self-employed without employees
☐ Unpaid family worker

2   **How many hours does your spouse/partner work per week (Please enter a number only)?**

29   **Detailed employed status (Page 5 continues)**

Page 35

1 What is your spouse's/partner's current study participation?

☐ Full time study
☐ Part-time study
☐ Not studying (e.g. retired or staying at home; for example, housewife)

Page 36

1   What is your spouse's/partner's current occupation?

2   What is your spouse's/partner's estimated personal annual income now (all ranges shown below are in NZ$)?

☐ Below NZ$5,000
☐ NZ$5,001 – NZ$10,000
☐ NZ$10,001 – NZ$15,000
☐ NZ$15,001 – NZ$20,000
☐ NZ$20,001 – NZ$25,000
☐ NZ$25,001 – NZ$30,000
☐ NZ$30,001 – NZ$35,000
☐ NZ$35,001 – NZ$40,000
☐ NZ$40, 001 – NZ$50,000
☐ NZ$50,001 – NZ$70,000
☐ NZ$70,001 – NZ$100,000
☐ NZ$100,001 – NZ$150,000
☐ Over NZ$150,000

3   Where is your spouse/partner?

☐ New Zealand
☐ China
☐ Commuting between New Zealand and China
☐ A third country (please specify which country):

Page 37

1   When did your spouse/partner start to commute between New Zealand and China (Please use the format DD/MM/YY, for example, 23/10/2003.
If you cannot remember the exact date, please give a roughly close date)?

DD MM YYYY   Date//

2   When was the decision made for your spouse/partner to commute between New Zealand and China while you stay in New Zealand?

☐ Before I/we/he/she applied for NZ residency
☐ After I/we/he/she arrived in NZ
☐ After I/we/he/she obtained NZ residency
☐ After I/we/he/she obtained NZ citizenship
☐ Other time (please specify):

3   How often does your spouse/partner commute between China and New Zealand?

☐ Less than once a year
☐ once a year
☐ twice a year
☐ three times a year
☐ more frequently

4   Who made the commuting decision?

☐ Me
☐ My spouse/partner
☐ Both mine and my spouse's/partner's decision
☐ Joint family decision
☐ Someone else (please specify):

Page 38

1   **Is any of your immediate family member(s) still in New Zealand (you can choose more than one answer)?**

- My spouse/partner ○ My child(ren) ○ My parents ○ My parents in-law
- My sibling(s) ○ None

2   **What is the main reason that you (and your family) returned to China (You can choose more than one answer)?**

- I can earn more and the cost of living is low in China
- I cannot find a satisfactory job in New Zealand
- I have business in China to run
- There are more and better opportunities for my career development in China
- I have more familiar and wider social and professional networks in China
- I just feel more comfortable in China
- My parents and many relatives are in China
- I feel China is where I belong to
- Other reasons (please specify):

3   **Have you visited New Zealand since you left?**

☐ Yes   ☐ No

Page 39

1   How many times have you visited New Zealand since you left (Please enter a number only)?

2   How often did you visit New Zealand since you left?

☐ Less than once every 3 years   ☐ Once every 3 years
☐ Once every 2 years   ☐ Once a year
☐ Twice a year   ☐ Three times a year
☐ More frequently

Page 40

1   Have you had a student loan in New Zealand?

☐ Yes   ☐ No

Page 41

1   **Please select the following statement which fits you:**

    ☐ I have repaid my loan
    ☐ I am in the process of repaying my loan
    ☐ I have not repaid my loan but I intend to do so later on
    ☐ I have not repaid my loan and I do not intend to repay it anyway

Page 42

1 **Do you have any plan to go to another country to work or live?**

☐ No   ☐ Yes (please specify which country):

2 **Where do you intend to settle down ultimately to live or work for long term and when?**

☐ I'll always stay in China
☐ I'll stay in China for the next few years, but go back to New Zealand to
   live afterwards
☐ China, after my retirement
☐ New Zealand, after my retirement
☐ Somewhere else, after a few years
☐ Somewhere else, after my retirement
☐ Don't know
☐ Other plan (please specify):

Page 43

1   My/Our family money flow situation:

☐ Money remittance is mainly from China to New Zealand
☐ We/I do not have any significant money transaction between places
☐ Money remittance is mainly from New Zealand to China

Page 44

1   **My/Our family money remittance situation:**

☐ Money remittance is frequent
☐ Money remittance is occasional
☐ Other patterns of money remittance (please specify):

2   **Reasons for money transaction:**

○   Regular business/investment transactions
○   Regular family/personal transactions
○   Occasional business/investment transactions
○   Occasional family/personal transactions
○   Other reasons (please specify):

Page 45

1 Do/does you/your spouse have/has property in New Zealand?

☐ Yes   ☐ No   ☐ I/we/she/he used to have, but sold it out later on

2 If you/your spouse have/has property in New Zealand now, what is its current value (Please provide NZ$ number only)? (Optional question) NZ$

3 Do you/your spouse have/has any other investment in New Zealand (for example, investment in share market)?

☐ Yes   ☐ No   ☐ I/we/she/he used to have, but sold it out later on

4 If you/your spouse have/has other investment in New Zealand now, how much is it (Please provide NZ$ number only)? (Optional question) NZ$

5 Do you/your spouse/partner have property in China?

☐ Yes   ☐ No   ☐ I/we/she/he used to have, but sold it out later on

6 If you/your spouse have/has property in China now, what is its current value (Please provide NZ$ number only)? (Optional question) NZ$

7 Do you/your spouse have/has any other investment in China (for example, investment in share market)?

☐ Yes   ☐ No   ☐ I/we/she/he used to have, but sold it out later on

Page 46

8   If you/your spouse have/has other investment in China now, how much is it (Please provide NZ$ number only)? (Optional question) NZ$

Page 47

1 **In general, your experience in New Zealand is/was:**

Pleasant and valuable
Unpleasant but valuable
Pleasant but not valuable
A waste of time

2 **Do you consider yourself as a:**

☐ Chinese ☐ New Zealander   ☐ Both   ☐ Other (please specify):

3 **Are you proud to be a Chinese?**

☐ Yes   ☐ No

4 **Are you proud to be a New Zealander?**

☐ Yes   ☐ No

5 **When China is doing well on the international stage (in economic, political, or major sporting fields), do you feel:**

☐ Proud   ☐ Jealous   ☐ Envious   ☐ Resentful
☐ Don't care

6 **When New Zealand is doing well on the international stage (in economic, political, or major sporting fields), do you feel:**

☐ Proud   ☐ Jealous   ☐ Envious   ☐ Resentful
☐ Don't care

7 **I feel a sense of belonging to:**

☐ New Zealand
☐ China
☐ Both New Zealand and China
☐ Not any country in particular
☐ I don't want to deal with this question
☐ Other (please specify):

Page 48

8 **Do you agree with the statement, "It does not matter to me which country I am a citizen of, as long as I can maintain a high standard of living"?**

☐ Strongly agree   ☐ Somewhat agree   ☐ Neutral   ☐ Somewhat disagree
☐ Strongly disagree

9   Please rate your feeling towards the below countries:

New Zealand: Love absolutely, Like, Neutral, Dislike, Resentful
China: Love absolutely, Like, Neutral, Dislike, Resentful

Page 49

1   When did you start to commute between New Zealand and China
    (Please use the format DD/MM/YY, for example, 23/10/2003. If you
    cannot remember the exact date, please give a roughly close date)?

    DD MM YYYY   Date//

2   **When did you make the decision to commute between the two countries?**

    ☐ Before I/we/he/she applied for NZ residency
    ☐ After I/we/he/she arrived in NZ
    ☐ After I/we/he/she obtained NZ residency
    ☐ After I/we/he/she obtained NZ citizenship
    ☐ Other time (please specify):

3   **Who made the commuting decision?**

    ☐ Me
    ☐ My spouse/partner
    ☐ Both of mine and my spouse's/partner's decision
    ☐ My parents
    ☐ My spouse's/partner's parents
    ☐ Joint family decision
    ☐ Someone else (please specify):

4   **How often do you commute between China and New Zealand?**

    Less than once a year
    Once a year
    Twice a year
    Three times a year
    More frequently

5   **What is your current status in labour force?**

    ☐ Employed full time
    ☐ Employed part time
    ☐ Unemployed
    ☐ Not in Labour force (e.g. retired or studying or staying at home; for
      example, housewife)

Page 50

1   **What is your current status in employment?**

   ☐ Paid employee
   ☐ Employer
   ☐ Self-employed without employees
   ☐ Unpaid family worker

2   **How many hours do you work per week (Please enter a number only)?**

Page 51

1   **What is your current study participation?**

☐ Full time study   ☐ Part-time study
☐ Not studying (e.g. retired or staying at home; for example, housewife)

Page 52

1   What is your current occupation?

2   What is your estimated personal annual income now (all ranges shown below are in NZ$)?

☐ Below NZ$5,000
☐ NZ$5,001 – NZ$10,000
☐ NZ$10,001 – NZ$15,000
☐ NZ$15,001 – NZ$20,000
☐ NZ$20,001 – NZ$25,000
☐ NZ$25,001 – NZ$30,000
☐ NZ$30,001 – NZ$35,000
☐ NZ$35,001 – NZ$40,000
☐ NZ$40, 001 – NZ$50,000
☐ NZ$50,001 – NZ$70,000
☐ NZ$70,001 – NZ$100,000
☐ NZ$100,001 – NZ$150,000
☐ Over NZ$150,000

Page 53

1   Which city/area are you living in when you are in China?

2   Which area are you living in when you are in New Zealand?

☐ Northland Region
☐ Auckland Region
☐ Waikato Region (Hamilton)
☐ Bay of Plenty Region
☐ Gisborne Region
☐ Hawke's Bay Region
☐ Taranaki Region
☐ Manawatu-Wanganui Region
☐ Wellington Region
☐ West Coast Region
☐ Canterbury Region (Christchurch)
☐ Otago Region
☐ Southland Region
☐ Tasman Region
☐ Nelson Region
☐ Marlborough Region
☐ Area outside Region (Such as Chatham Islands etc)

3   Have you had a student loan in New Zealand?

☐ Yes   ☐ No

Page 54

1   **Please select the following statement which fits you:**

☐ I have repaid my loan
☐ I am in the process of repaying my loan
☐ I have not repaid my loan but I intend to do so later on
☐ I have not repaid my loan and I do not intend to repay it anyway

Page 55

1   Do you have a spouse/partner?

☐ Yes   ☐ No

Page 56

1   **What is your spouse's/partner's current status in labour force?**

☐ Employed full time
☐ Employed part time
☐ Unemployed
☐ Not in Labour force (e.g. retired or studying or staying at home; for example, housewife)

Page 57

1   What is your spouse's/partner's status in employment?

    ☐ Paid employee
    ☐ Employer
    ☐ Self-employed without employees
    ☐ Unpaid family worker

2   How many hours does your spouse/partner work per week (Please enter a number only)?

Page 58

1   **What is your spouse's/partner's current study participation?**

☐ Full time study ☐ Part-time study
☐ Not studying (e.g. retired or staying at home; for example, housewife)

Page 59

1   What is your spouse's/partner's current occupation?

2   What is your spouse's/partner's estimated personal annual income now (all ranges shown below are in NZ$)?

☐ Below NZ$5,000
☐ NZ$5,001 – NZ$10,000
☐ NZ$10,001 – NZ$15,000
☐ NZ$15,001 – NZ$20,000
☐ NZ$20,001 – NZ$25,000
☐ NZ$25,001 – NZ$30,000
☐ NZ$30,001 – NZ$35,000
☐ NZ$35,001 – NZ$40,000
☐ NZ$40, 001 – NZ$50,000
☐ NZ$50,001 – NZ$70,000
☐ NZ$70,001 – NZ$100,000
☐ NZ$100,001 – NZ$150,000
☐ Over NZ$150,000

3   Where is your spouse/partner?

☐ New Zealand   ☐ China
☐ Commuting between New Zealand and China with me
☐ A third country (please specify which country):

Page 60

1   Is any of your family member(s) in New Zealand (You can choose more than one answer)?

My spouse/partner
My child(ren)
My parents
My parents-in-law
My sibling(s)
None

2   What is the main reason that you are commuting between China and New Zealand (You can have more than one answer)?

- I have business to run in China
- I want my child(ren) to grow up and be educated in New Zealand
- I want my partner or other family members to stay in New Zealand
- I want to settle down with my family in New Zealand in the future
- I can benefit more financially while keeping in contact with my family in New Zealand
- Other reasons (please specify):

3   Do you have any plan to go to another country to live or work?

☐ No   ☐ Yes (please specify which country):

4   Where do you intend to settle down ultimately to live or work for long term and when?

☐ China, after a few years
☐ New Zealand, after a few years
☐ China, after my retirement
☐ New Zealand, after my retirement
☐ Somewhere else, after a few years
☐ Somewhere else, after my retirement
☐ I enjoy commuting and will not settle down
☐ Don't know
☐ Other plan (please specify):

Page 61

1   My/Our family money flow situation:

☐ Money remittance is mainly from China to New Zealand
☐ We/I do not have any significant money transaction between places
☐ Money remittance is mainly from New Zealand to China

Page 62

1   **My/Our family money remittance situation:**

   ☐ Money remittance is frequent
   ☐ Money remittance is occasional
   ☐ Other patterns of money remittance (please specify):

2   **Reasons for money transaction:**

   ○   Regular business/investment transactions
   ○   Regular family/personal transactions
   ○   Occasional business/investment transactions
   ○   Occasional family/personal transactions
   ○   Other reasons (please specify):

Page 63

1 Do/does you/your spouse have/has property in New Zealand?

    ☐ Yes   ☐ No   ☐ I/we/she/he used to have, but sold it out later on

2 If you/your spouse have/has property in New Zealand now, what is its current value (Please provide NZ$ number only)? (Optional question) NZ$

3 Do you/your spouse have/has any other investment in New Zealand (for example, investment in share market)?

    ☐ Yes   ☐ No   ☐ I/we/she/he used to have, but sold it out later on

4 If you/your spouse have/has other investment in New Zealand now, how much is it (Please provide NZ$ number only)? (Optional question) NZ$

5 Do you/your spouse/partner have property in China?

    ☐ Yes   ☐ No   ☐ I/we/she/he used to have, but sold it out later on

6 If you/your spouse have/has property in China now, what is its current value (Please provide NZ$ number only)? (Optional question) NZ$

7 Do you/your spouse have/has any other investment in China (for example, investment in share market)?

    ☐ Yes   ☐ No   ☐ I/we/she/he used to have, but sold it out later on

Page 64

8   If you/your spouse have/has other investment in China now, how much is it (Please provide NZ$ number only)? (Optional question) NZ$

Page 65

1   **In general, your experience in New Zealand is/was:**

Pleasant and valuable
Unpleasant but valuable
Pleasant but not valuable
A waste of time

2   **Do you consider yourself as a:**

☐ Chinese ☐ New Zealander ☐ Both ☐ Other (please specify):

3   **Are you proud to be a Chinese?**

☐ Yes ☐ No

4   **Are you proud to be a New Zealander?**

☐ Yes ☐ No

5   **When China is doing well on the international stage (in economic, political, or major sporting fields), do you feel:**

☐ Proud ☐ Jealous ☐ Envious ☐ Resentful ☐ Don't care

6   **When New Zealand is doing well on the international stage (in economic, political, or major sporting fields), do you feel:**

☐Proud ☐ Jealous ☐ Envious ☐ Resentful ☐ Don't care

7   **I feel a sense of belonging to:**

☐ New Zealand
☐ China
☐ Both New Zealand and China
☐ Not any country in particular
☐ I don't want to deal with this question
☐ Other (please specify):

Page 66

8   Do you agree with the statement, "It does not matter to me which country I am a citizen of, as long as I can maintain a high standard of living"?

☐ Strongly agree   ☐ Somewhat agree   ☐ Neutral
☐ Somewhat disagree   ☐ Strongly disagree

9   **Please rate your feeling towards the below countries:**

New Zealand: Love absolutely, Like, Neutral, Dislike, Resentful
China: Love absolutely, Like, Neutral, Dislike, Resentful

Page 67

1   When did you go to the place you currently settle to live (Please use format DD/MM/YYY, for example, 21/10/2003. If you can't remember the exact date, please just give a roughly close date)?

DD MM YYYY   Date//

2   When did you make the decision to leave New Zealand and step into the country you currently live in?

☐ Before I/we/he/she applied for NZ residency
☐ After I/we/he/she arrived in NZ
☐ After I/we/he/she obtained NZ residency
☐ After I/we/he/she obtained NZ citizenship
☐ Other time (please specify):

3   Who made the decision to move to the country you are currently in?

☐ Me
☐ My spouse/partner
☐ Both of mine and my spouse's/partner's decision
☐ My parents
☐ My spouse's/partner's
☐ Joint family decision
☐ Someone else (please specify):

4   Which area had you been living in when you were in New Zealand (you can choose more than one answer)?

- Northland Region
- Auckland Region
- Waikato Region (Hamilton)
- Bay of Plenty Region
- Gisborne Region
- Hawke's Bay Region
- Taranaki Region
- Manawatu-Wanganui Region
- Wellington Region
- West Coast Region
- Canterbury Region (Christchurch)
- Otago Region
- Southland Region
- Tasman Region
- Nelson Region
- Marlborough Region
- Area outside Region (Such as Chatham Islands etc)

Page 68

5   What was your employment status in New Zealand immediately before you stepped into the country you are currently living in?

☐ Paid employee
☐ Employer
☐ Self-employed without employees
☐ Unpaid family worker
☐ Unemployed
☐ Not in labour force (studying)
☐ Not in labour force (retired or staying at home; for example, housewife)

6   What was your last occupation in New Zealand before you stepped into the country you currently live in?

7   What was your estimated personal annual income in New Zealand immediately before you Stepping into the country you currently live in (all ranges shown below are in NZ$)?

☐ Below NZ$5,000
☐ NZ$5,001 – NZ$10,000
☐ NZ$10,001 – NZ$15,000
☐ NZ$15,001 – NZ$20,000
☐ NZ$20,001 – NZ$25,000
☐ NZ$25,001 – NZ$30,000
☐ NZ$30,001 – NZ$35,000
☐ NZ$35,001 – NZ$40,000
☐ NZ$40, 001 – NZ$50,000
☐ NZ$50,001 – NZ$70,000
☐ NZ$70,001 – NZ$100,000
☐ NZ$100,001 – NZ$150,000
☐ Over NZ$150,000

Page 69

1   Where are you living now?

2   What is the main reason that you (and your family) left New Zealand and stepped into the country you currently live in (you can choose more than one answer)?

- I can earn more here than in New Zealand
- The cost of living is lower here than in New Zealand
- I could not find a satisfactory job in New Zealand
- I found a better job with higher income here
- I have business to run here
- I just feel more comfortable here
- My parents and many relatives are here
- There are more and better opportunities for my career development here
- Other reasons (please specify):

3   Is any of your immediate family member(s) still in New Zealand (You can choose more than one answer)?

My spouse/partner
My child(ren)
My parents
My parents-in-law
My sibling(s)
None

4   What is your current status in labour force?

- ☐ Employed full time
- ☐ Employed part time
- ☐ Unemployed
- ☐ Not in Labour force (e.g. retired or studying or staying at home; for example, housewife)

Page 70

1   **What is your current status in employment?**

   ☐ Paid employee
   ☐ Employer
   ☐ Self-employed without employees
   ☐ Unpaid family worker

2   **How many hours do you work per week (Please enter a number only)?**

Page 71

1   What is your current study participation?

☐ Full time study ☐ Part-time study
☐ Not studying (e.g. retired or staying at home; for example, housewife)

Page 72

1   What is your current occupation?

2   What is your estimated personal annual income now (all ranges shown below are in NZ$)?

☐ Below NZ$5,000
☐ NZ$5,001 – NZ$10,000
☐ NZ$10,001 – NZ$15,000
☐ NZ$15,001 – NZ$20,000
☐ NZ$20,001 – NZ$25,000
☐ NZ$25,001 – NZ$30,000
☐ NZ$30,001 – NZ$35,000
☐ NZ$35,001 – NZ$40,000
☐ NZ$40, 001 – NZ$50,000
☐ NZ$50,001 – NZ$70,000
☐ NZ$70,001 – NZ$100,000
☐ NZ$100,001 – NZ$150,000
☐ Over NZ$150,000

3   Have you had a student loan in New Zealand?

☐ Yes   ☐ No

Page 73

1   **Please select the following statement which fits you:**

☐ I have repaid my loan
☐ I am in the process of repaying my loan
☐ I have not repaid my loan but I intend to do so later on
☐ I have not repaid my loan and I do not intend to repay it anyway

Page 74

1 **Have you visited New Zealand since you left?**

☐ Yes   ☐ No

Page 75

1 On average, how often do you travel back to New Zealand?

☐ Less frequent than once every 3 years
☐ Once every 3 years
☐ Once every 2 years
☐ Once a year
☐ Twice a year
☐ Three times a year
☐ More frequently

Page 76

1   **Have you travelled back to China since you immigrated?**

☐ Yes   ☐ No

Page 77

1 **On average, how often do you travel back to China?**

☐ Less frequent than once every 3 years   ☐ Once every 3 years
☐ Once every 2 years   ☐ Once a year
☐ Twice a year   ☐ Three times a year
☐ More frequently

Page 78

1 **Do you have a spouse/partner?**

☐ Yes ☐ No

Page 79

1 **Where is your spouse/partner?**

☐ New Zealand   ☐ China
☐ Commuting between New Zealand and China
☐ A third country (please specify which country):

2 **What is your spouse's/partner's current employment status?**

☐ Paid employee
☐ Employer
☐ Self-employed without employees
☐ Unpaid family worker
☐ Unemployed
☐ Not in labour force (studying)
☐ Not in labour force (retired or staying at home; for example, housewife)

3 **What is your spouse's/partner's current occupation?**

4 **What is your spouse's/partner's estimated personal annual income now (all ranges shown below are in NZ$)?**

☐ Below NZ$5,000
☐ NZ$5,001 – NZ$10,000
☐ NZ$10,001 – NZ$15,000
☐ NZ$15,001 – NZ$20,000
☐ NZ$20,001 – NZ$25,000
☐ NZ$25,001 – NZ$30,000
☐ NZ$30,001 – NZ$35,000
☐ NZ$35,001 – NZ$40,000
☐ NZ$40, 001 – NZ$50,000
☐ NZ$50,001 – NZ$70,000
☐ NZ$70,001 – NZ$100,000
☐ NZ$100,001 – NZ$150,000
☐ Over NZ$150,000

Page 80

1   **Do you have any plan to go to another country to live or work?**

☐ No   ☐ Yes (please specify which country):

2   **Where do you intend to settle down ultimately to live or work for long term and when?**

☐ I'll settle down here
☐ China, after a few years
☐ New Zealand, after a few years
☐ China, after my retirement
☐ New Zealand, after my retirement
☐ Somewhere else, after a few years
☐ Somewhere else, after my retirement
☐ Don't know
☐ Other plan (please specify):

Page 81

1 **My/Our family money flow situation:**

☐ Money remittance is mainly from where I/we am/are to New Zealand

☐ I/we do not have any significant money transaction between where I/we am/are and New Zealand

☐ Money remittance is mainly from New Zealand to where I/we am/are

☐ Other money transaction pattern (please specify):

Page 82

1 **My/Our family money remittance situation:**

  ☐ Money remittance is frequent
  ☐ Money remittance is occasional
  ☐ Other patterns of money remittance (please specify):

2 **Reasons for money transaction:**

  ○ Regular business/investment transactions
  ○ Regular family/personal transactions
  ○ Occasional business/investment transactions
  ○ Occasional family/personal transactions
  ○ Other reasons (please specify):

Page 83

1 Do/does you/your spouse have/has property in New Zealand?

   ☐ Yes   ☐ No   ☐ I/we/she/he used to have, but sold it out later on

2 If you/your spouse have/has property in New Zealand now, what is its current value (Please provide NZ$ number only)? (Optional question) NZ$

3 Do you/your spouse/partner have any other investment in New Zealand (for example, investment in share market)?

   ☐ Yes   ☐ No   ☐ I/we/she/he used to have, but sold it out later on

4 If you/your spouse have/has other investment in New Zealand now, how much is it (Please provide NZ$ number only)? (Optional question) NZ$

5 Do you/your spouse have/has property in China?

   ☐ Yes   ☐ No   ☐ I/we/she/he used to have, but sold it out later on

6 If you/your spouse have/has property in China now, what is its current value (Please provide NZ$ number only)? (Optional question) NZ$

7 Do you/your spouse/partner have any other investment in China (for example, investment in share market)?

   ☐ Yes   ☐ No   ☐ I/we/she/he used to have, but sold it out later on

Page 84

8   If you/your spouse have/has other investment in China now, how much is it (Please provide NZ$ number only)? (Optional question)

□ Yes   □ No   □ I/we/she/he used to have, but sold it out later on

9   Do you/your spouse have/has property in the place you are currently in?

□ Yes   □ No   □ I/we/she/he used to have, but sold it out later on

10 If you/your spouse have/has property in the place you are currently in, what is its current value (Please provide NZ$ number only)? (Optional question) NZ$

11 Do you/your spouse have/has any other investment in the place you are currently in (for example, investment in share market)?

□ Yes   □ No   □ I/we/she/he used to have, but sold it out later on

12 If you/your spouse have/has other investment in the place you are currently in, how much is it (Please provide NZ$ number only)? (Optional question) NZ$

Page 85

1 **In general, your experience in New Zealand is/was:**

Pleasant and valuable
Unpleasant but valuable
Pleasant but not valuable
A waste of time

2 **Do you consider yourself as a:**

☐ Chinese ☐ New Zealander ☐ Both ☐ Other (please specify):

3 **Are you proud to be a Chinese?**

☐ Yes ☐ No

4 **Are you proud to be a New Zealander?**

☐ Yes ☐ No

5 **Are you proud to be a resident of the country you are currently in?**

☐ Yes ☐ No ☐ I am not a resident/citizen of the country I am in

6 **When China is doing well on the international stage (in economic, political, or major sporting fields), do you feel:**

☐ Proud ☐ Jealous ☐ Envious ☐ Resentful ☐ Don't care

7 **When New Zealand is doing well on the international stage (in economic, political, or major sporting fields), do you feel:**

☐ Proud ☐ Jealous ☐ Envious ☐ Resentful ☐ Don't care

8 **When the country you are living in is doing well on the international stage (in economic, political, or major sporting fields), do you feel:**

☐ Proud ☐ Jealous ☐ Envious ☐ Resentful ☐ Don't care

Page 86

9 **I feel a sense of belonging to:**

☐ New Zealand ☐ China ☐ Both New Zealand and China
☐ The country I am living in now
☐ All countries (NZ, China and current country I am living in)
☐ Not any country in particular ☐ I don't want to deal with this question
☐ Other (please specify):

10 **Do you agree with the statement, "It does not matter to me which country I am a citizen of, as long as I can maintain a high standard of living"?**

☐ Strongly agree ☐ Somewhat agree
☐ Neutral ☐ Somewhat disagree ☐ Strongly disagree

11 **Please rate your feeling towards the below countries:**

New Zealand: ☐ Love absolutely ☐ Like ☐ Neutral ☐ Dislike
☐ Resentful
China: ☐ Love absolutely ☐ Like ☐ Neutral ☐ Dislike
☐ Resentful
The country I am living in now: ☐ Love absolutely ☐ Like ☐ Neutral
☐ Dislike ☐ Resentful

Page 87

We'd love to hear your story or comment about your immigration experience. Comments about this survey are also welcome.

1 **If you like, please enter your comment below (or you can skip this page by clicking "next").(Final page)**

Appendix 8

Table 1 Long term and permanent arrival and departure of New Zealand (NZ) citizens born in China (including Hong Kong) between NZ and China, by age, in the period of April 2001 – April 2015

Age	Arrival from China	Departure to China	Net gain from China to NZ
Under 5 Years	341	38	303
5–9 Years	193	62	131
10–14 Years	182	57	125
15–19 Years	167	67	100
20–24 Years	140	557	–417
25–29 Years	413	607	–194
30–34 Years	474	336	138
35–39 Years	466	274	192
40–44 Years	472	232	240
45–49 Years	388	205	183
50–54 Years	287	196	91
55–59 Years	232	175	57
60–64 Years	178	121	57
65–69 Years	89	79	10
70–74 Years	58	40	18
75–79 Years	34	25	9
80–84 Years	15	9	6
85–89 Years	2	3	–1
90–94 Years	1	1	0
95 Years and Over	0	0	0
Total	4132	3084	1048

Table 2 Long term and permanent arrival and departure of NZ citizens born in Taiwan between NZ and Taiwan, by age, in the period of April 2001 – April 2015

Age	Arrival from Taiwan	Departure to Taiwan	Net gain from Taiwan to NZ
Under 5 Years	102	15	87
5–9 Years	70	65	5
10–14 Years	132	63	69

Age	Arrival from Taiwan	Departure to Taiwan	Net gain from Taiwan to NZ
15–19 Years	96	49	47
20–24 Years	115	417	−302
25–29 Years	257	382	−125
30–34 Years	192	127	65
35–39 Years	125	85	40
40–44 Years	101	78	23
45–49 Years	125	104	21
50–54 Years	190	148	42
55–59 Years	209	124	85
60–64 Years	170	45	125
65–69 Years	45	12	33
70–74 Years	22	7	15
75–79 Years	12	2	10
80–84 Years	8	1	7
85–89 Years	2	3	1
90–94 Years	2	2	0
95 Years and Over	0	0	0
Total	1975	1729	246

Table 3 Long term and permanent arrival and departure of NZ citizens born in South Korea between NZ and South Korea, by age, in the period of April 2001 – April 2015

Age	Arrival from ROK	Departure to ROK	Net gain from South Korea to NZ
Under 5 Years	60	7	53
5–9 Years	25	11	14
10–14 Years	18	14	4
15–19 Years	18	53	−35
20–24 Years	82	267	−185
25–29 Years	154	205	−51
30–34 Years	69	59	10
35–39 Years	40	27	13
40–44 Years	43	39	4
45–49 Years	46	64	−18
50–54 Years	45	57	−12
55–59 Years	27	39	−12
60–64 Years	21	16	5
65–69 Years	8	4	4
70–74 Years	0	2	−2
75–79 Years	5	1	4
80–84 Years	0	0	0
85–89 Years	1	1	0
90–94 Years	0	0	0
95 Years and Over	0	0	0
Total	662	866	−204

Table 4 Long term and permanent arrival and departure of NZ citizens born in India between NZ and India, by age, in the period of April 2001 – April 2015

Age	Arrival from India	Departure to India	Net gain from India to NZ
Under 5 Years	64	17	47
5–9 Years	27	52	–25
10–14 Years	72	70	2
15–19 Years	60	44	16
20–24 Years	37	71	–34
25–29 Years	53	82	29
30–34 Years	64	169	–105
35–39 Years	103	194	–91
40–44 Years	69	83	–14
45–49 Years	51	68	–17
50–54 Years	51	57	–6
55–59 Years	50	57	–7
60–64 Years	44	35	9
65–69 Years	25	17	8
70–74 Years	9	19	–10
75–79 Years	13	8	5
80–84 Years	10	6	4
85–89 Years	1	3	–2
90–94 Years	0	0	0
95 Years and Over	0	0	0
Total	803	1052	–249

Table 5 Long term and permanent arrival and departure of NZ citizens born in Fiji/Tonga/Samoa between NZ and Fiji/Tonga/Samoa, by age, in the period of April 2001 – April 2015

Age	Arrival from Fiji/Tonga/Samoa	Departure to Fiji/Tonga/Samoa	Net gain from Fiji/Tonga/Samoa to NZ
Under 5 Years	169	24	145
5–9 Years	259	51	208
10–14 Years	485	94	391
15–19 Years	546	116	430
20–24 Years	264	108	156
25–29 Years	204	89	115
30–34 Years	200	86	114
35–39 Years	166	103	63
40–44 Years	167	92	75
45–49 Years	179	116	63
50–54 Years	184	130	54
55–59 Years	173	95	78
60–64 Years	162	62	100
65–69 Years	92	108	–16
70–74 Years	84	48	36
75–79 Years	76	52	24
80–84 Years	36	20	16
85–89 Years	10	11	–1
90–94 Years	5	2	3
95 Years and Over	0	1	–1
Total	3461	1408	2053

Table 6 Long term and permanent arrival and departure, by age, of Chinese citizens, between China, including Hong Kong, and NZ, in the period of April 2001 – April 2015

Age	Arrival from China	Departure to China	Net gain from China to NZ
Under 5 Years	1750	82	1668
5–9 Years	2195	221	1974
10–14 Years	3736	173	3563
15–19 Years	29300	1768	27532
20–24 Years	26382	9621	16761
25–29 Years	10157	7924	2233
30–34 Years	7324	2348	4976
35–39 Years	5677	960	4717
40–44 Years	4071	743	3328
45–49 Years	2466	711	1755
50–54 Years	2021	642	1379
55–59 Years	3314	741	2573
60–64 Years	3219	646	2573
65–69 Years	2186	621	1565
70–74 Years	1315	412	903
75–79 Years	524	199	325
80–84 Years	134	62	72
85–89 Years	21	14	7
90–94 Years	6	1	5
95 Years and Over	1	0	1
Total	105799	27889	77910

Table 7 Long term and permanent arrival and departure, by age, of Taiwanese citizens, between Taiwan and NZ in the period of April 2001 – April 2015

Age	Arrival from Taiwan	Departure to Taiwan	Net gain from Taiwan to NZ
Under 5 Years	91	16	75
5–9 Years	187	40	147
10–14 Years	532	61	471
15–19 Years	887	234	653
20–24 Years	1024	562	462
25–29 Years	2206	650	1556
30–34 Years	660	307	353
35–39 Years	253	82	171
40–44 Years	367	56	311
45–49 Years	297	51	246
50–54 Years	263	70	193
55–59 Years	162	44	118
60–64 Years	106	10	96
65–69 Years	44	4	40
70–74 Years	21	1	20
75–79 Years	20	2	18
80–84 Years	15	3	12
85–89 Years	3	2	1
90–94 Years	1	0	1
95 Years and Over	0	0	0
Total	7139	2195	4944

Table 8 Long term and permanent arrival and departure, by age, of Fiji/Tonga/
Samoa citizens, between Fiji/Tonga/Samoa and NZ in the period of
April 2001 – April 2015

Age	Arrival from Fiji/ Tonga/Samoa	Departure to Fiji/ Tonga/Samoa	Net gain from Fiji/ Tonga/Samoa to NZ
Under 5 Years	4147	213	3934
5–9 Years	4339	521	3818
10–14 Years	4457	547	3910
15–19 Years	6931	778	6153
20–24 Years	5863	1595	4268
25–29 Years	5518	1244	4274
30–34 Years	4296	1003	3293
35–39 Years	3394	821	2573
40–44 Years	2900	671	2229
45–49 Years	1711	589	1122
50–54 Years	1188	529	659
55–59 Years	1040	406	634
60–64 Years	714	331	383
65–69 Years	490	283	207
70–74 Years	252	215	37
75–79 Years	134	131	3
80–84 Years	52	65	–13
85–89 Years	17	28	–11
90–94 Years	7	4	3
95 Years and Over	0	0	0
Total	47450	9974	37476

Table 9 Long term and permanent arrival and departure, by age, of Indian citizens,
between India and NZ, in the period of April 2001 – April 2015

Age	Arrival from India	Departure to India	Net gain from India to NZ
Under 5 Years	3082	174	2908
5–9 Years	2510	196	2314
10–14 Years	2055	128	1927
15–19 Years	10708	220	10488
20–24 Years	25993	1887	24106
25–29 Years	15493	2546	12947
30–34 Years	7247	1194	6053
35–39 Years	3870	586	3284
40–44 Years	2264	304	1960
45–49 Years	1459	205	1254
50–54 Years	1094	197	897
55–59 Years	1120	252	868
60–64 Years	1183	261	922
65–69 Years	859	234	625
70–74 Years	519	162	357
75–79 Years	275	74	201
80–84 Years	90	36	54
85–89 Years	22	11	11
90–94 Years	6	3	3
95 Years and Over	3	3	0
Total	79852	8673	71179

Table 10 Long term and permanent arrival and departure, by age, of South Korean citizens, between South Korea and NZ in the period of April 2001 – April 2015

Age	Arrival from South Kore	Departure to South Korea	Net gain from South Korea to NZ
Under 5 Years	599	251	348
5–9 Years	2026	1604	422
10–14 Years	4451	4730	−279
15–19 Years	3135	3091	44
20–24 Years	4647	2681	1966
25–29 Years	3197	2293	904
30–34 Years	1410	1207	203
35–39 Years	1843	1792	51
40–44 Years	1798	1706	92
45–49 Years	914	932	−18
50–54 Years	470	497	−27
55–59 Years	338	232	−106
60–64 Years	202	111	91
65–69 Years	173	86	87
70–74 Years	141	77	64
75–79 Years	66	44	22
80–84 Years	24	32	−8
85–89 Years	9	13	−4
90–94 Years	1	2	−1
95 Years and over	2	1	1
Total	25446	21382	4064

Notes

* Dalziel, L. *Skilled Immigration Policy Announcements. Media Statements and Briefing Notes.* 1 July 2003, Office of Minister of Immigration, Parliament Buildings, Wellington.
* See literature by Bedford, R., E. Ho, and J. Lidgard. "From Targets to Outcomes: Immigration Policy in New Zealand, 1996–2003". In *New Zealand and International Migration: A Digest and Bibliography, Number 4*, edited by A. Trlin, P. Spoonley and N. Watts, 1–43. Palmerston North: Department of Sociology, Massey University, 2005. p13.
* See literature by Bedford, R., Callister, P., & Didham, R. (2010). Arrivals, departures and net migration, 2001/02–2008/09. In A. Trlin, P. Spoonley, & R. Bedford (Eds.), *New Zealand and International Migration: A Digest and Bibliography, Number 5* (pp. 50–103).
* See literature by Bedford, R., Callister, P., & Didham, R. (2010). Arrivals, departures and net migration, 2001/02–2008/09. In A. Trlin, P. Spoonley, & R. Bedford (Eds.), *New Zealand and International Migration: A Digest and Bibliography, Number 5* (pp. 50–103).

Index

306 *Index*